Kodak *elegy*

Kodak Park. Courtesy of the author.

Kodak *elegy*

A COLD WAR CHILDHOOD

William Merrill Decker

SYRACUSE UNIVERSITY PRESS

This is a work of memory. Names have been altered and situations condensed.

∞ The paper used in this publication meets the minimum requirements of the American National Standard for Information Sciences—Permanence of Paper for Printed Library Materials, ANSI Z39.48–1992.

For a listing of books published and distributed by Syracuse University Press, visit our Web site at SyracuseUniversityPress.syr.edu.

ISBN: 978-0-8156-0972-8

Library of Congress Cataloging-in-Publication Data

Decker, William Merrill.
  Kodak elegy : a Cold War childhood / William Merrill Decker. — 1st ed.
     p. cm.
  ISBN 978-0-8156-0972-8 (cloth : alk. paper) 1. Decker, William Merrill—Childhood and youth. 2. Rochester (N.Y.)—Biography. I. Title.
  CT275.D32544A3 2012
  974.7'89044092—dc23
  [B]   2012010231

Manufactured in the United States of America

For Tom: First, Best, Truest Friend

"... a storm is blowing from Paradise ..."

—Walter Benjamin

Contents

Illustrations

Three children. Courtesy of the author.

Prologue

For a child of the fifties there would be no dearth of primary images: the two-toned sedan parked in a suburban driveway, the mahogany black-and-white television set with hourglass people in its porthole screen.

Peaceful routines revolving around a mother's homemaking, a father's imminent return. Neighbors and elderly relatives visiting late in the day for tea and a chat. Regular sight of military aircraft low overhead, occasional boom of fighter jets flying so fast and high they had ceased to be visible. Glad reunion of family toward evening. President Eisenhower, bald and beaming, on the front page of the afternoon *Times*—a benign and eternally babylike visage.

To have begun life in a middle-class home in a southeast suburb of Rochester, New York, entitles a person to generic memory. Ours was a family of four embarked on a rising tide of disposable income: plenty of money to go on vacation, celebrate holidays, remodel the house. Already we owned a second car and every year traded the old one in. Life proceeded as a festive round of birthdays and promotions. My father snapped a picture or two while my mother cut the cake.

The camera came out on every occasion. Consequently, there are a lot of photographs. Since my father worked for Eastman Kodak, we always had the newest easy-to-use model. By the late fifties we had color prints. Desirous of clean, utopian images, we'd await development of a roll of film, eager to behold this proof of our life's perfection, but there was seldom anything we hadn't already seen. Year after year the same old Christmas, winter snowfall and summer backyard, birthday, picnic, and lakeside vacation, children lengthening and grownups going a little more gray. None achieved the ideality of what was called the "Kodak Moment," but we seemed content. Once maybe every three years we'd take down the album and reminisce about good family times. In truth we had such times.

The snapshot album, the carousel of slides, present but a shell of bygone life. The child suspended on the backyard swing hears forever the drone of propellers aloft. There's nothing to fear and everything to love, yet a chill pervades the late afternoon as the swing set's shadow spills over the grass.

Already this child can hear the words: Escape. Escape if you can.

Kodak *Elegy*

1

Leaving Walden Road

My earliest memory recalls an event that could only have been a dream. I am on the floor in front of a fireplace examining the weave of an immaculately white carpet. Dad and Tom on their knees beside me do likewise. There's something wrong with the state of our house, and we're determined to know what it is. The log in the fireplace has shrunk to a carcass of embers. A window stands open, and cold, heavy air pours over our backs. In the kitchen my mother's voice twice calls my name. Suddenly, a flame leaps from the carpet. First there is one, but already there are several. They multiply beneath my father's hand as he tries to slap them out. Throughout the living room, every way I turn, I see the same little flames: scaling the drapes, mounting the furniture. They close ranks and begin to march as in a Disney cartoon. They leave scorch marks that look like a kind of writing. Wholly concerned with my own welfare, I get up and run ahead of the others through the wood-paneled den where the TV speaks vacantly. Then I cross the kitchen to the heavy back door with its stiff-turning knob. Here I am stopped, or perhaps simply checked, but in any case at dream's end—left, now as then, to puzzle over the after-sensation: a panic at being entrapped, a manic intent to break free.

Fire was my father's great phobic object. What else might a prosperous man at midlife, secure in his family and professional standing, fear with a primal, unreasoned dread? I take this dream as evidence of that dread, and of the part a father's fear may play in a son's formation. His own first memory was of a midnight blaze in the Boston row-house neighborhood where he began life. Still an infant when his father found work in the old Eastman shops, prompting the family's move to Rochester, he drew this recollection from his parents' reminiscence. It was nevertheless a memory

1

Slated for demolition, Penfield Road. Courtesy Brighton Municipal Historian Collection.

to build upon. As the man who for a quarter century oversaw Kodak Park's coal-fed generators, his attitude toward fire bespoke a dispensation in which servants were never permitted to usurp their masters. He'd quote the old proverb: a good servant but a bad master. Totally destructive when left to itself, fire admitted of rational and productive application. It served at the technocrat's confident beck. A professional engineer whose mind mirrored the solemn scientific mood of midcentury, my father took the optimist's view of force available in the Atomic Age. Genuinely moral and prudent men could adapt such force to a peacetime world. Every citizen stood to benefit from the results: safe and efficient fully manned factories, well-lighted houses, churches, and schools. Such order was menaced from without by communists and spoiled from within by politicians who misunderstood economics and human nature. Or, worse, understood those topics but sabotaged matters in pursuit of public careers, pandering to a raw, uneducable crowd whose narrow self-interest consumed the world.

He voiced these views with the air of a man who knew what it was to be crossed in a benevolent aim. The scene for me is fixed in hallucinatory vividness: my father and grandfather philosophizing in the kitchen before supper. Dad, still in his suit and tie, a tall, balding, contemplative man with mildly astigmatic gaze; Gramps, the companionable, white-haired gent, taking his sip of bourbon midsentence. My world took necessary shape from their words. Nature is predictable and so too are people. Most people at most times are rational: working together in a common purpose, they achieve high and even selfless ends. Some are destined to plan and lead, others to follow along. To be rational, however, is never enough, and wise men preserve a sense of humility. Let down your guard, and in no time at all your fire will turn and devour your substance. Its slight, unde-tected errant movement leads to the misrule of giant conflagrations. My father seldom questioned his belief that he was doing his level best or that he was fairly rewarded for his good stewardship. No one took greater sat-isfaction in the ordered disposition of work, home, family, nation. Reflect-ing, no doubt, the intensity of that satisfaction, my father's dread came out in a vigilance that verged on metaphysics and compulsion—an eye to the inevitably frayed end of cords, ashtrays heaped with my grandfather's pipe embers, matchbooks left in children's reach by workmen enlarging the side porch.

Our house, a center-entrance colonial at 68 Walden Road, never did burn down. Perhaps, as my mother alleged, it came close when at age five I lit a match inside my parents' closet so that I might see into its darkness. For punishment my mother made me confess this misdeed to my father when he returned from work. By then he had been informed of the incident and received my account with all-knowing calm. The house never burned, but as a child of six I imagined it vaporizing in the wave of an atomic blast, for ours was the first TV generation and we'd seen what atom bombs can do to wooden houses. Our minds were full of newsreel footage of London, Berlin, and Hiroshima under bombardment, as World War II reigned as the great defining public memory. Such images didn't seem to disturb us. We watched *Victory at Sea* and endless scenes of nighttime air raids, the TV screen gray with bursts of fire, sirens wailing beneath the continuous pop, little ashen people hustling for cover. We watched with the serene consciousness that America had won this war—that America won wars. No doubt we were learning that in ten years' time, the stakes had gone up. We watched mushroom clouds rising above Japan, Nevada, Bikini Atoll.

We watched communist troops spill into the streets of Eastern Europe and Southeast Asia. We watched airmen in oxygen masks wedge into jet bombers for combat in cold, moonscaped Korea. Then, going outside to play, we had the run of our isolated, tree-lined suburban neighborhood.

Walden Road is a semicircular loop that branches off Greenaway Road, rejoining it after an eighth of a mile. On both streets stand two-and-a-half-story wooden colonial and beam-and-stucco Tudor houses put up in the twenties, no two exactly alike, shaded by large oaks. The Tudor houses have steep roofs with eyebrow dormers that come into view as a treetop sways. Thick shrubbery and full-grown trees make for hidden recesses and blind corners. As children we had exclusive access to passageways, tunnels that ran through bushes planted along property lines, tree paths that led among interlocking branches. As a child I enjoyed the sensation of vanishing from the view of observers, real or imagined, into the bush. No one disapproved of what we did or set limits on our mobility within these circular precincts. It was simply play, unobserved and absolute, and the cellars and bunkers, hideouts and bedrooms of our undisclosed child-hood space remained (so far as we knew) unknown to our parents, who made no special effort to rule them. Once, when my brother was two, he disappeared for an hour. After a frantic search he was discovered in an upstairs room of the house across the street, playing with a wooden train set. No one had been at home, and he had simply let himself in. But this is the only instance I recall when extraordinary measures had to be taken to locate a child. My mother had a police whistle, and two long blasts gener-ally served to fetch us home.

Not that our streets weren't bounded by what a parent would consider hazards. To the south was a heavily trafficked country road that was fast becoming a suburban thoroughfare. To the north, down an embankment that defined the limit of the Greenaway Road backyards, lay the New York Central mainline right-of-way. To the west were streets and houses like our own, including a house that was supposed to be the boyhood home of a former US senator. Up that way lived enemy bands of boys and girls. No demographic difference distinguished the neighborhood's east from its west end, but the feud persisted and an occasional skirmish called one to frontline duty. To the southwest, beyond some backyards, lay what to a child's mind was an undefined area overgrown with bushes and trees. This marked a corridor that had first been a deer and Indian path, then a migration route for early settlers, then a secret spur of the Underground Railroad. Or so an elderly neighbor once explained. Now it lay fallow, with a narrow roadway and what appeared to be gravestones dissolving into vegetation. Legend flourished in this rank tract. Wasn't there, far back among the tangled trees and wild bushes, a tarpaper shack in which some crazy person lived? A raving person with long hair, neither man nor woman? A person, even, with dark skin, Iroquois or African? So ran the speculation. One November, when the leaves were down, and the great dry body of the underbrush lay dead on the hard ground, and you could see all the way to the construction sites on the other side of the corridor, we searched for this neighbor. Except for a hole in the ground with the charred remains of a campfire, we found no trace of a hidden resident.

The New York Central right-of-way, scene ever of astounding visitations, was the great captor of juvenile attention, and anxious parents worried about kids ducking the fence and skipping down the embankment. One mother told horror stories of a boy whose foot had become lodged between rail and wooden tie. It was hard for anyone to reach the tracks without a parent yelling and a phone call placed to the child's home. Such casual surveillance evidently worked. Most of my playmates had ventured once, but only once, down to the tracks. When we saw boys from other neighborhoods walking the rails, they seemed strangely orphaned, pathetic in their lack of parental oversight. The trains came frequently and fast. Passenger trains bound for Buffalo and Chicago and, in the other direction, New York City shot by in an aluminum streak.

At the edge of my friend Pete Radner's backyard, I sat in a tree that overlooked the embankment and gazed at the gleaming rails. These were, we'd been warned, *live* tracks, and the longer I gazed the more I could see that they vibrated with premonition, intelligent of arrivals more or less imminent, while the wires overhead shone and hummed with electric talk. The sunlight itself smelled of creosote. I was drawn to the embankment as to the verge of another world. The one time I cleared the fence and stepped down to the right-of-way marked a first acquaintance with forbidden euphoria, but the half-minute spent tight-walking the tracks sufficed, for at the top of the embankment our neighborhood ended and the railroad belonged to an order of existence that suspended the guarantees of quiet streets and green backyards. I felt, that one time, as though I had literally gone behind my parents' backs, and the happy terror of treading the rail was quickly supplanted by the feeling of having strayed beyond the protecting body of my neighborhood. The New York Central mainline offered spectacle to the watcher but mostly danger to children compelled to place pennies, beer cans, or stones on the rails, or who lay down on the ties and pretended to sleep.

From the security of the tree I surveyed the vacancy of the empty tracks. I first felt and then heard, two or three minutes before the train's appearance, the thud of its approach, the engine's growl, the resonant whoosh of its passage through right-of-way a quarter mile off, the rhythmic clatter of miscellaneous freight. At last the lead engine came into view, floating above the track, its headlamp puncturing the afternoon haze. The engines arrived in a wave of brown air, hot gusts lifting the leaves palm upward, and as the plume cleared I kept close count as boxcars, tankers, hoppers, and flatcars shuddered and jarred and lurched by. They bore the distinctive colors and emblems of the many rail companies and regions, far-off places like Oregon, California, and Maine. Extraordinary trains occasionally passed by, some that carried nothing but scrap, hoppers of shredded tin, or flatcars bearing defunct gargantuan machinery: blackened shards of retired smelters, shattered gear wheels, jagged shanks of sheet-metal housing. Cattle trains offered more variety, the smell of manure melding with diesel fumes, a humanlike lowing of animals audible behind the moaning wheels. Most exciting of all were the trains loaded with military hardware: tanks with long cannon, armored personnel carriers, bulldozers painted in camouflage. They would be, we were sure, on their way to protect Western Europe. No one ever wanted to miss those trains.

The spectacle got into my sleep, and the waking exhilaration of train watching was matched now and then by a nightmare in which a coal train derailed into the path of a passenger express. Coal trains on those tracks were already a strange sight, for in waking life they passed infrequently by our neighborhood. We would see them on the lakeshore line when we visited my aunt Jane and uncle Johnny at their home on Lake Ontario;

the coal would be headed to my father's generators. As the dream played out, passenger coaches and coal hoppers smashed relentlessly, burst into flame, and piled on one another until they topped the embankment. I knew people were trapped in the cars even though I couldn't see them. The heavy wreckage plowed through the fence and into the Greenaway Road backyards, slashing the lawn and spewing coal everywhere, while I, mindful of sharp-edged debris, fought to step clear and dash home.

The strife of the railroad contrasted with the tranquillity of the pioneer corridor. Forming as it did the southwest border of the neighborhood, it seemed westward and frontierlike. We could go a little ways into the bushes and build a hut; we could look around and see nothing but stands of long grass encroached on all sides by volunteer saplings. Ghosts of the migratory and fugitive people who had passed this way peered from the underbrush. We could imagine an indefinite expanse of land stretching over a continent. Yet we were seldom more than a minute's walk from the supper table.

It was in that contained but mazelike, that unpredictably meandering, expanse, a moment's walk from the supper table, that I first got lost. No one but I ever knew about it. The day was overcast and chill, sometime in late May; an airplane circled absently overhead. I had been investigating the large ephemeral puddles found here and there in the turf, each with a vigilant frog or two that vanished in August when the pool dried up. I had been moving in reference to a roofline, losing sight of it when I took an unfamiliar turn around a group of trees that extended farther than anticipated. When I got by the trees, the chimneys presented what seemed a different look. I kept walking, taking another turn around a stand of saplings before finding myself inside it without having marked the entrance. Sunlight had begun to bore little holes in the low clouds that overhung the day, and these trees, erupting in the season's first featherlike leaf, were thick with it. I walked on, held in my progress by the light that shifted among the trees and moment by moment thickened.

The light intensified, and I could see that the wood fell away a short space ahead. The sky to the south shone blue, remote beyond the milky sheen that clung to this second growth. What lay before me at ground level was not yet clear. Small heaps of things—paper bags, newspapers, empty bottles—lay under the trees toward which the path had begun to slope, and farther down I saw a longer, man-sized heap wrapped in a ragged blanket, while the sound of cars announced the presence of the busy road to the south that we were under orders not even to think about crossing. I recognized a large stucco house on the other side of the road. This was far-off, unfamiliar territory, although still on the edge of home ground. I would need to start back. Yet, when I turned around, I saw that my path was one on which many paths converged, and I could retrace my steps only a slight distance before landmarks merged and I was left to map the return trip by inner eye. Vaguely, as I did that, I was aware of the possibility of panic, a paralyzing anxiety emanating from my knees as I longed to be home that very instant, certain that my father had arrived, that I had been looked for, called to, convinced that I was hearing the police whistle. The light had drawn back into the low angles of early evening, and the paths wound confusedly among long shadow and copper glance. This is what it was to be lost, to be unable to get there from here, to be where one didn't want to be. My parents were missing me, I was sure, and were themselves beginning to panic. I could be a heap in the underbrush and they wouldn't know. For maybe five minutes I walked in interlocking circles studying rooflines, yet the second I had my bearings I was as good as home. Going in through the kitchen door, I was greeted by the familiar sight of my father and grandfather sipping bourbon highballs and eating Limburger cheese while my mother cooked. They acknowledged my entrance with the usual interrogatory, unseeing, affectionate greeting.

In after years my wandering would press farther-flung boundaries and lose the trail among far more complicated borderlands—the story, really, of anyone's life. Even then there was home, or the idea, or perhaps simply the retrospect, to contemplate. Home was center and recurrence. As my father had had the foresight to buy the lot on the other side of our driveway, we possessed what to the child's eye seemed like rolling rural space enclosed by bushes and trees. He planted and cultivated shrubs and saplings. My brother and I grew radishes and tomatoes and set up a vegetable stand made of root-beer crates, imitating a common sight of the countryside between the villages. My father pruned his shrubs while Tom and I sat immersed in a great pile of sandy soil, creating roads and villages for our toy cars. From our shaded play area in the side lot we heard running water and a clank of pots in the kitchen, and my mother singing.

ONLY AS AN ADULT could I appreciate the fact that the neighborhood in which my life began was my parents' first freely chosen place, far from their original city neighborhoods. They had married late, my mother thirty, my father thirty-five, then had lived a year in my mother's large childhood home, newly converted into a duplex. The Depression, the war, care of old folks, care of siblings had delayed my parents' marriage. Their lives, when I was born in December 1951, were more nearly their own than ever before, and their life together was a happy condition that consciously refuted the diminished expectation each had formed as a young adult. They had succeeded in changing the plot of the story. Their happiness was ever mindful of the shadow from which it had emerged. Our material well-being, rather than inciting them to banish thought of hard times, caused them rather to conjure its memory. In prosperity they persisted in scraping out the residue of a mayonnaise jar, prompted by a reflex that regarded the cupboard's bounty as temporary if not illusory. My father drove nothing fancier than top-of-the-line Chevrolets from my uncle Johnny Heinrich's "Chevyland" dealership. The Walden Road household, as far as I could tell, never required pinching economies. We had new cameras every year and always enough film to waste on shots snapped before people were ready. For the time being the problems of life were solved.

Some of our relatives and many of my parents' friends still lived in the city, although more and more had been making the switch to suburban life. I enjoyed visiting city relatives and observing the large old two-and-a-half-story houses of the city neighborhoods, stacked in file with narrow side yards. I loved the sight of the small groceries, restaurants, and taverns, their glowing neon beer signs giving the day a nighttime quality. The Jewish delicatessens with their illuminated Hebrew characters spoke of remote and ancient realms. I wasn't very old before I associated those neighborhoods and their mix of peoples with the "Old World," the Europe of the two world wars, and was fascinated by the story of how my uncle Ott's family, owing to their German name, had found themselves the target of violence—stones hurled through windows, slurs scrawled on doors. Riding about the inner city, I enjoyed viewing the churches and synagogues, social clubs and union halls. But a block away from the major thoroughfares the city suddenly became cramped and angular, and there was the fearsome look of narrow streets where broken clapboards and busted screen doors hung from wooden houses, or where blackened windows and charred roof beams complicated the picture of an otherwise normal house with a Christmas wreath. Not yet schooled in racial vocabulary, I noticed that people who lived on those streets were often not white. Something was telling me that normality centered in my own neighborhood.

I was happy to live where we did. In this leafy, well-established near suburb, neighborhood ideals survived. No one would ever think of throwing a stone at someone's house. A resident of these streets might have any kind of name—German, English, Irish, Jewish. The grown-ups greeted one another and the children addressed them as "uncle" or "aunt." Most of the men in their prime worked for Kodak; accustomed to wartime gasoline rationing, they carpooled well into the fifties. The hospitality of the home complemented the sociability of the sidewalk. I could sense that our home, with its flexible inner space on a quiet street enclosed by huge trees, instilled ease in our guests. Adults had room to stretch their legs and enjoy their liquor, laugh uproariously, bellow as one or another struck out a tune on our parlor grand, or fall asleep in one of numerous oversized chairs. My father's reserve adjusted to his guests' boisterous merriment while my mother managed the refreshments and bridge games. No one went home early from this house where, on winter nights, good-natured folks gathered about the affluent blaze of our fireplace. On occasion, late-night revelers descended on our household. For my parents, the amusement and flattery of such visits more than compensated for the inconvenience.

Five days a week Harold A. Decker arose early and rode nine miles north and west to Kodak Park, as George Eastman styled the company's large Rochester compound. A world unto itself from which nonemployees were rigorously excluded, Kodak Park, with its interconnecting red-brick buildings, some as long as a city block, didn't condescend to a child's capacity: enough for me to know that the company commanded my father's loyalty and that our house, food, and clothing derived from the success of its cameras, film, and blue-chip stock. That was a connection I was made to understand early. The child in me who was becoming aware that a word did not always mean the same thing noted that Kodak *Park* was not a park in the sense that Mendon Ponds—with its sandy beach, muddy wading, and gushing water pumps—was a park. Flanking a mile or more of Lake Avenue and Ridge Road, Kodak Park presented the aspect of a walled city. Among its rational and immaculate spaces stood factories, cooling towers, smokestacks, in massive profile, entrance to and egress from which were regulated by gates and checkpoints. At certain times of the day people streamed in and out. At night the complex lay under a green floodlighted haze, smokestacks hung with red blinking lights, high walls vibrating with a constant, electric, silencing hum. A piercing smell, as of vinegary cooking, pervaded the Park's environs.

Children and families were not permitted to visit the offices, laboratories, and factories at Kodak Park. At nineteen I would hold a summer job there as a night janitor, filling in for regulars taking vacation time, and so finally have a good look inside the place. But while I was growing up there was no once-a-year "open house." Kids with non-Kodak dads spoke of those occasions in which they got to see the machinery their fathers handled. My dad would explain that the machinery at Kodak Park, his machinery at least, was very large. There was the matter, furthermore, of security, for Kodak had government contracts, and there were secrets the company had to keep from other film and chemical firms. Every employee, even a supervising engineer like my father, was required to present a large, laminated identity badge to gain admission to the Park. In the photograph on his badge, my dad, bald with horn-rimmed glasses, severely set in business suit and tie, bears a stiff, closed-mouth, in-the-know smile against a mustard background, the assertive yellow of Kodak's trade color. I would have loved to have seen his office, met Miss Gore, his "old-maid" secretary, and followed him on his rounds. From pictures in the company newsletter I knew that he might spend some of his day wearing a smock, safety glasses, and hard hat, that he might be engaged in examining blueprints or shaking hands with dark-suited middle-aged men from Pittsburgh or Chicago, representing a company from which he had bought a million-dollar boiler. And I knew, from visits to the lobby of a building on the Park's perimeter where we would sometimes stop to pick up a packet of photographs, that there were a good many middle-aged men similarly dressed who all smiled the same closed-mouth smile and seemed to assume the same attitude: a self-importance that expressed itself in practice, not talk, and that met philosophical challenge with baffled and haughty indifference.

When my father returned in the evening he never had much to say about his day. A boiler that needed replacing, a contract to buy more West Virginia coal: to these he would briefly allude when asked about the workday's agenda, as though to deprecate the notion that a story could be spun from such stuff. The nature of his work and the structure of his time always remained a mystery. I had to imagine the interiors of Kodak Park and my father's day there. At some point I formed the conception of his office as a large room with small windows, spare of furniture: a broad metal desk with a few papers on it, and metal filing cabinets, pale green in color, matching the walls. The atmosphere was vaguely military. One window admitted north light—the washed-out light of a Rochester winter—while a long glass inset on the other side looked down on a boiler room in which men tended furnaces, opening and closing a set of hatches that gave on to a fire. Under my father's supervision, the fire was maintained always at white heat. Miss Gore would step out of her cubbyhole office, papers in hand, and after a few seconds step back in. Other scenes I imagined included a long hall of turbine engines cast in emerald light where men dressed in white smocks monitored gauges, and a long wooden table at which my father convened with other managers in business suits. Sitting always at the head of the table, Dad calmly delegated tasks. Over the years I might revise these scenes, but they would always retain their basic features. During my summer as a night janitor I was never assigned my father's building. It was hard at the time to admit to myself that this was the summer's chief disappointment. To this day I picture my father's workspace with a small child's images.

Naturally, it was suggested that my brother and I would grow up, become engineers, and work for Kodak. But who, really, expected that?

Not my father, whose own father preceded him in the firm, but who never planned to be in Rochester past his eighteenth year. My grandmother fancied him enrolling at Harvard, a career in Boston or New York to follow. He himself just wanted to travel and, leaving worry behind, see Europe, California. My grandfather's death and grandmother's brain tumors, along with the Great Depression, put an end to those thoughts. My father would consider himself lucky to graduate from the University of Rochester and proceed directly to a position at Kodak Park. Promotions came fast, and by the time the United States had declared war, the military value of his civilian post (Kodak supported reconnaissance photography and helped develop ordnance) was too great for him to be drawn into the armed forces. So the variation and adventure of a commission were not his experience.

Not that he complained about the way life turned out. And not that he wouldn't have liked his sons to become engineers and join the firm. They might train for other professions and still work for Kodak, an organization of multiple mansions with places for individuals of various gifts. As a child I looked upon Kodak as the place where I would work one day, skipping ahead of those chapters that dealt with the occult details of maturation. It would always be easier to visualize the life my position at Kodak would entail—a good, clean, ordered, suburban existence—than to imagine the work itself. Through early and middle childhood, I took it on faith that I would have that life. Inside me dwelt a prefabricated adult who would one day awake, unfold, and possess all the strengths and capacities of my father, whose manifold duties and resourcefulness in meeting them I recognized without understanding. The process was unknowable, and in my puzzlement I thought of the mystery shrouding the metamorphosis of cicadas. From nowhere in late summer they burst into voluble winged life, abandoning their exoskeletons on fence palings and tree trunks like outworn toys. The adult *me* would emerge ready-made, educated, and able to explain himself. The years ahead might clarify that process, but the notion of working for Kodak would never become less remote.

My mother, Marion, was harder to know than my father. What did you need to know about someone who cooked your meals, sang to you, bathed and put you to bed, got you up, and dressed you in clothes exhaling a fresh laundry scent? Such a person might well prove to be as elusive as yourself, whose presence you likewise took for granted. A wife and home-maker whose own mother died when she was thirteen and who, owing to the state of the world, had her children late—at ages thirty-six and thirty-eight—she grew up the youngest of three daughters in a household of strong personalities. There was her father, George Culp, my own Gramps, beloved fixture of our dinner table, a man who had led a restless career as banker, adman, actor, and singer, and who had sailed a succession of gorgeous boats docked at the Rochester Yacht Club, where he served a term as commodore. He spent a year away from his family in San Fran-cisco, working for the Bank of Italy and performing in local productions of Gilbert and Sullivan. He answered to no one but his mother, a power-ful woman who had divorced her first husband (my great-grandfather, a musician who drank), painted china, penned newspaper poetry, invested in the stock market, and pronounced on all subjects. She ran the household during my mother's teenage years. Mooma (as she was known) dispensed sympathy in bulk measure, but she could also ask too much of tender youth, as when she retrieved a cousin dying of cancer from a small town in southern New York and established her in my mother's room as an elderly dying roommate. Although the family was Episcopalian, Marion attended Catholic school from which she graduated at age sixteen nearly at the top of her class. Out of school the following fall, she had just worked up courage to ask her father to let her enroll in the small Catholic college when, in October, the market crashed.

Trim and attentive, she watched at the window for my return from half-day kindergarten, the bus depositing me on the corner. She met my homecoming with an elaborate lunch and conversation directed to my school activities, interests, and opinions. After lunch I watched TV, *Our Miss Brooks,* perhaps, or *The Millionaire,* with the deep but semiconscious recognition that my mere presence for her was a source of happiness. She would monitor my departure when, as a first and second grader, I walked the half mile to Indian Landing Elementary. There was a stretch of that walk—from the railroad underpass to the crosswalk opposite the school—that worried her, but I know she understood the pleasure I took making my way in the morning light. She herself spoke of the joys of solitude, home alone or off by yourself. When I returned from school she was always there at 68 Walden as though she and the house were one. But some of my most vivid memories concern her absence in the late afternoon or for a whole day in June or July. She'd go off to play bridge or join a ladies' excursion to Canandaigua Lake, and my brother and I would be watched by one of two old women: Mrs. Ameele, a Dutch lady who lived just inside the city limits, or Mrs. Frye, who occupied the mother-in-law wing of her daughter's Walden Road house. They'd tote big handbags containing whatever they happened to be knitting. Mrs. Frye followed soap operas—when she wasn't actually watching one, she checked the clock in anticipation. Mrs. Ameele sneered at the idea of soap operas. From this we learned that not all adults, and not all old ladies, were alike.

UNTIL I WAS EIGHT all outbound paths ultimately reversed direction: one ventured so far and then came back. In season and out, home held us in its deep gravitational field. The summer I was three, my mother was thought to be terminally ill, and my father hired a succession of housekeepers. But I have no way of knowing to what degree, or even whether, those circumstances fostered a premonition of loss. When I was four my paternal grandmother died, but her death hardly changed what for me had always been her status as a white-haired deceased person in a redbrick nursing home set among trees and a crystal brook, reached only after an intolerably long drive. Well might such a place, in all its remoteness, serve as an image of heaven. I recall scenes but no necessary progress. Three times in my first eight years I underwent abdominal surgery. My stays in the children's ward acquainted me a little with other people's suffering. The boy in the next bed had been scorched by burning gasoline; once during an adjustment to his dressings I caught a glimpse of buttocks all purple and black. The nurse who administered enemas thought I should know about the wing set aside for children with polio—such knowledge might encourage more fortunate children to count their blessings. I can still hear the bleatlike wail of a girl in the ward across the hall. But my own constitution, the only real concern, remained sound. My bones grew in my sleep. Faculties quickened as childhood threw off layers of somnolence. As I woke to some things, I fell asleep to others. All this was normal.

The photo albums document a conventional process of growth: eyes and mouth gathering definition, legs gaining spring. I had no reason to be aware that my parents got older, little reason to suspect that their life had a story, perhaps many stories, unfolding in the bland repetition of days.

But lives change, people have stories, one goes from here to there. On my eighth birthday, just after supper and our customarily frugal opening of gifts, my parents told me about the new house. My brother looked on; he'd heard this presentation a few hours earlier. Very simply but to me quite shockingly: our current house was now the old house. We would be leaving it.

My parents had been plotting this step a long time. From earliest childhood I'd been aware of construction projects along the roads leading to our neighborhood. High-rise apartments newly flanked East Avenue on the other side of the pioneer corridor. The country byways that connected the villages south of the city had become thoroughfares. Where the eye was accustomed to rolling meadow one suddenly noticed housing tracts, ribbons of bright, newly laid concrete lacing shorn ground, houses framed, roofed, and landscaped over the course of months. The villages had surrendered their rural character. None of this had much affected us in our neighborhood, long established and set in its own little wood. But now an expressway was to be built between the suburbs to the south and the city to the north, and it was to follow the pioneer corridor.

Twenty years later, discussion of the expressway's routing still roused my father's ire. During college he had worked as a civil engineer, and thus in his view he could expertly criticize the way city and county politicians rammed the inner and outer loops—as they are called—needlessly through neighborhoods, requiring unnecessary demolitions and excavations in rocky substrata. There had been, to his mind, easier, cheaper, more reasoned solutions. Not that he was displeased at having moved. My parents had planned all along to custom-build a house when finances permitted. It was the large-scale, coordinated imbecility that galled him, the typical stupidity of public officials and government bureaucrats imposing their schemes. In 1959 my brother and I sensed his displeasure, but we were naturally caught up in the excitement of heavy machinery and, somewhat later, the anxiety and sadness of the move.

The first sign of change, long before the arrival of the giant yellow equipment, before the endless warnings not to trespass the construction site and, if we did, not to pick up blasting caps, before the noise and dust and unctuous smell of machines gouging earth and rock, was the abandonment of several large houses on the busy road that bordered our neighborhood to the east. The expressway was to pass not through those sites exactly, but beneath them, on a right-of-way scooped out twelve feet below the level of the cellar floors. I remember balking, before demolition commenced, at what seemed the abstraction of that proposal. Not just the houses but also the lots would go, and the earth would be reshaped, as though made of putty. The site engineer, in hard hat, dress shirt, and tie, confirmed it all. You could remake anything with the right kind of machinery. The mess would go away as quickly as it came. After the earth was recontoured and landscaped, you wouldn't hear the traffic, wouldn't know there was a highway there, unless you looked. My father (the bigger and smarter engineer) wasn't having any of that. Their homes bought out from under them, the families one by one packed up and left.

Large elms bordering the street were reduced to stumps. What had been well-maintained wood-frame and stucco houses with flowers in the yards stood vacant. The grass grew wild. Soon windows were broken in—first isolated panes in the lower stories, but eventually those too in the highest dormers. Six weeks later we witnessed the spectacle of seeing the houses razed, an experience more thrilling, if disturbing, than watching houses rise, a sight just as common in those years. (*Raze*, I remember thinking, was another word that spoke contradictory things—for what then could it mean to raise a barn or be raised from the dead?) While the houses stood vacant they became the haunt of boys and girls too old to prevent from crossing the road, and accounts circulated about how in one house so-and-so's former bedroom was trashed or of how, in another, a glass gallon jug of bleach found in the basement was carried to the third floor, from which it was returned to the basement through the laundry shoot: the jug exploded, it was said, just like a grenade. Catching the spirit of this activity, but not yet ready to cross the road, I attended meetings of the Bottle Bashing Club, a group of kids who got together in the little forest of saplings beside the road along with what empty beer, wine, and liquor bottles we had scavenged. There was a certain connoisseurship to be absorbed from the older boys at such gatherings. The gin bottles from Mr. Benson's trash can, we agreed, produced the most satisfactory pop.

Such knowledge had its price. You would go home and for the first time not have much to say about how you had spent the last two hours. An eight-year-old cannot help but be flattered when older children confide their outlawry, but I sensed the grimness beneath the brag. There was something not right about the fun of breaking glass or smashing bathroom fixtures, of urinating in someone's kitchen or writing obscenities on someone's walls, exploits related with a brittle, dismissive, breathy laugh. The boys who obeyed the call to destroy the insides of the condemned houses felt, no doubt, that there was something horrific about visiting the rooms of a house much like their own—a house that they had once entered as guests—and permitting themselves to go wild, now competing, now cooperating in projects thoroughly destructive. They must have been horrified by the idea that everything on the lot was to be annihilated anyway so their piecemeal destructions couldn't matter. When the facade of the big stucco house was chipped away I could see, in the exposed master bedroom, a strange word, "*Kazi!*" scrawled in tar on the large floral wallpaper. I never found out what the word meant, but the *K* had a stooped-over look, as though it were trying to pose as an *N*. The effect was to suggest *Nazi* and *Kamikaze,* words at the time very much in a child's vocabulary, as well as *Kodak,* alpha and omega of all *K* words. This was my first exposure to the shadow writing known as graffiti. What pleasure could be taken in the condemning of these structures had thus been named.

Finally those houses came down. A week of work in the driest stretch of summer: a crane swinging a wrecking ball against a chimney, a bulldozer fixing its mandibles on a bit of wall, pulling away chunks to be loaded, semimasticated, in the back of a truck, a parched vapor of disintegrating plaster rising from the debris. As I watched them come down I formed an idea of how much material went into a house. Half-razed, the houses brought to mind a photograph in the *World Book Encyclopedia* of war-damaged houses in Belgium. A sound like a ripping thunderclap accompanied the collapse of a big wall, and the ground shook. Spectators gathered on the west side of the street and cheered. This offended my father, as did the fact that many of these people were strangers who came to gawk, having nothing better to do, parking their cars up and down Walden Road. While he didn't forbid our watching the demolitions, he thoroughly disapproved of our doing so. At some point I felt weird and embarrassed to be so interested in the process and didn't watch anymore.

After the houses were leveled, the lushly wooded pioneer corridor went—*everything:* trees, bushes, soil, substratum rock. In its place lay the wide trench that ran all the way to downtown Rochester. It branched, and while one segment proceeded downtown, another wound north and west to Kodak Park and Lake Ontario. The houses across the street from us would stay where they were, a chain-link fence running along the border of their truncated backyards, beyond which, below man-made cliffs, the expressway, Interstate 490, would pass. The houses remained, but the neighbors did not: the two families across from us moved, as did we, before the expressway opened.

IN NOVEMBER 1959 we left Walden Road for Whitewood Lane and the experiences, private and public, of the sixties. We moved two miles south and west but to a very different world: one where houses stood apart and residents affected a lordly mien. That fall, except for the half-dozen structures rising in stark novelty, Whitewood Lane and environs were a wide-open tract. A quarter mile west of the new house lay a stretch of abandoned canal and trolley right-of-way. In four years' time it would be cleared and paved so that the whoosh of continuous high-speed traffic existed as a permanent sonic ground once the line of suburban settlement passed and the land all about us was thick with houses and saplings.

During the first month on Whitewood Lane, I must have missed the interiors of the old house, but what I chiefly remember is that I couldn't look in the direction of Walden Road from my new bedroom's large double window. This window faced west: raw stretches of dark yellow land, a horizon of dull November trees with somewhere beyond it the county airport, a sky empty but for the lights of arriving and departing aircraft. When I recall my first year in the new room, I see above all that vacancy of prospect. In summer the sky was hazy, like a TV screen between programming. Reading on my bed in the hot afternoons, I might doze and dream of its blankness or of invisible words that came into view just as I awoke. In the years ahead the sky from those windows would exist for me as a field of contemplation on which to imagine a future life. Seldom, gazing out at it, did I think of the past.

2

Whitewood Lane

Whitewood Lane loops off Clover Street just south of its sister tract, Indian Spring Lane. I liked the idea of living near a spring, but nowhere, amid the digging and clearing, could you find anything so guilelessly storybook. A red-haired boy no one much liked claimed to have found an arrowhead, but all he produced by way of evidence was a piece of sandstone with a straight edge. Probably, as he said, the Seneca Nation had camped in the vicinity, but nothing made that street especially "Indian." Nor was the origin of "Whitewood" obvious. Perhaps it referred to the fast-growing sycamores planted in the neighborhood's deep front yards, the tract set in a bare expanse that before the war had been the Rochester Country Club's polo grounds. When we occupied the new house, Whitewood Lane was a contractor's work in progress: a street sign (white letters on a green ground), a quarter mile of fresh white pavement ending in a circle, and twenty-two half-acre lots—some graded, some with foundations, and six or seven with completed houses and the rudiments of landscaping. The houses were painted white, but so too were those on Indian Spring. South of Whitewood Lane is an older tree-lined street named Old Mill Road, on the far side of which runs Ebenezer "Indian" Allen's Creek, but no one remembered a mill. I think I knew even then that these names, if not meaningless, bespoke nothing you could touch.

The sycamores have long since matured, the houses assuming the look of dwellings that have stood fifty years and served three generations, but when we moved, Whitewood Lane marked the frontier of Rochester's suburban expansion. All spring and summer, driving over from Walden Road, we watched the house go up. What a difference between the cool shadiness of the old neighborhood and the crude exposure of this new

125 Whitewood Lane. Courtesy of the author.

place, where one ventured through mud and blowing dust and everywhere met direct sun. Still, its lack of solid form was exhilarating; getting atop the dirt pile at the border of our lot, Tom and I could see for what seemed miles. We played in the basement when it was no more than a hole in the ground. Amid great shifting pyramids of dirt (the excavations of basements of houses to be), we followed the progress at our own site: the pouring of concrete, laying of floorboards, erection of the maze of two-by-fours that defined rooms, closets, stairwells. Everything seemed new, from the blond two-by-fours to the virgin nails and nickel-size slugs punched out of the metal boxes that would hold our electrical outlets. Then came the stacks of shingle, gleaming copper wire and pipe, windows, cabinetry, and kitchen hardware. The unvarnished floors echoed with our footsteps, the walls with our voices, which seemed new in this house, awaiting the definition life here would bring.

For several years after we moved in, the smell of newly cut wood and fresh paint lingered in the house. It took almost as long to dampen the echoes. The newness of that house is one of my most permanent of vivid impressions. A colonial ranch with all but the boys' bedrooms and bath on the ground floor (in hale middle age my parents anticipated their years of incapacity), our new home was not so much large as spacious. It was solidly built, and my parents had reason to be pleased, although they'd forever cite little imperfections, small inconveniences they should have had foresight to avoid. They planted our half-acre lot with trees: oak, maple, birch, crabapple, peach, and a well-considered variety of shrubs. When my mother sold the house twenty-eight years later, a forest greeted the new owners. They might not guess that for the first two years the walls stood exposed to wind, dust, noise—dirt blown from nearby construction sites darkening our screens, sifting through the den's corner jalousie windows. Not much you could do about that, or the dogs that romped through our yard day and night, defecating in the new grass and digging in freshly planted beds. We felt at times more encamped than in residence. That first spring my brother and I would come to the back door lacquered in clay from sliding down rain-slickened dirt piles. From dawn to dusk all summer long the pop of hammer and buzz of power saw lived in our ears like tinnitus. Three years passed before Whitewood Lane had its full complement of houses with unbroken green sward growing about them.

But within the first year we enjoyed the amenities of a 1960s upper-middle-class development: a neighborhood newsletter, a bomb shelter, a gregarious family with a pool (my father believed in trees and privacy, and would have had to become another person to install a pool), Christmas

Eve carolers, rival child cliques. My mother renewed acquaintance with a number of old friends migrating to Whitewood and Indian Spring Lanes, former residents of the genteel city neighborhood of her childhood. Quite a few of the middle-aged men worked at Kodak and were my father's colleagues. Thus, many of the neighbors, on the surface at least, were our copy. Yet there was also, very subtly, the presence of another class: the not-quite-middle-aged offspring of Rochesterians with "old money," who spent winter vacations skiing in the Adirondacks and summer weekends boating on Canandaigua Lake, and who possessed a bit more of what passed in those circles for style. These families held membership in the Rochester Country Club. The husbands were bankers, contractors, or Xerox executives, the wives Junior League activists. My two newly minted neighborhood best friends were of this sort. In fact, my first experience of class consciousness came as the guest of these boys at the Rochester Country Club. They had the run of the pool, shower room, and concession stand at which they were entitled to charge drinks and snacks to the family account. But I could feel comfortable only in their proximity, and only half-comfortable then, eyed by other children who were country club members and who recognized me from church or school and knew I didn't belong.

The golf course lay just beyond the backyards of our neighbors across the street. It too felt like foreign terrain, although the low wooden rail that marked its verge encouraged children to prowl at will. In the Walden Road neighborhood the railroad exerted a similar attraction, but the golf course was quieter and offered no such brutality of spectacle. A golf course at the backyard's edge gives a home the feeling of a beachfront residence. Sand traps along the fence help with the impression. Here was this green, affluent, oceanic expanse, navigated by dour men transacting business. The course made little covelike indentations toward some of the backyards where golfers sought shade from the afternoon sun and sat at white wooden tables sipping Canadian beer. In summer there was a pervasive odor of pine emanating from little stands of forest that dotted the course like islands. By dashing from one wooded hillock to another, kids could deeply penetrate the course, and there was a pleasure to be taken in the long perspectives that would open at every doglegged turn. When you stepped from the course into a strange backyard you had the sensation of arriving from a forbidden distance. You could cross this ocean at a particular angle and end up in one of Rochester's wealthiest suburban neighborhoods where the houses resembled Norman castles. My two best friends knew a boy who lived in one of those castles. Calling at his deeply shaded turreted residence one afternoon, we were escorted through a dark wood-paneled hall to an immense kitchen where we were halted before a freezer devoted to ice cream bars. We were instructed to have whatever we wanted—to take two. The boy seemed normal until he sat down at a piano and played the opening of a Beethoven sonata. Performance over, we retired to his ordinary bedroom and read from his stack of *Spider-Man* comics.

Eventually, my family would join a country club where the money was not so ancient and the members not so fashionable, where my parents could meet old friends and form new friendships with people whose experience paralleled their own, and where the golf course, in my father's estimation, was superior. Such distinctions were in any case slight. Superficially—perhaps profoundly—the residents of Whitewood Lane led much the same life, give or take a privilege. Their investment portfolios would have been simple variations, net worth falling within a fairly narrow range. Although there could be no such conscious nuance in the naming of Whitewood Lane, this nevertheless was the whitest of white suburbs. The idea that persons of color would find themselves in the financial position to live on Whitewood Lane was at the time so unfathomable that the question of deliberate exclusion might not have crossed anyone's mind. Yet there must have been something that discouraged Jewish residence and that turned away the newly upper-middle-class Italians in the area. By contrast, the old Walden Road neighborhood had been a mix: the Mendelsohns, whom my mother once described as "patrician Jews," lived two doors up, while over on the corner of Greenaway lived the Radners. Everyone knew the story of how they had escaped Poland at the last possible moment. Once, when I was seven, I observed to my mother that it was truly a shame my playmate Pete Radner couldn't ever be an American. She gently set out to correct my views as to who could and could not be an American and made it clear that Pete, native born, was as much a citizen as I. But surely my theory that being Jewish made for a national difference had not been my invention—had been assimilated from something in the background of our lives. Just off Greenaway lived another Jewish family, the Rosenbergs. At some point I became aware of a middle-aged couple of the same name executed in our very own New York State electric chair for passing secrets to the Soviets. I even saw a picture of them—average-looking grown-ups with European immigrant spectacles. There were all sorts of ways for kids to absorb unspoken attitudes. Still, the working assumption of the old neighborhood was that difference is life as life is given. The elderly couple who lived next door on Walden Road were Catholic German Americans, their house filled with little crucifixes and Mary figurines. Next to them lived a large Irish family, the O'Shaughnessys; Timmy O'Shaughnessy, just my age, was blind. Whitewood, on the other hand, was uniformly WASP, and half the street appeared Sunday morning at Saint Paul's Episcopal Church. No one was especially old; everyone seemed able-bodied and some were assertively athletic. I felt the contrast, but years would pass before I'd understand it.

But already at some level I had grasped the notion that here, on Whitewood Lane, we found ourselves among our triumphant, undifferentiated kind. Our large, happy, dominant group had chosen to live on streets like this. Our lawns were deep, our driveways long, and we all had backyard patios. As motorists, bicyclists, pedestrians, we would always smile and nod. In this regard it was a friendly neighborhood, especially considering that we lacked front porches and certain residents preferred that you not walk on their grass. Several households socialized grandly, and once or twice a year somebody invited the whole neighborhood over for cocktails. My mother always wanted to go, and my reserved but not quite reclusive father would usually come home pleased, after all, they had made the effort. One fine September evening, a yellow school bus hired by the county Republicans came by the houses and picked up nearly everyone on the street, and we all went downtown to hear Governor Rockefeller introduce Richard M. Nixon, candidate for president, who spoke to the assembly's heavily prompted cheering.

It wasn't characteristic of my father to attend a political rally, even of his own party. He abhorred crowds of all description, abhorred politicians and public figures generally, supported but rarely cared to attend the Episcopal church to which we and our neighbors belonged. He felt at ease only at Kodak Park, at his club, and in his own home. Yet here was his home, built to his specifications, among so many others built to the nearly identical specifications of like professionals. There he was, mowing his lawn in the long, muggy summer evenings resonant with lawn mowers far and near. There he was on that bus! And there were we, caught in the demographics of our time and class, swept up into patterns of consumption and desire hard to distinguish, at a certain remove, from those of our neighbors. If we have a story, this is the ostensible—and from some perspectives the essential—part of it. There we were, investigating the new shopping plaza, and there, to compare notes, were our neighbors. There we were, maps in hand, on the road to Florida for spring vacation, and there, when we arrived, were our neighbors. Year in and year out the fathers arose and went to work, the mothers kept house and chauffeured the kids, morning and evening the paper arrived with news of strikes and colonial war. The years ran away: there I was, one September morning, at the small liberal arts college in Ohio, seeing the same faces from suburban Rochester, not differing at all from the faces of kids who had grown up in suburban Cleveland, Detroit, Indianapolis. There we were, with our mixed aspirations and student deferments, downing beers in the college bars, or sitting, with lengthened hair, on the dorm-room floor, passing a joint and comparing notes.

On closer view the picture changes. My family was helping to realize a postwar idea of the good life, an idea that called for two or three children, biannual vacations, frequent car trade-ins, a move at some point to a bigger and better house (yes: even if the expressway hadn't come through, we would have moved from Walden Road). It was a life of highly structured and studiously casual socializing—golf and bridge, ladies here, gents there, occasions for mixed company, planned and unplanned doings for the kids. A more utopian existence couldn't have been imagined by most of the Whitewood Lane residents, or so I scornfully reflected in my teens. Our life was as committed to the positive outlook as were the lives of the Nelsons and Cleavers. Intellectually, spiritually, nothing could have been emptier, and the children who didn't grow up to lead the same life ran off to the barroom, New York City, the university, the Peace Corps, in one or another combination. Yet for my parents and for people of their class and age, what seemed to be denial of the darkling breadth of human experience was by no means unfamiliarity with tragedy. Their every provision affirmed tragedy, and their defensive attitudes proceeded from a lasting store of sorrow. Theirs was always life on the other side of the Great Depression, recompense for sufferings patiently borne, with little expectation that life might hold such ultimate affluence. The child of this house who would one day announce that he had walked the streets north of Main Street and had seen a multitude excluded from this bounty, or who, daring further, would make bold to assert that Bobby Kennedy ought to be New York State's US senator, couldn't get much of a hearing. My parents had traveled too far to Whitewood Lane and were of no mind to see this carefully prepared, this comfortable repose disturbed. I couldn't know that as a teenager. Nor could I appreciate the extent to which the repose was already disturbed by my parents' growing anxiety over their sons, by "what the country was coming to," by my father's slow but steady physical decline, by the vacancies that descend on life's afternoon, the small, sharp panic of seeing the sun pass meridian. These were the stories that developed alongside my parents' survival of the Great Depression, their splendid realization of upper-middle-class ideals. As for my brother and me, the move to Whitewood Lane didn't so much unsettle us (the transformation of Walden Road accomplished that) as complicate the process of passage.

The photo albums from these years present our lives as a cycle of vacations and holidays. Except when caught unawares, we do what we can to look festive. But ready or not there was always an aesthetic flaw; none but my mother would ever succeed as an artistically rendered subject. Year after year we're shown to be opening the same basic gift or stiffly seated with relatives at dinner. In a five-year span my great-aunt Emma, grandfather Culp, and uncle Elwood drop out of the picture. Just after the yearly Christmas collage come the middle-aged guests in zany pose from my parents' annual New Year's Eve bash. Vacation photos depict my mother, brother, and me grouped on the beach or by a roadside vista impatient for the shutter to click. Others document the house through the seasons;

over the course of several years they show a luxuriant maturing of land-scape. The backyard patio with peach trees in bloom made for a striking snapshot to send out-of-state relatives or my mother's English cousin. It even made a setting suitable for a Kodak magazine ad, and one day in late spring a photographer and some professional models descended upon the patio for a shoot. The models—a man and woman, boy and girl, none related—were posed in a series of American Family attitudes. My mother thought I, with my preteen red cheeks, might have what it took to be a boy model and to my mortification asked the photographer for his assessment. The photographer admitted he could always use talent and positioned me by the patio wall. Smile! He promised to phone, and perhaps he did but there was not to be a call back.

If Whitewood Lane answered to anyone's idea of utopia, no one could deny that it existed amid a troubled world madder in reality than anyone wanted to contemplate. Our first four years in the new house corresponded with a turbulent chapter of national experience. In what chronologically is a short stretch of time the country witnessed a presidential election, a Cold War face-off, and a presidential assassination. John Kennedy's election already represented a crisis in the order of things if your parents voted Republican and had an aversion to the Kennedy family based on old-city neighborhood animosities (they were "lace-curtain Irish") combined with a resentment of how savagely they had mastered the capitalist system ("Joe Kennedy would sell his own grandmother"). I saw that Jack Kennedy was a man nine years younger than my father and that he spoke for a world younger than that of my parents: a "new generation" to bear "the torch." What would their world do to ours? Blinding icy winter light flooded the jalousie windows of our den the morning of the inauguration. Home from school with strep throat, I watched the proceedings on television, heard Robert Frost recite "The Gift Outright," and shivered in my sickness as the wind—nearly silencing the elderly Frost—buffeted the cloaked public figures and set about erasing the world as we had known it. That same wind blew about our house. The rawness of our new neighborhood seemed the appropriate if repellent setting for the present tense the Kennedy administration urged upon the country. I had absorbed, as ever, my parents' dread. Everything under Kennedy would be new, except my parents, who were increasingly middle-aged, who distrusted FDR and his Irish movie-star heir, who abhorred the word *charisma,* and who had never been able to hear the music in "Fanfare for the Common Man."

My father had valid as well as irrational objections to "Jack Kennedy and his crowd." One such objection seized upon the contradiction between the president's egalitarian politics and the wealth that environed a Kennedy as though it were as naturally occurring as water and air. No doubt there was something amiss with a country that took such pleasure in the aristocratic posture of its democratic heroes, that loved the marriage of folksiness and haute couture celebrated every week in *Life* magazine. And, later, the idea of the stylish president and his visionary advisers plotting an invasion of Cuba and nearly bungling a missile confrontation troubled my father in ways that he preferred to keep to himself. How could you hope to preserve your family's sense of normality when public events required you to meet with a neighborhood committee concerning the readiness of the bomb shelter and to think about how the street might look in the aftermath of a nuclear exchange? I had strep throat recurrently during the Kennedy years. In the delirious half-sleep of one of my fevers I dreamed that the bombs had come and caught us before we could get to the shelter. I couldn't be sure I was alive or dead, but if alive I had taken new form as an invertebrate being, plasma without border, bone having liquefied and skin burned away, an amoeba in a two-dimensional, blindingly pink, postnuclear world.

The assassination occurred in what memory, although not chronology, makes out to be much later, when I was in seventh grade: the young female social studies teacher took a call from the intercom, then announced with quavering voice that the president had been shot in Dallas an hour earlier. I learned of his death when I got home. There would be no lesson that night at Miss Botsford's ballroom dancing school. Although John F. Kennedy had always been an object of resentment in this household, the mood at home was somber, and my parents felt nothing but sympathy for Jackie Kennedy and her two small children. We followed events on a TV newer and larger than the one on which I'd watched the inauguration. I was much older in the lapse of three years, and this first of several assassinations seems more like a preface to the series of events that would form the background of adolescence than the final chapter of the Kennedy era. But no: I wasn't yet an adolescent and couldn't grasp the political meaning of such things. Public life remained spectacle. I was watching TV when Jack Ruby shot Lee Harvey Oswald, and so were my two best friends. One friend in particular, in our elaborate reenactments of the assassination and subsequent events, imitated Oswald's death yelp with stunning accuracy.

SUMMERS AND SCHOOL VACATIONS made for the best times, or so memory facilely suggests. But what was my actual inward state? I recall a person pathetically aware that his childhood existed as a temporal allowance—a meager and ever-diminishing allotment of summers and holidays—but whose assets were sufficiently ample to put off thought of the end. My neighborhood friends, Kip and Scotty, provided good if unremarkable boy companionship. We did boy things: bicycled freely within a two-mile radius, trespassed the golf course, swam in a neighbor's pool or in the larger and busier country club pool, visited a widow on Old Mill Road who was always good for chocolate bars (a bit stale), camped out in Scotty's backyard playhouse decorated with beer and whiskey labels, caught crawfish in Allen's Creek, and haunted the narrowing strips of suburban woodland. We conceived projects. Scotty's father was the builder of Indian Spring and Whitewood Lanes, and in the side yard of their large wooded residence lay a pile of cinder blocks with which ten-year-olds could freely conjure. One summer we erected a three-story hideout concealed by trees and underbrush. Another project, inspired by *The Untouchables*, involved fashioning toy tommy guns out of wood and sheet metal. We used these to mow down imaginary Mob rivals, making sure first to line them up evenly against the wall. Kip's family had a cabin on Canandaigua Lake, while Scotty's had a cabin and campground in the Thousand Islands. On occasion I'd be drawn into weekend excursions to these places. The boating and cold-water swimming provided great and thoroughly uncomplicated pleasure.

For an hour or so after my return, I experienced everything from a distant perspective, as though a part of me were watching from the water's far side. Once, coming home from Canandaigua Lake, I formed the idea that I was stepping back into a body—my home body—that never left the house and that consequently had been vacant the previous forty-eight hours. Perhaps the core of me couldn't bear to be apart from my parents. Or perhaps I was moved by the recognition that my absence grieved them, happy though they were to see me circulate. When you went away and came back, you saw not only your family but also a bit of the frame that held your lives. A year or so later, returning from another excursion, I was struck by the fact that the frame didn't have to be the way it was. Beyond anyone's explanation—anyone who formed part of this household, at least—it was just that way, and they (but not I, not now, never again) accepted it as inevitable. Suddenly it seemed to me that my parents leaned on that frame at their peril.

I had gone away and come back. Nothing really had changed in my absence, but there had been a passage of time. If nothing had changed, we were nevertheless closer to the moment when things must change. One Friday in June a week before school let out, I went up to the islands with Scotty's family. We fished, boated among the small islands, crossed over to Canada to buy firecrackers, and on Saturday night Scotty's dad set off a fireworks display from the riverbank. Back in Rochester my grandfather was in the hospital. I knew it was serious; I'd overheard my mother pronounce the word *cancer* with an oddly afflicted timbre. I had a great time with Scotty and his fun-loving dad, but all weekend long I maintained a blankness at my mind's center, an empty screen that represented my refusal to think about what I knew must be happening at home. Soon after I returned Sunday evening, my mother drew me aside to tell me my grandfather would not live through the week. In fact, he died the next day.

When as a family we went away and came back, the frame was visible in small details everywhere. Here was our house just as we had left it, and here was the mail, boring stuff mostly: the Kodak employees' newsletter, good for lining the bedroom wastebaskets, the monthly calendar from Saint Paul's Church, bills and bank statements, the latest *Life* magazines: this week Caroline Kennedy, last week Peter Fechter. We would go off, always by car, to the Adirondacks, Quebec, Boston, Ormond Beach, Myrtle Beach, all places that afforded contrast, and when we came back, there, at 125 Whitewood Lane, was the box that held our lives—for the time being. On the return trip from Canada late in August when I was eleven, I awoke in the green neon–lit penumbra of the motel room to thoughts about endings—the end of summer, the deaths of older relatives, the perishability of childhood.

I could see the brevity of childhood in my brother who, as a young teenager, had already left the world of amusements that continued to occupy me in his absence. I profoundly missed his companionship as playmate. He knew more than I, he was larger and better looking, he was confident and authoritative and personally magnetic, whereas I was none of these things. He was exciting to be around, although the price you paid to share his company—if you were a brother two and a half years younger—was a sense of total inadequacy. But he had grown too big to mix with kids my age or even a year older in pickup football games, and he would be embarrassed to play with the electric trains even if he had wished to. He spent a summer of transitions hanging out at a Sunoco station a mile from our house, pumping gas for customers as though he had a paying job. Every so often I bicycled by, but he gave me the impression that it would be better if I didn't. So when neighborhood pals were unavailable I fell back on solitary activities: reading, watching TV, or messing around with my chemistry set or microscope. I'd go off for a sample of pond water and prepare a slide, or prick my finger for a droplet of blood. I spent hours peering into the world of microorganisms, living blobs that wandered about under the lens, combining and dividing before I got bored and rinsed them down the drain. Maybe I'd grow up to be a medical researcher and discover antidotes to pathogens communists put in our water.

Neither my brother nor I took very well to our new schools. Tom ran with wild, problematic boys, precocious smokers interested in fast cars and beer. For a while it would be important for me to hold aloof from him and figure out who I was in addition to being someone's little brother. That would not be easy. Always the second or third youngest in the class, I could assert little physical presence at a point in life when social standing is determined by strength, swiftness, and athletic skill. I drifted by myself or in the company of other unassimilated kids on the classroom and playground peripheries. One spring day during gym class my first year at Council Rock Elementary, I happened to look up: I was playing left outfield with a borrowed mitt, and, barely emerging from my accustomed daze, I picked a ball out of the air like an apple off a tree. That won the game for the group of anonymous boys who were my team. And as though I were living out a fable, for the next two days I was able to smack the ball smartly through the hole between second and third base. But my streak ended as abruptly as it began, and I reverted to the ignominy of the nonathlete. I had fun while it lasted, but it wasn't as if I had petitioned the gods for playground skills.

The classroom was no different. As a student I was erratic, inattentive, sleepy, bored. In moments of alertness I might call out the right answer. Without meaning to, I had put a space between myself and my classmates. My desk was a mess of copying exercises and tests scored and interlineated with blazing red ink. One morning during study hall a sympathetic Jewish girl named Jessica wrote a long letter in careful script and handed it to me just before gym class. Jessica fascinated me: I liked to watch when late in the day she recopied her Hebrew lesson, the deft hand rapidly working right to left, and I figured that anyone acquainted with a language so deeply recondite would have something valuable to say in English. I put the letter in my desk to read later but never afterward succeeded in extracting it from the tangle of papers. Perhaps she had thought better of her outreach and retrieved it after I'd left the room. What message had she so labored to convey?

There were the momentary companions of middle childhood with whom friendship progressed a little way before something in the friend's character or family made further association impossible. A boy named Fred liked to host sleepovers. There'd be milk, cookies, lights out at eleven, but then he'd make us get up at three, sneak outside, and pass silently through a half-dozen backyards to a neighborhood park. Once there, we were to smoke cigarettes, overturn trash cans, and urinate against hydrants ("Let's see who can pee farthest," he whispered. "I bet I can"). A girl named Lee who wore boy things and spoke boy words despite the fact that she was pretty and petite brought me one day to her parentless house to play a game called "Father Says No!" My role was that of a dad administering corporal punishment to a girl unafraid to fight back. Then there was my sort-of friend Rick with whom I sometimes studied math.

He lived in a large white house by the school where kids could always pop in for snacks. One day we arrived to find his mom, dressed as though on her way to a party, mopping the kitchen floor. "Our nigger woman didn't show today," she explained with venomous cheer, in a voice that had no southern inflection to excuse the phrasing. I had thought no person could use that word, not in the polite spaces through which I moved, or at least no one I was obliged to respect. Rick just chuckled and said, "Lazy slut": language you weren't supposed to use in your mom's presence! Right then and there I'd had enough of Rick. On many occasions I'd return home thinking: I don't need friends; I don't need school.

Thinking: I can be lonely. I can bear loneliness; I can live simply to think and read. What if a person went through life missing, at every turn, moments of contact with ideal friends, and what if, friendless at ten, that person were just as friendless at twenty, thirty, forty, until the question expired in a solitude that actively repulsed companionship, a world with room for one person, period? And what was companionship all about anyway but getting together with others to nurse the pathetic satisfaction of not being alone, of imagining all those out-of-it folks stuck in rooms not having fun, lonely losers acutely conscious of the fortunate ones out with their friends? The parties to which my classmates were invited had as their one unifying feature my very personal exclusion. I knew there were individuals, boys and girls, who were never alone, and whose satisfaction in party-going had nothing to do with fear of exclusion, classmates with flowing hair, hard faces, confident carriage. But I was not one of them— not yet. I would start with the face.

I first heard the word *underachiever* in reference to myself. It was an odd term that faulted yet flattered. But I was the younger brother and retained absolute right to determine my place so long as I preserved some minimal role in the social pantomime. Deaf to the gospel of school psy-chologists and guidance counselors, I created for myself a life apart— from my schoolmates, my brother, my parents. Perhaps most kids at that age create such a life and do so with the sad conviction that their own isolation is unique. Too much raw world gets obtruded on an ego with too little power to press the world back. From eight to twelve one constantly struggles to achieve perspective. For brief periods you may conspire with someone cast in the role of best friend, but ultimately it's you and whatever space you learn to impose between self and world. You learn that the eye is in fact the first circle from which you must form the horizon. Sometime in middle childhood I stood before the narrow, arched windows in one of the classrooms at Saint Paul's Church. For some reason I was alone in that room, and the experience of beholding *one* green lawn through *three* identical windows impressed me with what a window can do for one's viewing. I was able, at will, to dissolve that lawn into three related but different lawns and then merge them back together. Vaguely, I was aware that three of anything in a church setting referred to our Trinitarian God, which I'd always accepted as a natural fact, but now that too seemed simply connected to ways of seeing. There were powers to my mind that didn't so much come *from* as *through* me; such powers were not mine to control, not yet. Later I would develop an exercise in which I closed my eyes and saw my life in the world as though monitored on a television screen: first I'd appear and then disappear from view. A variant of this was to imagine a window that looked onto an overcast sky, a gray sea, a field of snow. From this it was a mere step to visualize a blank sheet of paper.

There were various methods visually to shove the world back. But a person had also to invent ways of blocking the schoolroom's incessant chatter, the compulsive haranguing of grown-ups, the radio playing top-forty hits. It helped to have an archive of music and movie dialogue in your head or to be able to hear the needle's drift at the end of the record. A person constantly had to look for remote points of focus. One winter my father and I built a small shortwave radio. In my large upstairs bedroom I draped blankets over a card table and inside this shelter scanned the airwaves for urgent, exotic, incomprehensible speech.

I loved and feared what I visualized as the night sky's lethal asteroid space. In an episode of *Adventures of Superman,* a wicked ventriloquist somehow projects an enormous face onto the night sky. By this contrivance he terrorizes his victims who, attempting to flee the inescapable, drive too fast and plunge off cliffs. I knew better than to fear such phantoms, but I was well acquainted with my mind's irrational and imaginative vein. Sufficiently excited, it operated by its own persuasions. I was terrified by the idea of a huge, bulbous face speaking from the sky to my darkened room: God or his Successor in the grip of a rampage bearing the visage of an animated cinder. I had related horrors of opening the curtain only to see the hands and face of an escaped convict pressed against glass, or the blank-eyed stare of some poor soul shot while scaling the Berlin Wall. No superman existed to police apparitions that emanated from within. But then no supreme being, I was convinced, would lift a finger to prevent the United States and Soviet Union from exchanging missiles while the world slept. While I remained sleepless.

At night in my darkened bedroom, before the trees grew in, I could look to the north and see red blinking lights on the radio towers atop Pinnacle Hill and, to the west, make out the more distant towers near the airport. In their silence they seemed cognizant of schemes, decisions, powers—convergences that remained invisible until the precise moment I'd come in contact with their annihilating force. What if mine were the sole wakeful intelligence correctly ascertaining a threat? On cloudy nights the airport's pale-green searchlights swept the sky. Out in these new open tracts, the sky was large and sound carried. The nights were dark. I recall half waking to the wail of sirens and being frustrated by my inability to judge whether, in their remoteness, they were approaching or receding. I would fall back asleep and then startle awake to utter silence. There was always the terror of that slightly lower-pitched, more drawn-out wail that was the Civil Defense siren. Several times in those years I went down to my parents' bedroom and roused my father for his opinion. He listened carefully before reassuring me that it was a fire engine. I had trouble sleeping during the first years in the new house. One night, in a vivid dream that followed hours of insomnia, I stood in the far corner of our backyard. Day had broken: large canvas fire hoses traversed the lawn, and firemen placed a ladder beneath my bedroom window.

Threat supplied the world's fascination as well as its bedrock terror. The normal world was the world just before the conflagration broke out. The threshold between an ordered existence and one instantaneously deformed was everywhere. The placid look of suburban houses on a warm afternoon belied the fact that anyone and anything might suddenly be thrown into chaos. Longtime residents of Brighton told a particularly unsettling story: one spring morning in the late forties, homes in a quiet neighborhood near the high school started to explode—first one, then the one behind it, then the one next door, and so forth down the block, until the invisible leak in the gas supply was detected and plugged. In one of the wealthy older neighborhoods just off Clover Street, the palatial residence of a chain-store magnate burned as a result of a faulty incinerator. And then, inside the circle of familiarity, my pediatrician's combined home and office caught fire late one summer night. The newspaper described the house as "gutted," and Dr. Evans had been hospitalized with burns on his hands and face from a failed attempt to rescue his wife, who had fallen asleep with a lighted cigarette. Then there was the Wegman Warehouse fire, two miles north of Whitewood Lane: a broad, furry plume of smoke blackening the clear summer sky in the silence before the first siren.

But it wasn't just fires and explosions that changed the world. One evening Scotty and I were walking the shoulder of Clover Street, he on one side, I on the other. We were scavenging for interesting items that turn up on the roadside—car parts, odd bottle caps, coins, you never knew what. Suddenly, I heard the squealing tires of a vehicle in a panic stop and looked over to see a car nose downward and Scotty thrown to the pavement. And then Scotty, screaming, hauled up by his shoulders and placed on the backseat of the car, which took off with yet another squeal of rubber. He was gone as though he had never been! I drifted on, an irrelevant bystander, and had to explain, on reaching home, why my pants were wet and my face drained of blood. On quiet afternoons and early evenings, I would bicycle past these sites with the exhilarating thought that all places on earth were candidates for such visitations.

For a three-month period I caught myself in a recurrent daydream of watching the junior high burn. Flames leaped from the roof as the block-long structure "became engulfed" (as the papers would read) by the fast-moving fire. Columns of evacuated children gazed transfixed from the playground. The vision came upon me as though I were a medium and this an inalterable future event. I myself secretly figured as the one who ignited the solvent-soaked rags in the janitor's closet. But I was blameless: the event had to be; I simply served a large, compelling, unknowable purpose. I hated this vision. Surely, normal people didn't have such thoughts! When it came I tried to blot it out by an image of snow and colorless waves breaking on the beach at my aunt's lakefront house. Over and over I sub-vocalized *radar,* finding a peculiar power in that word to clear my mind. Perhaps I was suffering from nothing more, and nothing less, than a rec-ognition of the damage anyone, even a child, can visit upon the world. What if I grew up and found myself in control of the missiles? Someone in my generation would inherit that charge, provided, of course, we made it to adulthood. Over the summer the vision left, and in mid-July, when I noticed its absence, I felt as though a cosmic weight had been lifted.

There was power in words, and while those passages of the Bible com-monly read in our Episcopal church seemed much the same to my inatten-tive ear, I suspected that Psalms 24 and 91 were written to assuage missile anxieties. One must walk indifferently through "the valley of the shadow of death" and need not fear "the terror by night" or "the arrow that flieth by day." *Arrow* I thought a wonderful word; a missile with nuclear war-head was nothing more than an elaborate arrow. But even more intriguing than Bible verses were commercial trade names, and "Kodak" naturally headed the list. The name itself was a charm, a gem, an incantation. It invoked the force field that guaranteed my family's well-being so long as the war remained cold; in order of importance, Kodak preceded God and country. *Kodak* felt more like the true Word of God than anything I knew from scripture. One day I thought I'd get to the bottom of *Kodak.* Taking a sheet of graph paper, I wrote the word over and over, in capitals, lower-case, horizontally, vertically, diagonally: lower left to upper right, upper right to lower left. What was it about words that begin and end with the same letter? They named entities that were self-enclosed, godlike, aloof from a world they nevertheless governed. *Xerox* worked the same magic. Both names were one letter off from qualifying as palindromes. I liked the crystalline quality of a word like *civic* or *level* and was sure that some-one had studiously engineered the off-balance of *Kodak* and *Xerox.* Pal-indromes belonged to everyone, whereas slight asymmetries reflected a powerful man's will. Asymmetry created the condition of leverage. But George Eastman, Kodak's demigod founder, had been dead for years, and the company was run by a cabinet of men slightly older than my dad. To judge from their group photo in the company newsletter, they all looked alike. Dad might easily blend in someday.

There was power in words, but there was a secret method to drain them of meaning, something I learned from a person I had greatly disesteemed. When Tom's friends congregated in his bedroom, they'd mill about and stroll through my room as though it were a lobby. I'd have to close the door if I wanted privacy, hard to do in mid-July when mucilaginous heat pervaded the upstairs. One time Jimbo (I thought of him as Dumbo, the dumbest of Tom's friends) appeared at the foot of my bed while I was trying to read. "Ever notice," he observed, "that if you say a word over and over it just becomes sound? Like this: glad, glad, glad, glad, glad, glad, glad . . . See what I mean? It means nothing at all!" I performed the experiment and found that it was true. With sufficient repetition a word became an empty shell, a deceased word. I had made a wonderful if frightening discovery. What was I supposed to do with that?

ALTHOUGH KIP AND SCOTTY made reliable companions, I spent much free time by myself in and about the soccer field that you reached by crossing Clover Street, the increasingly busy thoroughfare that bordered our tract on the west. I stood in the center of that field and studied the back of our houses; I noted my bedroom's dormer window among the assortment of rooflines. I contemplated the neighborhood with its fresh white paint and fledgling trees. Then I turned and self-consciously disappeared from view. On the far side of the soccer field was a railroad track that saw maybe a train a day and beyond it the broad swath of land that had once been canal and trolley right-of-way but was destined, like all such land, to become part of the environing asphalt corridor. While it was wild I explored this tract choked in mazelike second growth, and after it was bulldozed I visited the off-hours construction sites. Not just expressway, but houses, apartments, and office buildings would also eventually materialize in this space. The jumbled, half-bulldozed terrain was full of dangers: sinkholes brimming with dark water, junked cars from twenty years ago, sharp and rusty lengths of metal banding in the plowed underbrush. There were bushes that could reduce a shirt to ribbon. In a corner away from the early excavations, amid some bushes and tall grass, I built a shelter out of stones and board, a large, semiferal Siamese cat monitoring my activity. I had recourse to that shelter and that cat throughout a six-week stretch one summer, and once had the satisfaction of sitting through a thunderstorm there. One day in August I found it partly dismantled. Once it had been discovered it was no good as a hermitage, and I never afterward returned to the site.

The single railroad track that divided the soccer field from the canal right-of-way curved, on the one hand, south and east, while on the other it extended north a couple miles before looping west toward the city. The year I was eleven, one of my summer ambitions was to walk that track into the city, or at least until it arrived in some open stretch where I'd become too conspicuous and the project had to be abandoned. The day I selected for this trek was alternately hazy and sunny, hot by midmorning when it was too late to turn back. Yet how fine it was to set out after breakfast, a breeze stirring the dry leaves on the poplars that lined the track. How exhilarating to look straight ahead two miles down this narrow corridor that ran between backyards, slipped past a school, then loitered by the docks of a hardware store, lumberyard, and cement plant before veering toward the city. I could see traffic crossing the track at a nearer and farther street, and thought I could make out the exact point at which the track, just shy of vanishing, curved west. Within twenty minutes of setting out I had passed the school. As I crossed the second of the two streets I noted a first sensation of fatigue, but I was already to the hardware store. I was making good time.

Beyond the lumberyard and cement plant stood a large warehouse belonging to a local dime-store chain. On one of the docks a man stacking pallets looked up at me with evident suspicion. Although I felt sure he had forgotten me in the time it took for him to look down, it was enough to make me feel genuinely off-limits, as though I had now trespassed a remove beyond the familiar off-limits through which I had been treading all morning. His glance gave me to understand that henceforth I was not an accustomed sight. To be on the safe side I left the track and took a dirt path parallel to the railroad. It passed through a brushy lot littered with beer bottles and pages ripped from a girlie magazine. Beyond the lot were more warehouses but also large, boxy wood-frame apartment buildings with kids roaring in the backyards. I could hear the steady rush of traffic on the length of nearby expressway. The track had already curved into the city, the sun had come out to stay, the heat intensified, and the weed lots stank. I felt very strongly I did not want to go on. I had envisioned walking a deserted path that would permit me to observe without having to deal with brawny men and strange children. Before me the railroad angled away from the apartment houses and crossed a bridge over the expressway. The roaring had grown louder, and its source became more distinct. Two boys seemed to have gotten behind me, and I felt as though I were about to be pursued, and then I was:

"There's the fucker!" one of them said.

"He dies!" said the other, and set about hurling stones the size of tennis balls. I feared being hit in the back of the head. One stone bounced and struck me in the calf.

What had I walked into? I had given no thought to an ambush and hadn't the shred of a plan. I was running out of visual screens, not to mention hard shelter. Everyone knew that crossing a long, narrow railroad bridge was a bad idea, but for my purpose I was sure trains came through on that track only in the early morning. So I crossed the bridge.

The boys didn't follow. I found a small hollow beneath the far end and hid there a good half hour. I have no recollection of crossing back. Somehow I must have descended the bank and returned home by neighborhood streets.

When I told the story to friends, I emphasized the view of the city one got from the other side of that bridge: the very old canal buildings, the hotels and department stores, the skyscrapers under construction, the thoroughfares and quieter streets that led to downtown Rochester. I would even embellish the picture to include the blue rim of Lake Ontario some ten miles to the north, although in fact the sky that day was tan with haze and smoke. I wasn't prepared to narrate hostile encounters with boys I couldn't begin to understand. I was far too wedded to ideal notions of my little adventures.

Sometimes, in the strip beyond the soccer field and railroad track, I met kids from other new housing tracts, and occasionally an adult—surveyor or probable pervert—of whom it paid to be wary. A moon-faced, bald-headed man stepped out of an abandoned car one day and, seeing me, clutched his crotch and murmured, "Oooh, oooh!" like Officer Toody on *Car 54*. Another time I fell in with some slightly older boys. One of them merrily observed that it was against the law to be where we were and that at any moment the police might swarm and run us down to the station, where our parents would have to pick us up. "Not me," declared his buddy, displaying a large, evil-looking slingshot. At that moment I formed a conception of being on the other side of the law. We then proceeded to raid the grape arbor of a man who lived on the corridor's edge. As we retreated the boy with the slingshot took out a pane in the man's garage window. Laggard in theft, I returned home feeling guilty and transparent. I'd had a good time, and had thrilled to the sound of the windowpane's pop. But I wasn't cut out to be a hood.

I wasn't cut out to be a hood but, like most kids, was fascinated by the outlawry even good kids seem compelled to explore if only in small, symbolic ways. I felt, as surely all young people feel at regular intervals, something personally annihilating in my parents' system of life. But I figured that, whatever I might do, I'd never get caught, and with very few exceptions did rather safe things, like throw snowballs at fast-moving trains. With my best school friend (different from my neighborhood friends) I'd go into grocery stores and, when no one was looking, peel labels off beer bottles for my beer-label collection. Daring a bit further, we made off one day with some empty beer cartons, folding them up under our shirts. Deciding afterward that we had gone too far, I resolved next time only to swipe labels, but my friend had another idea. To my horror and amusement, there he was stuffing first one and then another bottle into his sweatshirt pockets. I stepped away and maintained a fixed distance, ready at a heartbeat to disown him. Lifting bottles was his decision and his crime. I was not, and had never been, a shoplifter, which I considered stupid and recognized as dangerously habit forming. Only later would I realize—long after we had opened the beer, taken a few swigs, and poured out the rest on the September ragweed—that his crime was directed at impressing me.

His name was Chris Bright, and he and I were best school friends on and off through elementary and junior high. We looked alike and were sometimes taken for brothers. If I were the second youngest in the class, he was the third. Teachers often spoke of his brightness, and when I first knew him he had an enthusiasm that made him seem a grade or two younger. He never scorned an idea you might share with him, however fantastic. He cried hard at a disappointment. One time his dad took us to the canal to fish, and whereas I landed a foot-long carp, Chris's fish got away. The whole way back to his house he whimpered inconsolably. His father, Dr. Bright, was a research chemist at Kodak, a man for whom my dad had great respect, despite what he vaguely alluded to as his personal oddities, which included his clipped manner of speech and his little, red sputtering Renault (normal people drove boat-shaped Chevies, Fords, Buicks). One day the telephone rang. Answering it, my mother froze to the spot and listened a long time. Chris's father had been electrocuted in an accident at Kodak Park. This was something new—someone my age losing his father! Some months later my dad, dismayed over what would prove to be only the first of Helen Bright's breakdowns, wondered aloud how such an easily preventable accident could have happened to such an alert man. I grappled with Dad's unguarded suggestion that this death was no accident. But I tried very hard not to think "suicide." Chris returned from this disaster an alternately sullen and wild boy—still my friend until, a summer later, when I returned from four weeks at camp, I learned that his home had completely dissolved and that he and his two brothers had been named wards of the state. It was as though they had left the world.

Chris stole beer and knew the location of an unmonitored cigarette machine. He had crossed a line but had not gone so far into that new territory that I couldn't accompany him on a parallel yet always technically legitimate track. I soon learned that grown-ups could ignore such fine distinctions. We had stopped at a downtown drugstore for gum when a middle-aged saleswoman came up to me and declared that my shopping was over for the day, wasn't it? Only slowly did it dawn on me I was being accused of shoplifting or (worse—because how could she prove it?) planning a theft. Chris, not up to anything that day, exited the store laughing and waited for me, all indignant, to follow, and laughed again as I cursed the saleslady and her security guard who stood by the door like Joe Friday. Soon thereafter, Chris initiated a series of successful raids on the girlie-magazine rack of a busy South Side mom-and-pop grocery. This started a trend among boys more genuinely bold than even Chris, and before long there was a library of such magazines: *Playboy* and *Penthouse,* but also a sampling of thin, cheap publications full of back-page ads for even clammier gazettes depicting girl-girl spanking and jailhouse trysts—all of it, I remember thinking, a corrupt if strangely compelling application of Kodak technology—hidden in the corner of one boy's garage.

Still this was comparatively tame stuff. It wasn't as disturbing as other things kids did. The studious and well-behaved neighbor girl who flashed her private parts in the woods near our school troubled and fascinated profoundly. A tenth-grade boy's incestuous relation with his ninth-grade sister imparted a nauseating stir to the cafeteria gossip. The world teemed with liberties there for the taking. For a while there circulated rumors of older kids sneaking out at night and gathering at someone's house to drink beer and play strip poker while the parents vacationed in Florida. One began to hear of high school dropouts obtaining prescription drugs and selling them like menu items. Everyone suddenly seemed deep in the woods or headed that way, and even some adults (parents of friends, former teachers) began to exhibit corruptions: a taste for drink, a reckless-ness with motor vehicles, a compulsion to philander, an interest in young bodies. Fathers disappeared from households. The mother of a school friend trotted out a new middle-aged "boyfriend" every month. Only my parents held steadfast, exempt from anything that might impugn their dull good character.

Something remained dangerously unappeased in the amenity of sub-urban living. The pretense to high civilization made everything worse. For me the chief symptoms, summer and winter, were claustrophobia and a sudden onset of hives. But didn't everyone feel it, this emotion somewhere between ennui and rage, a voltage uncontained in the circuit of sanctioned activity? Although I found ways to work it off, I too knew the sensation, as who doesn't—from age ten through one's teens—discern human order as so much bluff designed to mask an underlying chaos, derangement people are powerless to resist? Kids are only too aware of fire and acci-dent, war and disease. They have a premonitory idea of the soft meadows and fascinating chasms that lead to the river of death. Thoughts about the jagged edge could totally dominate your mind if you let them, driving you from scripted roles. A part of me clung a bit desperately to those roles.

Sometimes I didn't mind being home when the time came to be there. I liked my parents' companionship. I knew their reflexes and could amuse myself by starting them off on various tirades. They had a history that wasn't mine and had struggled and suffered honorably. They were losing their vision as I gained my own, but that (so I thought in philosophic mood) simply reflected an inherent flaw in the parent-child relationship. I could keep them company on long winter evenings playing gin at the card table set up in the living room. Escape! Yes—but the teenage urge to flee home confinement ruled my brother more than me. There was something solid to my parents' lives that didn't dissolve in the upper-middle-class medium. And I knew it was only a matter of time before I would leave.

One cold, bright Sunday morning during my eighth-grade year, my parents and I had just finished breakfast when we noticed two police cars and a cluster of neighbors in front of a house three doors down. This was the home of the least-typical Whitewood Lane residents, an elderly woman and her grown daughter. Each winter they spent a month in Florida, and they were there now. The house had been broken into and vandalized, and their car had been stolen. Later that morning the car was found a mile away, abandoned in a snowdrift. Other details emerged: upholstery had been shredded and ketchup flung on walls. These were acts that seemed absolutely to contradict the premise of a place like Whitewood Lane. As the longtime morning paperboy, my brother was summoned to the town hall to answer questions. A day later the detectives summoned him again.

My brother must have had a miserable two days of interviews and an excruciating third day before he stood in my parents' presence to be charged. He had been the accomplice of a boy a year older from Indian Spring Lane who was known to be wild. Later I would understand that Tom never actually entered the house and only reluctantly occupied the passenger seat when the other boy had backed the car out of the garage. It had been a matter of being too close to someone else's adolescent error, but proximities at such times always get blurred and adults seldom know the difference. Criminality, however, formed no part of the family profile. That must have been the perception of the town judge and even the Whitewood Lane neighbors, for my brother got off with a scolding and was permitted even to continue as paperboy. But inside our house there was much to process, and where and how do you begin? No one had much to say, no one felt like talking, confrontation was not my parents' way. I kept my own counsel. I would have to deal with this at school thanks to a spiteful neighbor girl who made it her business to give this tale a scandalous currency. Whatever anger I bore my brother was less memorable than the agonizing perception that he had become, so it seemed, a stranger.

I can see him still, standing before the mirror on the second-floor landing of the Whitewood Lane house, dressed for his court appearance in the cardigan sweater he had received at Christmas, a slight variation from the cardigan I too had received. Our mother's Christmas shopping proceeded by a rule of two: each son, and, later, each daughter-in-law, having to open the nearly identical gift simultaneously. But Christmas was well past, even though the snowdrifts and gray sky would last another month. I was alone in the house while they were away at the police station and alone again several days later when my brother made his court appearance. Whatever his fate, he had succeeded in altering our story. I remember feeling as though something had imploded in the order of things, that the placid outward appearance belied fissures pervading the supporting structures. I recall the large house in the dark afternoon, the somber pleasure of rooms submerged in meager daylight, the tomblike privacy of carpeted space that remained intact if I didn't think about it. When the three came home my mother went through the downstairs rooms, turning on lights and drawing drapes.

Thus, a level of normality was reaffirmed. Even so, my brother had become opaque, and I struggled with the idea that a member of our household had been some unknowable combination of witness to and participant in acts of pure destruction. But had it not occurred to me that I could find myself in that same place? Had I not sacked my gym teacher's closet, shredding his papers and snapping his pens, and had I not pressed my divider point through the principal's sidewall? Was there not something heroic in breaking free at any price? About this time I read in the Sunday supplement an article linking male adolescent outlawry to something called *Eros*. It was my first exposure to that word, and it introduced the thought of an uncontainable fire pursuing many objects only one of which was mindless sexual ecstasy. Eros, I understood, existed as a force within us all. It wasn't rational, it had a destructive agenda, and if in certain mature or gifted people it led to great accomplishment, it nevertheless, since the beginning of time, had set anarchy against order, frenzy against reason, son against father. Feeling, as I did then, a bit protective of my father, I recoiled from that idea. Yet, over the next several years, if not already, I noticed inside me a growing indignation with the ways of my elders, a desire to see the world of adult assumptions violated, a wish to live wholly in the utopian company of my contemporaries. The worst moments came when I was on my best behavior and universally taken for an exemplary youth. Over the next years there would be the customary resentments, shouting matches, and slammed doors, but no one in our household went in for extended quarrels. The sun was not permitted to set upon anyone's wrath. Such bad energy was required to find other outlets. Walking the suburban streets by myself or with a friend—comparing notes with respect to personal grievances—was one; driving aimlessly about the city or nerving myself to pass for eighteen in the bars would be others. We wished to rebel, we would succeed in so doing, but neither my brother nor I wanted to open a grievous, slow-to-heal breach. In opposing our father we preferred simply to absent ourselves from his world, to bid a good-natured and even sentimental good-bye, and to leave that world intact, lest it prove, after all, the only real one.

3

Brothers

My father habitually misspoke my name, as though a piece of my brother's permanently adhered to my own. Outside the home, according to formula, we were "big D" and "little D," and teachers assumed the younger sibling was simply the elder's mimeo. As tots we were sometimes dressed in identical outfits; as teenagers our clothes looked so much alike our laundry got confused. Reared in an era of eager conformity, we were destined to be interchangeable, and my efforts to differ might have the effect of proving ineluctable sameness. Yet from age ten I, for one, no longer confounded us, no longer saw anything but two insoluble meanings. Perhaps for that reason we forged in our teens a good, companionable relationship. We'd do things together—his things, mostly, since he was the one who could drive—but inside the world defined by his interests I was free to claim my own enjoyment.

He had his friends, sports, clothes, cologne, TV shows, records, magazines. I watched and learned from what he did. I always knew more about him than he would know about me. A younger brother, I recognized early, merits no more than passing notice. My life was adjacent to his and theoretically a variation thereof, just as my bedroom resembled his structurally but with my own signature mess. I didn't have to wish myself him to admire his superior qualities. He was well formed, strong, and strikingly handsome. He was quick to size up a situation and reduce it to a phrase. He could laugh in the face of anyone dumb enough to try to intimidate him. I was more hesitant, didn't always care to mix, and preferred to take life at a distance. He saw at first glance, I at second. Difference needn't set us apart. We could exist as complements.

I-494, Brighton. Courtesy Communications Bureau, City of Rochester.

We went separate ways. Since he was older he had opportunities for experience, good and bad, which he alone might enter, closing the door behind him. I'd miss him and mourn his absence. But then and ever he'd reappear when I least expected him, and just when I thought he'd deserted the ground of sibling origin he'd conjure it anew. Even in midlife he possessed that power.

AN ELDER BROTHER dwells in deep memory as a strong second self. His presence defines the sibling's existence as a condition of weakness. In savage phase he persecutes that weakness as if nothing that frail has a right to live. As the good second self he fosters the sibling, hoists him to his feet, observes the gathering strength in his arm. He protects the brother from older children, instructs him in the ways of combat, wards off disease and death. There was a boy in my kindergarten class, an only child, dying of polio, bones and flesh softening, falling apart, and this boy became my nightmare image of the prostrate form my own weakness took: my body after fever, surgery, or in backyard play thrown to the turf, inert, defeated. But here was my brother yanking me up, invigorating me with harsh words and affectionate roughness. We're on the same side, we face a common enemy, and our parents need protection. Smoke from a leaf fire lingers in the twilight, and stars have begun to appear. At the battle's close I lose sight of my brother around a neighbor's porch. I break into sweat beneath my fall clothing. Something irrational possesses my hold on the solid, recurrent ordinary world: young as I am, I suspect it proceeds from me. Yet only after I have mounted the steps and found him in the kitchen, red in the face with his jacket off, examining the casserole fresh from the oven, does my panic subside. Supper follows; my brother gets to go out for a while, but I must bathe. Outside the house, absolute darkness envelops our world, lamps and windows keeping it at bay. Reverie on themes of neighborhood play animates the night's long sleep.

Alone in the yard next morning, I study the day's reclamation of the world from the wilderness of night. My brother is permitted to walk through the dark to a neighbor's house at the end of the block, but I am not old enough: I have to content myself with shadows, while he gets to probe the night's black pocket. As the sun clears a neighboring roofline, I note how the night lingers in the weeds behind the garage, on the west side of bushes, in the long grass encircling a hydrant, how it persists in the cricket's chirp and mourning dove's coo. Twenty years later our dad will confess how hideous he finds the mourning dove's coo—as though its witless and interminable lament mocked a legitimate fear of death. But as the very young sons of his midlife prosperity, my brother and I have little to fear from the darkest night and even less from scattered nocturnal remnants continuing their work at the sunlight's edge, like fragments of dream a person recalls an hour or so into day.

Our world was full of such remnants.

Like most children of the suburban frontier we conceived a fascination for shadow worlds: hidden meadows containing junked cars, weedy
lengths of seldom-used rail line, causeways harboring limestone ruins of
Erie Canal masonry. The interest in retrograde sites went back to earliest
childhood and preserved the dream of uterine hollows that haunts the
infant mind. In the mound of sand on Walden Road we created scenes
remote from day-to-day life: secluded crossroads, hideouts accessible by
winding and dangerous paths, lakes that didn't appear on the maps. The
child-self seeks its solipsist realm in isolated fold, stretch of sky, or field of
water. Like a second womb, the Walden Road neighborhood held its children in elastic bond. Whitewood Lane, by contrast, compelled exploration
of territory harboring rusty and pointed objects. Beneath the hornet's nest
and poison ivy lay stones with fading inscriptions. A boy could explore
these oddly bounded yet borderless tracts as far as his nerve might let
him—do so, at least, before the last vacant patch vanished beneath highway and house. For my brother and me there were still time and world to
explore. Tom might abscond a while, then appear with news of margins
worth our inspection. They were commonly very near. He and I found
neglected loci in close proximity to domestic scenes where we needed to
be when a head count was made or people were called to supper.

We liked to return with tokens—license plates, taillight pieces, railroad spikes, bottle caps of exotic beer, shotgun casings, coins from the
interwar years, pages ripped from discarded books: paragraphs on knives
from an old Scout manual, an encomium to Aunt Gertrude's pies from a
Hardy Boys mystery. You could hold and examine such items and infer a
lost world where they once had a place. Our desk drawers and windowsills
were filled with such things. Thinking back, I am struck by the contrast
between the newness of the Whitewood Lane house and the antiquity of
those objects. Tom and I had this notion: somewhere along the township's
edge was an old rail line, and by walking that line a little ways you'd find
yourself in a village where time had stopped in the 1930s—our fantasy
emulating the kind of metaphysics we'd see every week on *The Twilight
Zone.* With our electric train layout down in the basement we tried to re-
create this changeless era—an epoch some thirty years out of reach. We
liked the past because the present kept changing, because time rushed

through it into featureless space, the unformed, exorbitant, annihilating future. There had to be something, however imaginary, that didn't change. Soon after the move to Whitewood Lane we acquired the hobby of assembling and painting plastic model cars. We were never much interested in '60s models, selecting those from the '40s and '50s. To make them look more authentic—more like the junked cars we'd spot in creases of unimproved real estate—we waited until Dad stepped inside for the platter of marinated chicken and then held our cars over the charcoal grill until the plastic softened and we could press dents into fenders and doors.

My brother's first word was car. This presaged a lasting fascination. As the second sibling I too must cultivate this fetish. I could no more resist the force of his interests than find another household. In the den stood shelves of bright picture folds surveying the field of motorized transport and storybooks featuring automobile protagonists. The jumbled assortment of cars, trucks, motorcycles, and jeeps occupied a shelf of its own. Some of these toys were large, plastic, and prone to breakage. But by the time I was four my brother had acquired die-cast, detailed, scale-model cars made in England. My eye was drawn to these smooth, cool, enameled vehicles that commended themselves to juvenile narrative. Soon I too began to receive this coveted article that went by the trade name Dinky Toy. Some replicated American makes—Ford, Plymouth, DeSoto—but most were British with steering wheel on the right. They arrived in yellow boxes accompanied by a catalog with instructions for joining the Official Club. It involved a currency conversion and a long wait, but eventually we became members in good standing with embossed certificates and lapel buttons we wore to family gatherings. At an early age we knew something of England, land of pounds sterling and inverse traffic.

In the long months between Christmas and birthdays we were sometimes treated to a special purchase, one each of equal value, and for this purpose Mom would drive us to a small toy store on a downtown side street. Behind the counter stood several shelves devoted to those yellow boxes. The mere sight of them induced in us an agony of choosing, as if all the wealth in the world were concentrated on those shelves. Upon our return we sat at the kitchen table and gazed at our acquisitions, setting up roads among the silverware as we ate our sandwiches and soup. The new vehicles assimilated to scenarios already in progress. In the side yard sand pile we fashioned roads and towns, elaborate worlds supporting complicated story lines. We had England but also Florida and California. We built and destroyed daily, quarreled over unauthorized demolitions, lost and found vehicles as the sand shifted.

The interest in cars was not simply a random fixation of my brother's infancy. Automotive interests abode in the extended family. Dreadfully puritan though my father was in matters of automobile taste, my grandfather had an eye for style and long experience in sales. He worked part-time in the business office of our uncle Johnny Heinrich's Chevrolet dealership. To have our cars serviced or to examine new models we drove up Lake Avenue to Johnny's lot north of downtown on the city's west side. The showroom was a realm of pure dream, the toy store people came to as adults. This was an epoch of flamboyant styling and theatrical unveiling of new model lines. Celebrating the arrival of the new model year in late September, Uncle Johnny set up searchlights and hired dancing "Indians." We were never there for the curtain rise, but by early October our nagging request for a showroom visit produced results, and once on site Dad conceded an interest in purchasing a new car. Our uncle or cousin came out from the office to guide our inspection of these fabulous machines that smelled of fresh wax and lubricants, a fragrance unsullied by the exhaust fume, cigarette butt, and motion sickness of real life. We sat in the Corvette and then studied its engine as though we knew what to look for. Later we went down a hall and up a back staircase to my grandfather's office with its stacked papers and aroma of pipe tobacco. This was his perch a little above the world's street-level commerce. He walked us to the Coke machine and bought each a bottle with change from his jacket pocket.

Beyond this special family connection, cars lured with irresistible association—youth, power, speed, girls, crime. They offered time travel, old models conjuring a quaint lost past, new models revealing a utopian future. Old and new alike might affect a futuristic look. They betrayed a desire to lift into space, explore the far galactic rims. Be it ever so prosaic, the car in the driveway spoke to every child's dream of growing up, starting the motor, studying the controls, backing the vehicle into the street, and driving away.

From age twelve my brother subscribed to *Hot Rod Magazine*. Once a month, after he had spent a lingering silent lunch over the issue, I'd devote a part of the afternoon to examining photos of candy-colored roadsters, dragsters, and funny cars, yellow or red or black with flames flaring up from the mud flaps, and immaculate chromium manifold and pipe. These vehicles cruised a habitat of boulevards lined with palm trees—Florida or California. When not a blur of pure motion, they parked athwart a beach of white sand. A young woman or two, tanned, blonde, bikini clad, nearly but not quite a candidate for *Playboy,* lounged on the hood, while the muscled and toothy owner sat at the wheel. "This is the life," his expression seemed to say. In places like Rochester, people drove family sedans vulnerable to the heavy salting of winter streets, and your average utilitarian vehicle exhibited perforations along the rocker panel. But even in Rochester, with its fleet of dumpy cars, you met the frenzy for automotive innovation—the yearly extension and elevation of fins, doubling of headlamps, massing of chrome, enhancement of speed. Yes: it was as though these vehicles were meant to fly, orbit the earth, probe outer space. Through the early sixties a florid imagination took hold of the garish metal death box. As preteens we loved to inspect, smell, and palpate the new cars at the annual downtown auto show and gaze at specimens far more exotic than anything on our uncle's lot. And once or twice, on morbid impulse, we bicycled up to Elmer's Garage to gawk at wrecks retrieved from the highway. We had read about this one—the fatal '57 Fairlane that had left the road at sixty miles an hour and slammed into an elm. The boy and girl had been on a date. Waves of force deformed the roof and even the rear fenders. The front end bunched right up to the windshield, concave grill drooled chunks of bark, steering wheel dangled from the column . . . and there, on the door, dashboard, and all over the front seat, was a mess of dried blood, like a spilled bowl of soup. Too late to avoid the sick metal odor! That day we had our fill of wrecks. Yet something incited our interest in the damaged body and junk phase of the automobile's life. It spoke truths all else conspired to mask.

One year in the mid-1960s, our family drove to Myrtle Beach for spring vacation. For winter-weary, flat-vowel folk from the Great Lakes, the Deep South presented a world of seduction, but everything there was a bit out of kilter, the price you paid for a warm climate and nightly shellfish dinners. Once you crossed into Virginia the roads worsened; old, slow-moving vehicles impeded our steady sixty-mile-an-hour clip. Recklessness put on a show: someone doing ninety in a big yawing convertible would take on a whole line of cars entering a curve. We passed wrecks along the highway—one in particular required an averted gaze, as here on the shoulder lay a rag-doll body doctored by country folk. Apparitional vehicles materialized from long dirt roads: a prison bus full of black convicts, farm trucks loaded with beat-up furniture, a hearse, and then another, and then a third. We breezed through small towns with old shiny cars parked along the courthouse square. We arrived at Myrtle Beach and saw many late-model northern cars with New York and Pennsylvania license plates. We were there several days before my brother discovered a junkyard within walking distance of the hotel—something to explore during the inevitable overcast afternoon. What would a southern junkyard be like? This one occupied a meadow surrounded by huge trees with wide arched trunks like ruined ancient temples. A girl Tom's age from Niagara Falls tagged along on this jaunt, and her self-conscious naughtiness heightened our sense of criminal trespass. She in fact was the first one in and insisted on draping torso and hip over the hood of a Packard coupe despite our warnings about broken glass. I remember thinking on that occasion: What if she were our sister? We'd have to look after her! This girl introduced troubling dimensions of anxiety and responsibility to what was otherwise boyish sport. She inserted, in short, sexuality, but given the setting's foreign quality, we already felt a bit out of depth. You couldn't be sure of the ground in the South, consisting as it did of spongy soil and viney growth. There had to be insects and snakes, mere mention of which brought our companion to her senses. The litter of car parts, windshield glass, and hulking bodies dumped in mounds, like skulls, made for hazardous trekking. We found what we were looking for at the yard's edge—a South Carolina license plate on the rear bumper of a Ford truck. We got it back to the hotel and hid it in our suitcase, and only afterward imagined the gun-toting watchman and Nazi guard dogs that would have loved to devour our vitals.

Over the course of several days we noticed that cars driven by blacks were generally total wrecks. They would sputter by on visibly bad tires, leaving a noxious plume in their wake. Eight or nine people might stuff the gills of an ancient sedan. Sometimes the vehicle was overlaid with ornaments or fitted with fins and flames, but it still seemed on loan from the junkyard. Accustomed to thinking everyone deserved equal treatment, more or less, it shocked us to see people deeply reduced. We discussed the matter and decided it was neither fair nor safe. Complimentary copies of the local paper were available at the resort office, and one afternoon the headline read "Negroes Die in Fiery Crash." Below the headline an indistinct photo of shredded metal and charred human forms completed the ghastly anecdote. I may have been wrong to think I was seeing incinerated bodies. But by age eleven I was a little aware of the horrific violence directed against blacks and sensed in that image something more than an auto wreck. That people should be forced to drive unroadworthy cars struck my brother as terribly wrong, and I readily absorbed his outlook. I admired the goodness in him that sided with the down and out.

AS BROTHERS TWO AND A HALF YEARS APART we'd do things together, then go separate ways, called by our respective peer bodies whose group personae exaggerated the difference between older and younger sibling. The car mediated this relationship—divided and then reunited us. A threshold appeared the moment one of his friends began to drive. When your brother has to go because a car is waiting in the driveway, his buddy incongruously at the wheel, you feel the age difference acutely. A year later he had his own driver's license. Our parents couldn't have been thrilled at the idea of our being in a car with my brother in control, but they liked to see fraternal relation. As a passenger in his car (not his car exactly but one of two family cars) I went places I wouldn't go with Mom or Dad. With respect to the vehicle, my brother revealed performance capacities our parents weren't apt to discover: how fast the Chevy V8 reached sixty, how nimbly the Impala's wide body wove in spite of the ride's general softness. Tom's driving put me on edge: he followed close and changed lanes abruptly. But I was eager to go places with him, anyplace, really, even just the dime store. I liked visits to the gas station, where he chatted with the owner while the tank filled, or to a used-car lot where we looked at vehicles (sports cars, pickup trucks) unlike anything our dad would ever own. At Christmas we might drive downtown to shop, but our travels generally took us to the far suburbs and villages along the Erie Canal. Here you would find centuries-old trees and Greek Revival houses, some constructed entirely of cobblestone, and creaky five-story wood-frame hotels, some of which predated the American Revolution. Lafayette, friend of the Republic, spent the night in one of those hotels. New York State historical plaques stood before half the buildings, and ancient iron and wooden bridges spanned the canal. We drove slowly through the villages in a mood of unspoken expectation. It always seemed we were on the lookout for the old, odd, obscure, and ghostly. I regretted that we could never just take the whole afternoon and follow a country road south to one of the smaller Finger Lakes where tourists might find, off some of the county highways, settlements clustered on gravel streets, and even (or so we'd heard) all-black or all-Indian hamlets. But Tom always had plans that placed a limit on our wanderings.

I fantasized setting out on a road trip, just the two of us. Our destination was a Pacific beach void of everything, including surfers and hot rods. One early Saturday morning we'd roll a Chevelle SS out of the garage and head south and west on country roads. We'd drive to the state border and cross, proceed to the next border and cross again. We'd go border to border, observant of each state's flower, bird, and tree. We'd stop at Stuckey's for pecan rolls. We'd gas up at Mobil stations with the old Pegasus emblem. The fantasy had a soundtrack consisting of two songs: "Theme from Route 66" for day, "Telstar" for night. In small towns we'd talk with country girls who would admire our out-of-state plates. When we reached Kansas and its sea of wildflowers I'd get to drive. My brother would teach me to drive those roads where there was no one to pull you over and ask to see a license. We'd cross the mountains and speed across deserts, winding through groves of saguaro cacti, trace of atomic test blasts hanging in the sky. We'd spend the night at motels made up of little detached cabins—lodgings our father always disdained, insisting we stay at the Quality Court, making reservations in advance. On the contrary, we'd drive all night and quit when we felt like it. We'd stop for scenic vistas, roadside museums, and frozen custard. We'd drive to California on vacant roads and see no one in the process.

A typical errand with my brother might start with a trip to a record store, the declared and authorized purpose. We'd swing by Wegman's and fetch something for Mom since we were driving her car. We'd make these stops, and on the way home Tom would take a detour.

Sometimes we'd find ourselves in Henrietta, one of the new sprawling suburbs southwest of Rochester just north of the New York State Thruway. In contrast to the winding thoroughfares that connected the villages, here major arteries ran straight and intersected at right angles. New neighborhoods weren't so much built as installed. In addition to identical looping tracts with the standard three-bedroom "ranch" there arose blocklike multifamily structures arrayed in rigid parallel phalanx. Out here the world was flattened and paved, new groundbreaking constant, construction frantic and awry. Like an aggressive metastasis, auto dealerships and shopping plazas rapidly environed these townships; in time the car lots would expand and consolidate, the plazas transform into elephantine malls with sylvan and floral names. The big warehouse marts were a decade away. Drive-in theaters and drive-through restaurants flourished in these spaces, as did miniature golf and go-cart parks. Here too you began to see large, cut-rate self-serve gas stations that dispensed with garage and mechanic. Some of the new restaurants—Tahitian Hideaway, Japanese Steakhouse, Taco Cabana—offered novel fare and fantasy ambience. Not long after came the gentlemen's clubs. From television shows set in Los Angeles (they were never set in places like Rochester) one knew that businesses like these had long been established on the West Coast. Now they were spreading to the suburban East. They ran promotions. They offered coupons. They aired endless repetitive advertising on WBBF, the local top-40 station, obligatory listening at pizzeria and public pool. Fearing grease and unwonted spice, our parents refused to dine at those restaurants. What was the attraction? The shopping plazas on the far rim had nothing you couldn't find close to home, and the discounts didn't begin to cover the gas and time it took to drive out there. Our dad believed that prudent motorists fed their engines a steady stream of name-brand gas, preferably from the same station and pumped by its owner. We were not to fill up at El Rancho Gasateria, where the fuel could be highly seasoned or otherwise contaminated.

We might cruise for twenty minutes through tracts of new housing and remnant farmland then pull into the driveway at the house of a girl who lived in one of these subdivisions. I sit in the car while my brother visits in the house. Fifteen minutes elapse; he has forgotten I'm out here, or presumes on my indulgence, with nothing to do but stare at the house and lawn and neighboring houses, variation of the standard suburban scene, and the girls between nine and twelve who filter through the yard, sidestepping the sprinkler's pendulum sweep. Whatever I do, I can't go in the house. Better to walk home two and a half miles along fierce thoroughfares in ninety-degree heat, better to be hit by a truck than go in and disturb that slow-motion colloquy. The twelve-year-old girl with the lank brown hair comes up to my window and stares. I may be in her driveway but I'm in my family's car, and with my juvenile grasp of eminent domain I resist her border-control scrutiny. Still, I find her troubling. As we don't have a sister, I find girls perfectly unintelligible, as though everything in the outward expression were divorced from the inward state. Still staring. What do I say? She's like a girl mannequin propped against the car door. At moments like this I imagine catastrophe: air-raid sirens steadily rising from the semiaudible ambient din, the sky filling with invisible missiles coming and going. We'll either die or survive together, this moment providing the basis of a long-term relationship. Finally, in the tone with which a person might propose the solution to a math problem, she asks, "Are you his brother?" For a moment I experience the familiar sensation of nonbeing: defined solely in relation to another, called by his name or hearing my own inserted as a second syllable, present by virtue of comparison. Sitting in a car in a strange driveway, on the ocean bottom for all my brother knows. In vain I swear to myself that I will never, ever, be put in this position again.

Or we might head to East Rochester, the industrial suburb southeast of the city on the New York Central mainline. There is something down here that interests my brother, but he's tight-lipped about what. We slow at the outskirts so he can scan the junkyard, then proceed down Main Street to the Shell station on the corner where two state highways intersect. We're not getting gas. He pulls in and parks away from the pumps, says he'll just be a minute. Along the side by the gas station's restroom sits the yellow, battered forties-era Ford coupe mounted on a racing chassis. He seems to want a close-up view of this car he has seen compete at a local track. The owner, a slender man in a gas-station jumpsuit, comes out of the garage, and he and my brother converse. The man's initial wariness dissipates, and twenty minutes or a half hour later they shake hands before my brother turns back to the car and we depart. At gas stations throughout the county you might spot these battered racers. On Friday and Saturday nights they converge on clay or asphalt ovals and roar well into the night. The program consists of a series of heats, a consolation race for the slower vehicles, a feature race for the fast. There are local heroes and Canadian challengers. There is a field of respectable also-rans. The drivers are semiprofessional at best. Most are strictly amateur and lead strenuous working-class lives. My brother, in his early teens, conceives a fascination for these home-tooled vehicles that absorb the passion of obscure lives and manage the urge to escape. He's come under the spell of the folk democracy of the regional stock-car racing circuit. There is beauty in this. I follow along.

Before he could drive, he lobbied our dad to take us to an occasional race at the county fairgrounds. Dad's willingness depended on various things—how exhausting the week had been, how much his back ached (the stands offered nothing but bench seating), and our mom's social calendar. He might derive a passing enjoyment from the entertainment but felt ill at ease among the chiefly uneducated crowd drawn to the fairground. I liked to go, and while I found the races exhilarating, the crowd in all its splendid variety held my abiding interest: leather-jacketed guys and their scant-clothed girlfriends under the lurid lights of the track, the gathering haze of dirt churned skyward by the parade of cars fishtailing through the turns. There were faces here you didn't see in the suburbs: middle-aged men with bulky tattooed forearms; big wives chugging cans of beer; country families toting snacks, drinks, and padded fold-up seats that mounted on the plank bench; scrawny, intense solitary men whom my brother had a knack for engaging in conversation. Sometimes the conversation revealed life stories—narratives of seafaring, street violence, incarcerations, work on various pit crews, just and unjust firings. There were the teenage couples on double or triple date, indifferent to the setting of their private affairs, confident that the race-in-progress commanded general attention. The girl in front of us nibbles her inattentive boyfriend's ear, then takes his hand and places it on her breast. She is on her third beer (I, voyeur, have been counting). Nearly everyone but the three of us brings a cooler or brown paper bag of beer, and as the night progresses the heavier guzzlers slump and sprawl or, intriguingly, become excitable. In the next section a quarrel breaks out between a guy in bib overalls and another in sleeveless T-shirt, and now one of them throws a punch. Two black-shirted security officers rush up the aisles and remove the offenders. An explanation slowly circulates: the matter concerns the track ethics of rival drivers. Yes: one of the drivers does bump overmuch, but there is general condemnation of the fracas on the part of these laid-back folks who have toiled all week and want to metabolize beer in peace.

Once my brother had night driving privileges, he and I and maybe one of his buddies would head out to an area speedway Friday nights. We'd stop at a grocery on the county line and purchase a six-pack of Genny Cream Ale, and I'd get to cradle the cold contraband in a brown paper sack moist with condensation. The beer was to stay in the bag until we got to the track, and my brother's driving seemed to improve with its incriminating presence. The traffic thickened as we approached the entrance where a brawny state policeman directed the flow, halting our progress to admit a dozen left-turners, but soon he waved us in and we found ourselves crossing the meadow that served as a parking lot. Tom liked to park by the meadow's edge, where you wouldn't get wedged between ill-parked vehicles and where trees provided alternatives to the pit toilets behind the ticket booth. We'd lock the car and follow the crowd to the spectators' gate and pay admission. Tom would then go to the newsstand and buy two of the weekly racing papers. Then he'd want us to walk rapidly to our accustomed place five rows up and seven paces to the right of the finish line. We'd settle, light our cigarettes, and pop open the beer. In July, as the long, brutal late afternoon gave way to evening, you could feel the heat of the day rising out of the wooden stands; you could feel the sweat on your shirt back cool. In an hour you might want a jacket. Just as we arrive a first few cars begin warm-up laps. Eventually, all have a turn, and some forty minutes after we have claimed our seats—during which time we get through a beer and read the newspapers while the bleachers fill up, same people in the same places, some of them greeting my brother by name—we stand for the two national anthems, and then the first heat begins.

One evening, in the lull between warm-ups and the first heat, a lanky cop with bristle mustache strode to the front of our section. I saw him fix an eye on Tom, too busy reading the racing news to notice. The cop then proceeded to mount, forcing his way through spectators sitting thigh to thigh just below us, until he shimmied toward my brother, who slowly met the ferret brow moving in for the kill. "Stand up, sonny," instructed the cop, "and let me see some ID. Now turn around. Let me see that jacket!" The confrontation came on so fast that neither of us managed to kick the beer under the bleacher, contingency plan for just such a pass, but clearly the man had something more serious in mind. "I want that roll of tickets," he barked, stabbing an index finger into Tom's shoulder, "and I want it now!" Standing erect, fronting the wave of the cop's halitosis, Tom said nothing, his expression frozen in initial surprise. I sat down, having stood for a second only to find myself nauseous and light-headed. Well, I reflected, we'll both go to jail—brothers in crime, whatever the accusation—and the thought seemed to rescue the moment. But then a female voice called from below: "Ernie! Ernie! That's not the kid! He's over here!" I looked to see the deadpan woman normally ensconced in the ticket booth pointing to someone in the next section. The cop's finger suspended its action; with a snort and the lift of an eyebrow he was gone.

When my head stopped reeling I saw the man who sat above us, a retired fireman known as Big Gus, wrap his arm around Tom's shoulders while his wife patted his hand. They were playing the part of emergency mom and dad. All the bench neighbors expressed indignation. A good citizen had been falsely accused by a bantam village cop. "Just be glad it wasn't a state trooper!" Mrs. Gus said. I ditched my tears before anyone noticed. A minute later we witnessed the cop strong-arm the real malefactor to the gate. "Fuck you! That's what I say!" the kid shouted to no one in particular. His mop of blond hair concealed half his face. He looked nothing like Tom.

This was the first of two memorable incidents from the times we attended together. Normally, evenings were sedentary and meditative.

The crowd stood for wrecks and close finishes but for the most part sat. There wasn't much point in cheering on favorites who couldn't hear you over the roar, but that didn't keep people from cheering. The glad monotony of circling cars encouraged abstraction of mind—at least in me. What was I thinking? I liked the strange peace and containment of this focused, repetitive event taking place in a pasture beyond city and suburban limits. We were back in time. I was neither reading nor mowing lawns nor stranded at home with parents on a weekend night. I savored the scent of exhaust and burnt rubber. I was in Tom's world, which was not really mine but which I liked because I loved and feared losing him—to misadventure, lunkhead friends, booze, wrecks. Here at the track I knew where he was, and because I was with him nothing could happen. By force of will I'd get him home. I had us under control.

Yes: it was on me to keep things together. My parents weren't up to the task. Parents never are: They seldom recognize there is a task. Or rather they misconceive it. This isn't their fault. They aren't in position to see what siblings see. I was the brother and I would do the keeping—or not— and it would be my anxiety and failure. It would be my weakness. Perhaps Tom felt the same about me, but I didn't take his kind of risks. Or at least I didn't think so.

Sometimes we'd go to a speedway requiring an hour's drive each way. We'd find ourselves deep in the countryside of New York State. The track might have been designed for horses and have a hundred-year history. The stands might be rickety and the French fries bathed in vinegar. The emergency vehicles on standby might be old. We liked these variations and especially enjoyed seeing the novel field of cars—drivers and rivalries we had read about in the back pages of the racing news. Some of these tracks sat spectators a little too close to the action, and we'd come away wearing a palpable layer of dirt. The crowd always seemed pretty much the same— middle-aged couples, teenagers on dates, whole families, and the vaguely Gypsy people who came and went on motorcycle. But you could never predict who might be seated beside, below, or above you: here was an elderly village pediatrician, there an aviation engineer. One time I sat next to a Catholic priest, an affable walrus who laughed long and hard when asked between heats to explain mortal sin (I thought it was only polite).

Near or far, the track—beyond the normal excitement of the races themselves—afforded the satisfaction of leaving the suburb and entering a sphere where social pretensions didn't seem to exist. Neither the world of the suburb nor that of the track much reckoned the existence of the other. Auto racing for most of our Whitewood Lane neighbors meant the Indianapolis or Daytona 500. My brother and I might watch these events on TV, but neither of us developed much interest in big-time racing. We liked the obscurity of local tracks that ran their races without national sanction. In remote venues a driver's celebrity consisted of weekly coverage in the regional gazettes and hometown fan recognition. A few drivers were objects of adulation. But the professional star didn't count for much. Nobody there could afford to attend high-dollar events. It was enough to make it to the Fourth of July weekend program. You budgeted to get to the weekly races and the annual race at the New York State Fair.

One month into the season, one week seemed much like another. The crowd settled in for an evening program in the mood of expectation spectators enter at all sporting events. You know what must happen and how it will unfold within a range of familiar surprise. Who will win and who will wreck and how competitive the contest will be remain open. All drama must transpire within those bounds. Spectator behavior was mostly the same, governed by the universal understanding that racing was a family activity. As the regular attendee knew (and the casual attendee sometimes did not), you wanted to see nervy driving, but it was bad form to avow a pleasure in wrecks. Most occurred when, spinning out in a curve, a car would be tapped, bumped, or walloped in the side—or, if it rotated 180 degrees, hit head-on. By then the unlucky vehicle would be rolling backward, mitigating the violence of impact. Sometimes a car would hit the wall, catapult, flip end over end, coming to rest just off the track. Yellow flags slowed the race; red flags halted it. There'd be a hushed moment before the driver climbed out the front or side window and waved to the crowd. Everyone cheered, relieved that three seconds of excitement hadn't been purchased by injury. Wrecks were not, so it seemed to me, accidents; they may be unplanned, but they were too frequent; they were incident to this kind of driving. Given roll cages, helmets, and safety suits, drivers seldom incurred injury. Death was extremely rare. As a self-respecting spectator you wanted to see competitive, aggressive racing but not smash-ups, for even when drivers emerged unharmed, wrecks entailed costly repairs for racing teams lucky just to break even. (I once asked Tom if the drivers carry insurance on these vehicles, and he gave me the look, boy, are you ever dumb.) But in the event of a wreck you were there to see it, and spectators were quick to rise from their seats if they sensed develop-ing action.

In truth we saw so many wrecks, most quite minor, that we didn't think much about it. Fire always got the crowd's attention, and so did detached wheels hurtling in the vicinity of a grandstand. Rain was some-times a problem, more for the asphalt than the dirt tracks, and races would have to be called if surfaces became liquid. But there was a fine line between a little and too much moisture. One year, on a misty evening toward the end of August, we attended races at the local asphalt track. The season was almost over: not many cars had shown up to compete, and the crowd seemed sated with this weekly habit that had gone on now for three and a half months. Darkness had set in noticeably early. The events went off with perfunctory regularity; we waited for the program to conclude so we could go home. Toward the end of the first consolation race (always the most boring), seven or eight cars entered the third and fourth turns. All night there had been problems with cars spinning out on the slick track. A spinout is one thing, but now one of the cars, in what appeared to be a defiance of the law of gravity, turned abruptly toward the fence and leaped out of the racetrack into the grandstand flanking the turn, and what we saw next was a void where the car had taken out five or six bleachers. Seconds earlier spectators like us had occupied that space.

The crowd around us froze and then, looking away, emitted invol-untary moans and whimpers. We knew at once there were people who hadn't survived. For an hour the crowd was held in the stands so that a parade of ambulances could remove the dead and injured. We learned that night that a twelve-year-old boy and his grandfather had been killed and another half-dozen spectators had been hospitalized; the morning paper would confirm the tally. On the way home my brother and I sat in silence. Generally when we drove some place together, we didn't converse but not because we felt speechless. It was hard to comprehend what we had just seen: not blood or mangled bodies but a car gone weird and then a hole in the night where people had been sitting.

We might have sworn off racing for the season, what little was left of it, but it seemed important to return to the track when it reopened two weeks later. There was a moment of silence for the dead and injured following the national anthems. What had happened, everyone averred, was pure freak. People volubly affirmed the doctrine that everyone—spectators, drivers, pit crew, and so on—was safer here than they were on the highway or in the taverns or anywhere, really, even one's home, where families become volatile after a long workweek and where psychologically it was dangerous to be on a weekend night. People felt terribly sorry for the driver, a nineteen-year-old kid who had to live with the guilt of something that wasn't his fault, who happened to be there at the fulfillment of what everyone tacitly accepted, in entering the gate, as a remote if probably inevitable fate. But some folks were also thinking: what if the track owner hadn't chosen to erect a grandstand (called the "new grandstand" even though several years old) in a place known to be hazardous, what if that grandpa had thought not to sit on a bleacher flanking a curve? There were reasons besides the inferior view that Tom and I never sat there. But none of this thinking changed the fact that all of us regulars had witnessed what we never expected, never imagined, never consciously paid money to see, and what in retrospect we could scarcely credit we had seen: a fatal accident, the abrupt and absolute end of the world for folks who held ticket stubs identical to our own.

Racetrack sensations normally fitted into a narrow fold of weekly routine, but this event defied relegation. I felt sure that I needed to think about what I'd seen, brood on it, appease this strange guilt that was mine because I had sat there and watched, but I made little progress and was left with a dull mental shadow that lasted about a month before my attention took up other things. Tom and I didn't talk about it. Words hardly exist for teenage boys to sort through such experience, and I had no idea what he was thinking. As we drove in the night—that night and others—we sat and gazed at the road before us, rural route and suburban thoroughfare. His eyes were fixed on objects, outer and inner, I couldn't discern; mine already were scanning horizons he couldn't know. We were called in different directions, and it wouldn't be long before I had my own license and nighttime errands, my own rapport with the mystic V8 beyond the Impala's firewall. We went our separate ways. It was sad to think I was diverging from someone with whom I'd shared a system of living, someone I knew with deep if qualified intimacy. But I had my own roads to identify and map. And at some point I must have coldheartedly decided I could not guarantee his well-being.

As respectable middle-aged men, we'd retrace our steps in suburban borderlands and resume the séance of vanished worlds. We'd take in a race together. We'd affirm boyhood as the first condition and brother love as a principal strand in a life's fabric. We'd take fatherly midlife perspectives on the lure night exerts over teen children. Age would bring an understanding of our father based on fellow feeling. But for now our ways had parted, and though our paths would continue to cross, years would pass before we'd reunite.

4

Camp

Three weeks into the long summer recess kids complained of nothing to do. The novelty of large free days had fled. Boon companions fell into quarrels, and biking the township required an effort. My preteen body succumbed to hot-weather lethargy. I was able to recite the TV schedule, channel to channel, sign-on to sign-off.

On my mother's wall-mounted planning calendar, the word *camp* with daisy squiggles encompassed two weeks of July. In August we might drive to Quebec, our typical late-season family excursion, but until then camp was the one escape. Renouncing inactivity wasn't easy, however, and the idea of a wooded lake with rocky glens did little to reduce the dread of those weeks as the hour of departure approached. Camp meant suspension of neighborhood contacts; it meant a day of homesickness and the noisy liquid presence of those unfamiliar children, one's fellow campers. It meant getting up early to dress in the cold and relieve oneself in a latrine made odious by other campers. It meant taking one's meals in the dining hall with its permanent odor of sour milk. In reflective moments just after taps, it meant the troubled recognition that so much summer has already passed, and only so much therefore remains. But by the time I was having those moments I had become attached to camp rhythms and didn't want to return home to a hot bedroom and repetitious suburban days.

Camp days had two distinct sides; together they formed a lesson in compensation. For the bad food and forced cheer and moronic songs at evening campfire, they offered moments that figured on no one's agenda. I might walk to the latrine at three in the morning, stars and planets illuminating a sky that pierced one with the thought of its visible boundlessness. Or I might find myself far out on the lake in midafternoon, the

Old camp: waterfront. Courtesy of Mary Smith, Hamlin historian.

canoe held by adverse currents, and entertain notions that no amount of paddling now could get me back to the inhabited shore with its known routines and roads that led home. Every two days a thunderstorm rolled in, echoing warlike through the lake valley, producing a torrent that dissolved the world as I had known it five minutes earlier. I'd wait it out in the barn or boathouse, and no one, at such times, might know where I was. But set activities dominated the day, and campers moved through the schedule by group. The Iroquois Confederacy provided team names. While Onondagas fashioned boondoggle knickknacks, Mohawks mustered for morning swim.

Thus, a nearly mindless serenity pervaded group and individual experience, but now and then something gratefully traumatic might occur. Late one morning I had just cinched a loop on a boondoggle key chain when I saw two counselors sprint past the pavilion toward the lakeshore. They were followed by the camp director and nurse, then other counselors and a parade of campers. Against orders to stay put, we all in turn rushed to the waterfront, where latecomers saw only the backs of other campers. Word circulated that a boy was receiving mouth-to-mouth resuscitation.

Soon the Penn Yan ambulance corps arrived, and then everyone caught sight of the boy, blue as egg white, carted off on a stretcher. Children intuit the law of probabilities: at some camp surely someone must drown, but there must also be numerous near drownings. Large trends if not individual instances are always beyond anyone's control. Routines picked up where they left off, and the boy, we learned later—barring "brain damage," for me a new term—was expected to make a complete recovery. But we never saw him again.

Here as elsewhere, everything seemed geared to the norm's rapid resumption. Amusement and boredom were justly proportioned. We had hikes and crafts, archery and rifle, swimming and free time, nearly every day. The trading post opened after supper for purchase of candy and pop. At the end of breakfast a handbell rang for the announcement of that day's activities, identical to those of the day before. Aside from the angel-of-death visitation, it was the unplanned, mostly private event that made for lasting impress. Day and night the lake's undulation worked a subtle hypnosis.

The summer I was twelve I went to a different camp, farther away and in a more rugged country. It was a difference between the rolling, rural, blue-bottomed lake country a half hour's drive from the southernmost suburb and the Adirondacks, a densely wooded, angular terrain requiring a five-hour bus ride, much of it over narrow uphill roads, to penetrate.

Going to camp in the Adirondacks required a commitment to be away four rather than the accustomed two weeks. It meant overnight canoe trips with strenuous portages; it meant learning to ride and care for horses and making sudden, steep, rocky ascents on horseback. The nights would be cold, the lake never warm. We would test those waters the first afternoon after getting our cabin assignments. Experienced campers knew when to scatter and rush toward the cabins and how to finesse duffel bags onto desirable bunks. Amid the chaos of occupying the log structure that would serve for a month as home base, we rapidly fished out swimsuits and towels. And in the total undressing that followed no one could help noticing that some of us had gone through puberty, some of us hadn't, and some were in between. The path to the lake was paved with sharp stones. But down we went to assemble on the swooning wooden dock where counselors stood by to tell us when to jump in and how far to go. On exiting the water we learned our status as swimmers, the verdict read publicly and recorded on clipboards. Although I had only just entered puberty, I figured I could swim as well and as far as anyone (some of the older boys, I was happy to see, floundered laughably). Pretending to misunderstand instructions, I threw in an extra pass, lest my proficiency go unnoticed. I emerged as a swimmer with full rights and prerogatives, cleared for canoe trips and the class in boatmanship. The whole induction had gone well, and I felt, within the first hour, something like reborn.

Next day, on our first hike, a two-mile trek to the far shore followed by a one-mile climb up the side of the neighboring mountain, I had fresh opportunity to prove the hypothesis that had begun to take shape inside: that I was not at core the younger son and little brother but my own man, someone who by sheer will could march ever forward and never be known to complain. In the first mile the sun lanced the heavy lake air that had made us shiver at the outset. And in a matter of minutes blisters began to form on both heels. The path wound among trees and boulders some twenty yards above the shore. Now and again we caught sight of the dining hall across the water, appearing more and more like a toy replica. We were far along but still a half hour from where we would stop for lunch. I tolerated the blisters; as my feet bumped the stones in my path there were many arduous sensations to register. Yet the experience of proceeding vigorously and in pain was new and, as I thought, manly. Short of exposure to physical torment, what chance does a twelve-year-old boy ever get to persuade himself that he is a man? When we arrived at our picnic site I found a smooth rock that allowed for upright sitting. This served to alleviate the strain, while the plain cheese sandwiches satisfied a wolfish hunger, and in a half hour's time I, for one, was ready to start up the mountain, happy for the pain I had learned to endure, pleased that I was not going to share the ignominy of the half-dozen boys who would have to wait below on the shore. The leisurely pace of the climb altered when the lead counselor determined that we had only enough time to go up, look about, go down, and head back before thunderstorms came on. So up we marched, faster now than anyone would have chosen, breathing hard in thinning air. With each step my heart thumped and my knees and quadriceps burned, but I was not going to turn off the path like some of the boys, whimpering in broken teenage voice, while the stronger kids pushed on. Suddenly, we spilled out onto a horizontal open promontory, and there below us stretched the lake, small from that perspective, and there, over in a corner, as though set up for dolls, was the camp. An hour and a half later we were back in camp, thunder barking from the slopes we'd just visited.

I occupied thereafter a respected place in the camp hierarchy, on good terms with the stronger and older boys who formed the elite, and in a position to note—for future reference should cause arise—their follies and frailties. I prized my status all the more given that Tom had other plans that summer and wasn't available for protection and counsel. Most of the boys who broke down the first day found ways of salvaging their dignity. The cohesiveness of the various subgroups didn't generally require a pariah. But this company had new things to think about. There were differences of neighborhood origin that hadn't meant much the previous years at the other camp but that now existed as a dangerous subcurrent. Some of us came from the affluent suburbs, but many were from city wards where the suburbs were viewed with suspicion. Some of the city kids talked so much about neighborhood matters that it was as though they'd never left home. The city speech added third-generation Italian inflections to the standard western New York accent, known for its flat a's and nasal i's. Not only what you said but how you said it placed you. A handful of the city campers were from Wards 7 and 3, the large inner-city black neighborhoods. The suburbanites wished to befriend this group they referred to as "the colored kids," but we proceeded in a confused manner that didn't know whether to patronize or to emulate. The black kids, on that score, knew the suburbanites better than we knew ourselves. Some were cordial, others remote, but they mostly kept to themselves.

The counselors, more aloof at this camp than their counterparts at the other, promptly intervened when a conflict got out of hand, as one did the second day when, just before lunch, a fight broke out between an Italian and a black kid after what to my ears had been an exchange of equally incomprehensible remarks. During lunch the camp director, normally present only at evening meals, floated along a side aisle. His was a striking figure: very tall with dense reddish brown hair and mustache, and a head that, from years of exposure to the natural elements, resembled a block of wood. He looked vaguely English and spoke with Canadian vowels. With impressive absence of severity, leading off with a canned joke he had no doubt told before under identical circumstances, he restated the "ticket home" policy to an assembly that had spent its lunchtime buzzing about the incident. Two days later the Italian kid, a confirmed sorehead who couldn't shake his anger, did go home, a good riddance.

A day would go by before it was clear that our cabin group had two counselors, and, except to lead outings, enforce housekeeping and timeliness, and quash fights, they didn't obtrude much on the world of the campers, although in privileged moments one or both might grant a camper some friendly conversation. They had their own quarters and kept their own hours. One of them had a car that I'd wake sometimes in the night to hear gearing down. One was white and the other black, and there was what struck many of us as a remarkable absence of clumsiness in their relationship.

I retain no clear memory of their names but have some sense of what they might have been. Somewhere there may still exist a box of letters I wrote home from camp, and as I would have had little to report to my parents but the names of counselors and an obligatory account of activities, there may be an exact record. Andy (it was one of those names that rhymed with something else, like *handy*) was a tall blond fellow with a clear ringing voice that silenced the campers the instant it began to sound. Quick-witted, he could, and would, one-up anyone who offered a challenge, and that along with his reflex decisiveness established him as a natural leader. But there were other sides of Andy from which a twelve-year-old might learn. Andy played guitar and sang. He played the classics—"Kumbaya," "Drunken Sailor," "This Old Man"—but more interestingly and subversively he knew Bob Dylan, whose music I was two or three years from discovering on my own. From the steps of the staff cabin on a ridge above the camper's bunkhouses, Andy would belt out "The Times They Are a-Changin'" and, more ominously still, "Masters of War." One night at campfire he sang "A Hard Rain's a-Gonna Fall." The lyrics took me all the way in: I, *I*, was the blue-eyed son. My sense that there existed anything like social protest, let alone a politics that might have any relevance to my generation, dates from my hearing those songs. "Masters of War" especially provided a hard new thought, one that brought with it a vantage from which to see the world with altered clarity. This song at a stroke cast the elders, my elders among them, in a harsh, inquisitorial light. It revealed the evil and indifference of old and middle-aged men who masqueraded as good, prosperous citizens, and it set the patriotic attitude (the home attitude, my father's attitude) in a new frame.

The other counselor went by a whole name, like James, William, or Jonathan—and this last will satisfy the requirements of memory. He was of average height but muscular and quick. Jonathan was unlike any black person I had ever known in that there was no trace of the South in his speech. I had not yet known any black people besides Eddie Mae, who cleaned our house once a week, and a gregarious singing fellow named Jesse who polished shoes at a resort in Ormond Beach, Florida. I was aware of black people in the national as well as the local Rochester news, aware of something called the Civil Rights Act, but to me Negroes—as they were still called—lived on another planet. Jonathan was something new. He spoke with classroom precision; in fact, he and Andy were both studying at the college in Cortland to be teachers. In a friendly, derisive way he would tell the campers how hard they could expect to work during next week's overnight canoe trip, how long and rugged some of the portages would be, and how you had better not even think of stumbling with a canoe on your shoulder. He said he didn't believe we were a bunch of pansies but he didn't know; we'd find out pretty soon. Jonathan inspected the cabin every evening at five and did so with a stabbing scrutiny that froze the cabin residents. But were anything awry he would point it out politely, as though it were enough for one gentleman to mention a problem to another to see it rectified.

The boys in the cabin, twelve and thirteen with a fourteen-year-old or two thrown in, were a mix of suburban and city, although city kids dominated. Besides myself there were two other suburbanites. City campers, white and black both, called us "the rich kids." But while the other suburban kids bonded, I, eager to shed place identities, buddied up with a boy from a neighborhood just over the city line from my home township.

His name was something like Greg or Craig; he was bland and companionable. The only other thing I remember about our acquaintance is that I visited him twice after we got back from camp and that on one of those occasions we were in his backyard when smoke started to billow from a nearby apartment house. Given what by then had been a summer of unrest, my first thought was, how close are we to the nearest black neighborhood? Slink (real name Ivan) and Howard were from the Seventh Ward. When he had anything to say, Slink spoke rapidly and in a monotone. He must have relished the effect produced by such words as *titty, pussy,* and *motherfucker,* but it was as though a machine spoke while the silent, inaccessible core of the person watched from afar. Toward the end of the first week Jonathan came in at the close of one of these performances and, taking Slink aside, "laundered his mouth." Howard, heavy set and self-confident, made it very clear that he was a prize scholar and graduate of leadership programs. He would berate Slink when he thought the whites were out of earshot. More than once, on the basis of their growing acquaintance with Jonathan and the two black kids, the white kids would remark to one another that all blacks certainly are not alike. But recognition had to start somewhere.

A group of pubescent boys must devote a share of its conversation to sex. This wasn't a topic on which I had much to say, but I was willing to listen. Perhaps that was true of most. Two or three boys, including Slink, set up as authorities. One of them spoke of an older sister with adventurous friends (the sister herself was not adventurous) who lounged about, boasting of their exploits. Having heard such talk, this boy affirmed that girls thought about sex as much as boys and spent their school days aflame with desire beneath their shy and passive exteriors. Also: in his sister's Catholic high school the girls would get so aroused that they'd have to sneak off to the girl's room at lunch for lesbian sex. Also: a couple of these girls were going to show him things when he got back from camp (his sister wasn't supposed to know). Another boy had a paperback with the title *Lil' Lipstick,* consisting of scene after scene of purple, explicit prose detailing the escapades of a reform-school runaway. The book nearly made the round of the cabin before it was removed from circulation. "What *do* we have here," Jonathan boomed during one of his inspections, having noticed the plateau the book made beneath a sleeping bag. Everyone at some time had gotten hold of *Playboy* or an imitation, but a few of the boys had stumbled upon some really wicked magazines that "showed everything." I myself had something to contribute to the discussion here in consequence of having a friend whose grandmother rented rooms to college students in her big old house in a southeast city neighborhood. Once while visiting his grandma, my friend and I were prowling about in the college kids' rooms when we found a clipping from a Spanish-language tabloid featuring a grainy, black-and-white photograph of a couple engaged in oral sex. Such accounts were exchanged among the larger cabin group, but an occasional private discussion touched more anxious issues. One rather nervous cabinmate (a short fellow with round tortoise-shell glasses) told me about the time he stumbled upon his mother and stepfather very nearly, but not exactly, in the act, while another boy a little older confessed that just looking at a German skin magazine once made him climax on the spot, and that he had felt both sick and excited. These revelations were intriguing, but with neither did I have any basis to volunteer counsel.

Sometimes, during open conversation, Jonathan or Andy would pop in, and one of the bolder campers would refer a question to the counselor's presumably broader experience. Neither rose to that kind of bait. But it was whispered that Andy didn't talk because he had some real life up in the cabin late at night. Between one and four o'clock Wednesday and Friday mornings, wakeful campers might hear the car come and go, and there was a girls' camp in the direction the car seemed to head. We found out later that it was almost a tradition for counselors of the boys' and girls' camps to see each other clandestinely. On Saturday afternoon the first week of camp, I was on my way to the counselors' cabin when I heard a girl's voice in the front room. Later on I saw bright girl-color clothes on the line in back. Two Saturdays later I caught a glimpse of the girlfriend herself.

But that was after the overnight canoe trip.

WE WERE OUT TWO NIGHTS ON THAT TRIP. After breakfast the second Monday we boarded a yellow bus that pulled to the end of the camp's long driveway, where it paused to let the truck hauling the canoes take the lead, and a half hour later we were parked just off the highway, unloading canoes and shouldering packs. The first portage led from the drop-off point to the moderately lively channel that flowed, after an additional portage, to Raquette Lake, on whose shore we would spend the first night. We would cross the lake, camping the second night on an island somewhere in what seemed its vast center. We traveled three to a canoe, the middle rider spelled from the paddle, the sight of which everyone abhorred as the day got on and forearms and shoulders ached with repeated motion. Once we were fairly embarked and canoeing became routine, we proceeded for the most part in silence, absorbed at once in the labor of paddling and the trance of a world that admitted you on strict terms: that required you to sit upright and alert in your narrow vessel but that relieved you of every other care. Among our group there was little difference of individual capacity. No one tripped during a portage, and no one whined on task. The novel settings and strenuous activity suspended distinctions and bickering. Routine conversation had little place. We were far from everything, including camp, itself already far from Rochester, and even near things—wooded shores, rock islands—arose from a cleansing overwater distance. A fish breaking surface or waterfowl circling low overhead counted as arresting and ponderable events. We reached camp the first night without incident, setting up tents on the shore of a lake that, compared to the normally small lakes of the Adirondacks, seemed like an inland sea. We bathed and floated in the enormous lake, culling the warmth of the upper layer that had lain all day in full sun. Suspended in that medium I remember thinking the lake's far shore must touch the world's authentic wildness and my body, no longer anything necessarily mine, was one with it. We ate the coarse canned food and sprawled on the earth already cooling after the long, sunny day. The scent of pine and charred firewood permeated everything. After we had spread our bags on the dry upper beach, the counselors made us withdraw to higher ground, so we had a night of lumpy sleeping under the fringe of trees.

Next day, just before sunrise, the morning stirred with color and light, as though here, where water, rock, and sky met, the world evolved each day from raw material. This cloistered fold of creation seemed indifferent to people. The lake surface, tranquil beneath a layer of mist, struck one as a wholly optical impression that couldn't exist as palpable substance, yet it was precisely into that vaporous mirror we'd venture following breakfast and chores. The two or three boys who felt compelled to halloo to the gulls were told to shut up. As we launched the canoes off the beach, our oars were the lake's sole source of agitation. The sun dispersed every shred of vapor within minutes of clearing the near horizon, a high forested ridge with remnants of a lookout tower. For the whole morning we hugged the shore. My waking seemed an extension of the night's sleep under stars, which in turn preserved something of my immersion in the lake the previous evening. As I worked the oar at the bow of the canoe I felt as though something beyond my agency communicated the motion. Such thought had entered my mind before but never with such force; this far from home and wonted routine, there wasn't the trivia of family living to thwart intuition. Morning became noon; we pulled up onto a gravel beach for lunch before crossing to the island. Viewing it from a distance I couldn't decide whether it was small or far off. Through binoculars I could see rocks in the water just off shore and waves radiating from them. I asked Andy how we were supposed to land the canoes. He explained to me, and then to everyone, that we would approach the island from the other side. We had our work cut out for us, and for another twenty minutes the counselors let us stretch and doze. The lake was restless when we resumed our way, but we launched the canoes like veterans.

The memory of the rest of the journey involves the idea of an open sea with the sky clouding and the waves deepening as we approached the island. The water increasingly resisted forward movement; our journey seemed uphill. With the many corrections we had to make to reach the cove we might have doubled the distance. We were exhausted by the time we tumbled ashore and stowed the canoes. The island was a rocky, narrow, inhospitable spine with a stand of pine, patches of sand, and no place to pee in private. One pine bore the long scar of a lightning strike. We made camp and had tents ready to go up should it rain. The water all about us was overwhelming in its weight and extent; it seemed miraculous that we had arrived without mishap. I felt as though I were up a tree with a storm coming on. After sundown we saw lightning to the west and north. That night I lay on a slope and fell asleep dreaming of sliding off the face of the earth.

Well after midnight a series of screams jolted us from our slumbers. We awoke to see a boy in the neighboring group stand bolt upright, his feet stuck in the sleeping bag, wailing and slapping his thighs. He stumbled and thrashed and sprang back up as though trapped in a swarm of ants. "They're on me! They're on me! They're coming! They're on me!" he shrieked. It took all four counselors to restrain him and another ten minutes to make him stop roaring. One of the campers whispered, "Night terror," and I instantly recalled the term as it appeared on the medical history page of the camp application. The chart listed a myriad of infirmities, from "abasia" and "bed wetting" to "zoophobia," and dead in the middle was "night terror." My father had explained: this was a condition in which a child cannot awake from a nightmare, but screams and thrashes and must be held down until he comes to his senses. It arises from something wrong in the brain. He caught my eye and said I needn't worry about night terrors, we'd know already if I had that condition, but I wasn't sure. The idea was horrifying, and I feared the power of suggestion. To be so enmeshed in the inner ghoul that the hard and sane exterior world ceases to exist—what ultimate madness that! This night's victim— Joey—was by day a very normal camper, a good rower and steady in portage. If he could have night terrors, anyone might. But the incident proved strangely cathartic. Settling back to sleep, I was glad it had happened, for I now formed the icy conviction that I myself would never have night terrors: this boy, thus afflicted, had satisfied a cosmic need for someone to crack from within, exempting the rest. A year or two earlier I'd have been afraid of the contagion of example, but now I felt cured. I'd retain control over bad dreams, and nothing from deep inside would show on my toughened visage.

Next morning was cloudy, and there were signs of storms rising in the West. The lake, wakeful throughout the night, had calmed, and campers were ordered to pack so that we could make our escape. Skipping breakfast, we got across to the lake's other side on the initial surge of our bodies' waking and there made a fire and ate while waiting to be picked up. We were back at camp in time for lunch.

Thereafter, to be in camp meant not being out in a large, ill-defined domain where it would be possible to get and stay lost and where each person, myself included, seemed strange, outside the normal frames of reference. But it was on the whole a very good strange. I had felt throughout a keen exhilaration, the euphoria of getting further outside the ordered zone of my parents' life than I ever had before. I'd had moments in which I'd not only felt confident but positively fearless. Yet there had been something unsettling in that euphoria, not concern for one's physical safety but fear of finding a larger reality that might prompt one to reject everything familiar and dear. Death might come easily and without the anticipated terrors in such a place. On one of our portages we had skirted a clearing in which the carcass of a buck sprawled in odiferous glory, and although I didn't care to study the process of decomposition—the sonorous fly mobs couldn't be missed—it seemed right to think that a creature could slump to its native earth and that time and the forest would take care of it. Human places and ways involved thought and planning, clear borders, the counting of heads, endless talk, pointless quarrels, hope, regret, resistance to change, horror of death. The Indians, I reflected, had been able to live on water and rock, although now they lived on reservations, small boxes appearing here and there on the map; you'd see one occasionally with shortened hair driving an ancient pickup. They were like everyone else now, only poor. After we had come in from the wild, camp seemed a petty and self-absorbed place, an extension of the Rochester suburbs.

I wanted to know exactly where we had been. After supper that first day back I went up to the counselors' cabin to look at relief maps. I had never studied such maps before and at first found the detail unintelligible—all this specificity in one sector twenty miles square! But Jonathan took a pencil and lightly traced where we had trekked and, recalling the lay of the land and water as we had passed through, showed how those features were represented on the map. How little of that country had we actually seen, and how vast this creased and vertical tract with its complicated watercourses. I was struck that cartographers had taken the time to measure the height of the least hill and could report the coordinates of the smallest creek. Reduced to so many boxes, this wild expanse was very well known, and human intelligence might fully digest it by means of such instruments.

"Is the map accurate?" I wanted to know.

"Mostly. But not completely."

The counselors cited minute but significant features that didn't appear; they told of creeks changing course and rock slides altering ground-level perspective. Earthquakes, frequent if minor, stirred the Adirondack bedrock, and every thousand years or so unmade whole mountains and lakes. But then your mood or fatigue or your memory of a place, if you've been there before, can also alter things. Nothing stands still to be mapped. The same place is a changed place. Before I left the cabin they brought out another map that showed the looping trails I would soon get to know on horseback. The previous year a downpour had washed out a portion of trail, and the detour was still under construction.

Horse camp commenced the next week. There was very little horse experience among the campers, and so the first few days were spent riding bareback and learning how to fall. With horses I had an established grievance. When I was eleven, a friend's mother placed me bareback on a spirited horse at their family's farm south of Rochester. At first I was amazed at how high one sat on the back of a horse. When the horse was released the large electric body proceeded to buck and kick so violently that, five seconds into my first ride, I lay in the dust surprised only that I hadn't been trampled as well as thrown. My friend's mom, conscious of her mistake, mentioned several times on the drive home that Indian boys ride bareback all the time, are constantly thrown, yet get right back on. Like you'd know, I remember thinking, my back and shoulder stiffening in pain, like you grew up on a reservation in the heart of the Rochester suburbs. For me, her comments even more than her actions precipitated one of the universal experiences of childhood—the recognition, sooner or later, that adults are stupid. This second experience with horses had to be more successful. The animals were generally even tempered. Before we got to ride we had to learn how to care for and talk to them, and regard them not as beasts to be feared (respect was something else) but as forces under command. Anything that big, that urinated such torrents, was a force to be reckoned with. It took a lot of time to care for horses before and after the ride, but such care formed relationship. These were valuable lessons. We were two days bareback before graduating to saddle. I wasn't thrown. Still in the bareback stage I made the discovery that, beyond the jolt of trot and canter, the horse entered a gallop, and in doing so drew the rider's body to its own.

I became a confident rider. I learned to speak to my old bay mare and pat her when her ears went back. These were trail horses, their personalities subjected to group discipline, but they still could get cranky and nip. The excursions grew longer and more complicated among woodland path and water crossing, with an occasional forty-five-degree plunge. To our everlasting boy amusement, the horses farted and defecated in stride. On returning from a ride we were told not to let them gallop the last quarter mile to the water troughs, but we did anyway.

Hiking, canoeing, and now horseback riding: I could do all of these and do them well. In my weekly letter home I wrote about these activities in a tumble of detail. I wanted my parents to be satisfied with the quality of my childhood experience. But I knew there was a story—though only half-formed—that I was keeping to myself. It had something to do with the fact that I had become lean. My hands were serviceably callused and my limbs tan and strong. In the bathhouse mirror my eyes returned something sterner than a mere child's gaze.

THEN ONE OF THE OLDER BOYS in the cabin evinced a peculiar animosity. Surly by temperament, he had it in him to be inexplicably abrasive, but when someone pins you against a wall two or three times a day, you begin to suspect something personal. His name was Ramon, which indicated already that he didn't come from my suburb. He had never been friendly, but he and I had always gotten along. We had crewed together on the canoe trip and had been paired for various chores. People can become infuriated when you just honestly ignore them, indifference construed as deliberate slight, but Ray had never exhibited any more acknowledgment of me than I of him. I had formed no conscious opinion of him; he existed in my mind as a set of two observations—that he sweated heavily, the collar and underarm of his shirt dark with moisture, and that he swam head upward with pummeling hand motions. To me he was a kind of blob.

"Hello, Brighton!" Ray hailed me by my township's name as I stepped into the cabin. "Show me your hands! Make a fist!" By this point he had wedged me between bunk beds, his forearm against my chest. He grimaced as though he were baring fangs and roared like a cartoon bear. At close range he smelled of baloney and sweat. The two campers on the adjacent bunk continued their game of checkers.

A little rough-and-tumble is tolerable, but his aggressive greetings had to stop. He outweighed me by fifty pounds, and his stink was worse than his weight. If I were to get him off me, I would have to turn his size to my advantage. I had once, to my horror and guilty satisfaction, floored my brother by punching him in the solar plexus. Could I repeat that action, could I floor Ray and avoid serious trouble? His own roughhouse stuff left no marks and might even have appeared playful to someone observing at a distance. Retaliation, if effective, would leave no marks.

"Hi, Brighton!" No sooner had I entered the cabin than Ray, leaning forward in the opposite direction, backed against me, using his butt as a battering ram. Then, holding me against the inside doorpost, he made a string of imitation farting sounds, palm athwart mouth. The five or six guys in the cabin, including my buddy Craig, laughed and laughed.

Retaliate I must. An elbow jab to the gut, for instance. That would surprise him, and the essential stupidity of the person would peer out at the world for all to see. But truly I wanted to knock him down, and the next scene of my revenge fantasy featured a second blow to the midsection and then a backhand to the forehead when he tried to get up. At that point he'd know what he was up against. I could walk away and wash my hands.

But just when I was primed for a physical confrontation, his attacks became verbal. At first I flattered myself that he had read in my body language a readiness to resist. To credit my antagonist with that perception, however, spoiled my theory that he was a stupid person with a stupid person's penchant for imaginary grievances, and it ruined that moment in the scenario in which he reeled in astonishment at what had just hit him. The verbal attacks took the form of one basic epithet tossed in passing: "rich shit." This confirmed my suspicion that his hostility derived from whatever problem he had with my being a suburbanite. Possessing little street-fight vocabulary, I couldn't form a response that referred to his status as a city dweller, which didn't seem blameworthy, and I couldn't call him "wop" for at least two reasons—he didn't have an Italian surname, and the use of slurs wasn't in keeping with my family's behavior. Also, I had no interest in defending the front lines of class identity, as I had begun to suspect (although I hadn't the precise words) that the suburbanite's social privilege was indefensible. So my comeback had to refer to something else, his heaviness or stupidity or some combination of the two, as in "lardhead."

But the readying of defense mechanisms didn't address the larger question of why he disliked me, a question one boy can never ask of another. I understood that not everyone wants to be your friend, but belligerence toward someone as carefully inoffensive as myself made no sense. Was there a simple explanation, external to our relations, such as his dad being laid off at Kodak? Why else should he dislike me with a vehemence that bordered on loathing? What was I failing to see? Did he know? And did he therefore know more than I? And, if so, did he know by virtue of being older rather than more intelligent? Had I, from first to last, underestimated him, and overestimated myself? Perhaps my obliviousness toward him had conveyed attitudes I thought I'd kept to myself. From the perspective of forty years I can see it: my existence was not for him—as it was for me—a condition of innocence and good intentions, but evidence of social crime. At the time I had very little feel for the situational dynamic of inequality. Obvious disparity—black and white—alone made sense. How much more prepared I should have been for Slink or Howard to decide I was the enemy. But Slink actually warned me once that Ray was lying in wait.

I hid a green switch in my bunk between mattress and frame. I would haul it out and whip his face if he jumped me again. Meanwhile, I resorted to the guerrilla tactics I had learned in the school for younger brothers. I sprinkled barely visible quantities of sand in his bedding. I referred to him as Ray the Ape as though this were an established phrase. I started a rumor that he was the one who never flushed the toilet (the real problem, as everyone knew, was the water pressure). I glared at him and entertained hateful thoughts. Then, passing through the dining hall door—I was leaving, he was entering—I laid an elbow to his big sweaty gut. And while Ray doubled over I was taken aside by two counselors from the neighboring cabin and issued the appropriately severe warning. Ray was similarly warned, and the feud went into cold storage.

NEARLY EVERY EVENING, now, I and one or two other campers went up to the counselors' cabin after supper to look at maps or hang out while Andy smoked and talked and played the guitar and Jonathan read aloud from the newspaper he had picked up that afternoon at the crossroads. In the summer of 1964 there would have been a variety of news, but the one story I particularly recall concerned the heat wave spreading to the East and the incidence of heat death among city dwellers. Our July days had been warm but nights were invariably chilly, so you wouldn't guess the rest of the country experienced abnormal summer. From St. Louis and Chicago to New York City, Washington, Atlanta, and Dallas, people awoke day after day to the same unmoving, hazy heat. Letters from home had begun to mention it. Jonathan, whose family lived in Brooklyn, described the kilnlike heat of the row-house neighborhoods. I could only imagine the conditions. Andy, from Westchester County, talked about what it was like in summer passing through Harlem on the train to Grand Central Station, the cars threading gaps between tenements on elevated track and pausing in front of open windows, "like there you are in someone's living room, man." I had not yet been to New York City, but I had a fair idea of what tenements looked like and could form some conception of street after street of dark, airless boxes with half-dressed people marking time in windows and on fire escapes. Tiring of the news, Jonathan turned to the sports page. Andy strummed the guitar and sang, alternating between love ballads and songs of ominous prophecy. The boys had begun to tease Andy about his girlfriend, and no one believed his claim that she was his sister.

During the third weekend half the campers and counselors were out on a canoe trip. The camp director and his assistant led a corps of the oldest boys in some roadless stretch of wilderness. The horses were in pasture. Except for swimming and reading, Saturday afternoon remained unstructured. Jonathan was away, Andy in and out. I went up to the counselors' cabin about midafternoon. Before I knocked on the screen door I saw the young woman there by herself.

For several years thereafter I wanted to believe that something happened other than the fact that a twelve-year-old boy approached the cabin of his twenty-year-old counselor, established, through a screen door, wholly unanticipated eye contact with a young woman, and, mechanically, without saying a word, as though drilled to do so in the academy for cautious children, turned and retreated. The young woman hadn't been in the least embarrassed; she smiled and very likely said hello. In the weeks that followed I couldn't determine what all I had seen. She sat by the cabin's large west window in a patch of sunlight, so I could hardly pretend I hadn't seen her. I knew she had registered our fleeting eye contact, and for me to remember my sudden aphasia was mortifying. I had formed an idea of what she looked like from the two occasions on which I'd seen her clothes hanging on the clothesline: first a red top, later a yellow swimsuit turned inside out. She had shoulder-length streaky blonde hair and deeply tanned arms and legs. I had come upon her in the act of dressing, and the sunlight draped her brown shoulders and white secret flesh.

"Sorry!—I was looking for Andy."

"That's okay, give me a second . . . All right, come on in. He should be back any minute. I'm Kim."

By this point—in the fictive remembrance I'd return to again and again, always to give it some further refinement—she had on a light cotton robe. She seemed pleased to have a visitor and conversed as if used to having guys around while she dressed. She pulled her hair back and brushed it. She smelled heavily of skin cream, vanilla, and her own mysteriously scented self. You might close your eyes, inhale, and believe her aroma was the only reality. In strict loyalty to this memory I would never confide it to anyone.

EVERYONE WAS BACK IN CAMP for the last four days. Our thoughts turned toward home and what we'd be doing in the narrowed margin of summer vacation. Then came news of the riot, although first we heard simply that Rochester was on fire. In his supper-time announcements throughout the last week, the camp director refrained from using the word *race* or *riot*. Instead, he called it a "disturbance" and insisted that authorities had it contained. But white kids who called home heard something else: blacks were rioting and Rochester was burning. The blacks were looting stores and assaulting police and had even shot down a helicopter. The National Guard had been called in. As columns of smoke rose above the inner city, suburban residents armed themselves. Bands of black youth had been seen fanning out toward the townships. The race war had begun. It had begun and for once not Washington, DC, not New York City, not Los Angeles claimed the nation's attention, but dowdy, provincial Rochester. An excitement that was also a sickness ran through the body of the camp. I felt the sickness but remained skeptical about some of the reports. Several white kids raved on and on. Even a fellow child could see that fear and bigotry degraded their thinking. They were not themselves, and you could see at a glance evidence of parental hysteria. Moved by fear, it took very little for grown-ups to embrace the stupidest notions—like black teens invading the suburbs to rape girls and poison dogs. Even if there were a war, I had never seen enough black people in Rochester to be persuaded that whites didn't hold an overwhelming numerical advantage. Jonathan spent most of his time with kids from the Third and Seventh Wards whose homes were in the path of the flames and who had become physically ill with anxiety. Still the camp director insisted there was no war. Despite developments at home, the talent show would proceed as planned.

And so it did, and was memorable not simply because talent shows are supposed to be fun and this one came at a time when everyone talked and thought about troubles back home. The black kids, quiet in any case at this mostly white camp, and for the last few days withdrawn from all but themselves, provided most of the talent, performing a cappella in church-trained voices with an elaborate choreography of step and hand clap. As soon as an act would commence, the black kids not onstage popped up and performed in what to the whites was a mysterious audience role. This was new—people behind you out of their seats and shouting in your ear as though they and not you knew how to behave at an entertainment—but those onstage encouraged it. And there on the far side of the dining hall stood the camp director, beaming and stiffly clapping his hands. This was the last night of camp. At the show's conclusion he took the stage and in his crisp manner, never visibly ruffled by the thought that some of these kids would be returning next day to a war zone, reviewed the highlights of the last four weeks. He recognized various boys who had placed in archery, rifle, and swimming competitions or who had manifested courage and leadership. He talked about life's challenges, the need for people to build bridges, and the solace of nature. He talked about the friendships he personally had formed in the past four weeks. I wasn't recognized but I didn't care. I had soured of camp. I didn't want to go home; I wanted to go to New York City! How was it possible I had lived twelve and a half years and had never been there? But really there was no place I particularly cared to go.

The bus ride home held none of the splendid anticipation of the journey out. We retraced the path out of the upcountry down the narrow, curving roads to the New York State Thruway and the hazy swamp flats between Syracuse and Rochester. In the heat and traffic the camp world we had left after breakfast rapidly became a memory apart. Remembering it in that first retrospect, I seemed at once to be recalling a dream from which I had just awakened and an experience that provided a clarified window on all that in life and death was enduringly real. Against a backdrop of boundless forest and innumerable lakes the undraped body of the girlfriend arose like a special revelation. As the bus turned off the thruway at the first Rochester exit, the campers emerged from their group daze, everyone alert to what we would see as the convoy rolled toward the downtown Y only a few blocks from one of the torched neighborhoods. Some of us were clearly going to see a lot more of it than others, but everyone would have to develop a sense of living among battle lines. Other cities would soon be in flames. It was an election year, and the television news was beginning to reveal a world of small war that sent you again and again to the atlas.

But for the time being I was back in my bedroom among the stage props of an earlier life, watching the square black-and-white TV that had belonged to my grandfather. It would serve for a time as my window on the world. Amid the spectacle of burning cities, Malcolm X entered my room and Vietnam slid the more fully into view. And the little girl, daisy in hand, annihilated by the hydrogen bomb: an image, I thought, of near future probable. All else in the house seemed directed at reassuring its occupants that time and change were illusory, yet to be aware of that effort was already to sense its failure. Like any twelve-year-old, I was used to such rents in the fabric of childhood. Already I had a past to forget as I moved forward in experience. With the fresh memory of physical exertion I admired my callused hands and deeply tanned arms, certain that my limbs had hardened and lengthened. I would outgrow this room, this house, and the little-brother role. That understood, I could turn off the TV and open the windows. And with the sound of distant expressway traffic fading toward points unknown, I could sleep contentedly under that roof.

5

School

Day after day the cicadas' chant rises to a frenzied pitch. Their noise enters the open window, making the woodwork buzz. Sick of the stagnant indoor heat, I step outside, close my eyes, and let the ruckus abduct my mind. For a moment I find the deaf center in all that riot of sound. Then I'm back in the heat and shrill.

Summer, grown stale, needs to end. Leaves already have begun to fall, and cicada bodies, done with copulation and egg laying, litter the sidewalks. The season has no further use. You think, as a kid, how nice to be grown, to look freely forward to the season's turn, silence and sun of the first killing frost, but September approaches like an appointment with doom. Now commence the back-to-school sales. Labor Day, total sham, is worse than no holiday. Within the week kids are up at an unwonted hour, before the cicadas have warmed to their labor, and gathered on the corner where the residential lane joins the township artery. Five minutes behind schedule, the yellow bus shrieks to a halt, and we mount the steps burdened with the day's fetish paraphernalia: new school clothes, freshly shaved pencils, notebooks on which no mark has been made. This virginal state won't last the week. Passengers already seat themselves mindful of past animosity. Block by block, starting and stopping, collecting bodies in visible flux, we yaw our way through the town's ruled streets to the long three-story brick structure. And now we're there. Like kids arriving in the half-dozen buses ahead of us, we disgorge at the curb and file toward the doors. From every quarter children's voices drone and ring like cicadas'. Against the crosscurrents of hallway traffic we find rooms, teachers, classmates.

Junior high: exit wing. Courtesy of the author.

This year I resolve not to be cowed. I decline the supporting role. They can stage the circus on a distant planet for all I care. I wear the hard face that bespeaks zero interest.

But on Day One of a new school year, nothing exempts even the principled skeptic from reading the mix of known, half-known, and unknown faces, taking the measure of their unequal power. How obvious this classmate's need, how enviable the edge of that one's phrase. There's safety in being aloof but only if you fix your eyes on cool, distant, imaginary objects. I had succeeded in willing the condition of impermeability, or so I thought, and looked about to see who else had mastered the trick. Girls with transformed bodies created a new kind of troubling fascination. Quite a few had grown tall over the summer, were now just as tall as I, curving at the hip, and swelling a little, maybe a lot, under the shirt.

This year I'd be the one to impose requirements: Rolling Stones and James Brown. Recognize the towering superiority of this music, and sneer at the British pop groups. These shall be my terms of friendship, take it or leave it. By week's end I have one friend, someone who, entirely on his own, has arrived at identical conclusions, and between us we have one convert. The three of us sit at lunch with two girls who adore the Beatles. Such predictability makes one puke. But the girls are cute, and in their presence we agree to relax such doctrine as we heartlessly inflict on each other. One of the girls dips her tater tot in the blob of ketchup on Mitch's plate. "Mitch" is a good name; it should have been my name, rather than the Chamber of Commerce name (Bill) I was stuck with. Gary, the convert, eyeing the tater tot, rattles off a list of Beatles hits he's ready to call "great." At Miss Botsford's Academy the year before, a girl I wanted to dance with remarked, "I bet you hate the Beatles." To which I replied, "Actually, I think they're great!" The girl had been right: I hated the Beatles. They were not great, they were sometimes okay, they passed for great among those who lacked credentials to judge, who couldn't tell true from sham. I knew that then, and I knew that now. Sometimes you'd hear a mom exclaim, "I think they're great!" Remembering my lie makes me cringe and rethink my friendship with Gary.

This year there were options. You no longer needed athletic prowess to swagger. For instance: you could purchase cigarettes from a machine just inside the rear entrance to the supermarket across from the school. A brick wall of ambiguous jurisdiction provided a place for kids to meet. You could go over there and hang out, and no one would bug you, unless you had an older brother jealous of encroachment, in which case you needed to time your appearance. If kids got into fights, it involved two guys over a girl or two girls over a guy and didn't involve disinterested parties. Kids didn't taunt just for entertainment.

The year before, at recess, two confident boys had questioned my ability to beat up one or both of them, had questioned whether I could beat up anyone—whether, even, I could pin Kenny, small but wiry, a favorite with the girls, who treated him like a pet. I took the bait. Kenny had repeated jokes at my expense; he had won every academic and citizenship prize and was commonly thought to serve as informer. He had just emerged from the back door and for once, happily, wasn't carrying an armload of books, which I'd have had to tumble to the ground. I respected books and was glad they wouldn't figure in this incident. I could topple and then pin Kenny, and it would all be over in seconds. I said as much as I seized him—gently, I thought—by the shoulder: this is all fake, so just play along. But beneath my palm his shoulder pivoted and drove at my chest, his whole body mobilized against what had begun as halfhearted aggression. And then I was motivated. With a sweep of my foot I took out his legs and, falling against him, managed to fasten his wrists. I had him pinned. Then, as I got up, I noticed the stunned eyes and mouth and tried to take his hand, to help him to his feet in a gesture of renewed civility. He got to his knees, turned, and vomited. What could I say? "I'm sorry, I'm really sorry." To which he replied, "It's okay, just leave me alone." Ropes of vomit saliva hung from his mouth. The two boys who had instigated things had danced away, laughing. This was my mess. It was not in my character to do such things; it was someone else's act. The sight, the stink of vomit, stayed with me. All afternoon I waited for my summons and just wished the ordeal to be over. Why couldn't school officials do their jobs? Between classes I overheard one girl ask another, did you hear what happened to Kenny? My villainy was out. Was there not some penance I could do? But admission of anything was like death. I had to convert my shame to indifference. When I reflected that Kenny was Jewish I felt worse: deep inside me was this Nazi goon. But nothing happened, and outwardly I got off scot-free.

So this year I met kids at the wall to smoke or fake smoke, to discuss music and hear high school girls and boys converse. These were kids of an alternate pattern; here was education of a sort.

The boy with stringy black bangs proclaimed, "I got a pen and a bag of Cheetos."

"Well," answered the boy with blond mop, "I got this" (a beer can raised an inch from a sweatshirt pocket).

They had just come from a shoplifting expedition at the poorly managed supermarket across the street. They chatted a while about one of their friends who had run her mom's car into a row of garbage cans, and everyone laughed. Then a high school girl, tough and pretty, with dark streaks in her yellow hair, exhaling smoke from mouth and nose, spoke: "That guy at Rollo's said he'd give me thirty dollars to pee on him." Rollo's was an outlet for cheap, trendy clothes.

"You gonna do it?" They wanted to know. The girl wore an expression: I'm considering my options.

"It's thirty dollars."

"That's really sick."

"Does he get to pee on you?"

"No, but he gets to pee on *you*."

Gym class, a daily humiliation preceded and followed by the terror of an unsupervised locker room, was not quite the horror it might have been. I had learned at camp how to undress without calling attention to myself, to align with the bigger and stronger kids, and to avoid getting bushwhacked in the gang shower. They'd get a kid down and put soap in his eyes and then snap wet towels at his privates. The kid would put out a falsetto wail until Mr. Briggs, the gym teacher, burst in to break it up. He'd linger to chew out the victim for being such a patsy. But the boys who bullied were a subelite. Just knowing that afforded a degree of protection. Being good at something, anything, in the realm of physical boy activity secured a rung other than the lowest in the male hierarchy. I could never do anything to alter the fact that I was younger than nearly all my classmates ("When are you going to grow hair on your balls?" Mr. Briggs, total asshole, asked in sixth grade before the whole class), so I just had to stay on alert. Chris, smaller and weaker than I, was exempt by virtue of his outlaw fame. Our friendship had brought me a line of credit, but after sixth grade he was gone. Some of the friendless older boys made overtures to the younger, and thus I had once indulged the acquaintance of a boy named Arthur Frueg. Among the slick set his name converted to Farter Frog. He was sad to the point of pariah-hood, a born slob in a constant sweat, glasses riding the tip of his nose, but he had magnificent coin and comic book collections and his grandmother was friends with my mom. Mysteriously, he lived with the grandparents: evidence, there, of something organically wrong. The question of whether I could continue this friendship in junior high was thankfully mooted when he moved away. Throughout elementary my strategy had been to avoid being tagged weakest and most pathetic. I had succeeded at that and now, in seventh grade, looked to ascend. In the annual President's Fitness Test, I scored badly on the pull-up and rope climb, but in the top percentile on agility and endurance. "Need to work on that arm strength," remarked one of the stronger boys, as if to say, "We can see you're coming along."

Over my shoulder and upper arm I visualized a thickening muscle shield. Puzzling over the objectified image standing before me in the mirror, I thought I detected encouraging signs.

The boy's bathroom in the basement west wing had four stalls, trough urinal, and two sets of sinks and mirrors on opposing walls. You'd catch sight of your unsuspecting profile in multiple receding frames. Here as in public restrooms everywhere, flushing was optional, and the place stank at high decibels. In addition to receiving normal waste, the stalls were depositories of vomit and diarrhea. It was probably too much to expect sick people to pull the knob. Just be happy they made it to the bathroom. I'd had an abdominal spasm once, and it was only by miracles of timing and privacy that I didn't have to be sent home. Then, in the sixth grade, I was at my desk, one row from the window, when I heard the sound of heavy liquid hitting the floor and almost simultaneously caught the scent of sharp and sour cheese. A boy on the window row had stood right up and heaved his all. No preamble, just spew. The class was evacuated fire-drill style and moped in the hall until the mop brigade had done its work and we were informed the classroom was safe to reoccupy. But a trace vomit odor hung in the air; it was there next day and indeed every day until the end of the year, and anyone present that morning would know that the odor had become a permanent part of that room's character. Another time a little kid barfed in the cafeteria, and the joke of course was that no one even noticed. We must have all known, at some level, that every body had the capacity of making some liquid public stink, and so everyone saw his or her fate reflected in these victims. Girls with their menses had an additional liability; we got to hear about that in Health. The nurse worked admirably to reassure us. Body fluids, girl fluids and boy fluids, were normal, and the problems they posed could be approached with confidence and cheer. Pimples likewise afflicted adolescents through no fault of their own, but it was best to leave them alone or let a dermatologist determine a remedy. But a pimple just beneath the jaw is not like the pimple in the middle of your forehead. You can worry it with your thumb and forefinger and not be accused of the social crime of popping a zit in public. The body's strong ridding reflex renders all but irresistible the manipulation of lesions. The object, in keeping with the ideals of John F.

Kennedy—namely, to stay fit and make our world a better place—consists in isolating and eradicating abscess. With the right amount of pressure a pimple explodes with ejaculatory force, and the pus and blood can be wicked away in a discretely wadded Kleenex.

BUT JFK HAD DIED THE YEAR BEFORE. That was part of what felt different. Everyone hardened in accord with the national trend. The goal this year was to be cool and stay out of trouble. Better, socially, to err on the side of cool. Yet nothing was worse than for school authorities to haul you down by the scruff of your neck. Schools are ruled by fake-friendly adults who express an unctuous institutional concern, thinking thereby they can mask their profound personal satisfaction at nailing you, but in vain. I spent two weeks hanging out at the smoking wall, listening to the drivel of older kids destined to quit school and commit misdemeanors, before discovering the more sustainable company of low-profile rebels my own age who wanted to talk about bands and books but who cared about getting good grades. It was possible to get into trouble without wanting to, even so. You could engage in inaudible talk and still get called out.

"You, Dexter!" the vice principal boomed as I flowed with the crowd from afternoon assembly. "What have you there?" He seized therewith my spiral notebook and thumbed until he found the page on which I had written the words to "Not Fade Away." Rather than listen to Boy Scouts yammer about merit-badge projects, Mitch and I had spent the half hour parsing Stones lyrics. In his shoe-box office the VP proceeded to explain that not paying attention when a classmate speaks is disrespectful in the extreme. It practically qualifies as antisocial behavior. Above the lined brow he sported a Fabian pompadour; his office stank of Brylcreem and breath mints. Then: "What's this?" he asked, pointing to a graffiti-like glyph—the word *crap* all by itself on the center of a page.

"*Clap.* I know my writing's pretty bad."

"And this?"

"*Pack your self.* Assembly was over. But we didn't want to talk out loud."

I could tell he was dubious.

"What does this mean?" He had turned to a page with the James Brown line "You got to live for yourself! Yourself and nobody else!"

"You have to listen to the whole song . . . ," I began.

But by now he'd flipped back to "Not Fade Away" and softened, confiding, "Personally, I prefer the Beatles. Their lyrics make you think."

You might bring something to school, like a book of matches, clear sign of criminal intent. You could be caught with a book inappropriate for children, like the Harold Robbins novel confiscated from my homeroom desk. One time Mitch came to school with a pocketful of Trojan prophylactics. It wasn't anything like what the VP would have thought had Mitch been caught. He had found them in his recently deceased grandfather's apartment, although what his granddad was doing with them he didn't know. He was embarrassed by the idea of his mom stumbling upon them. So he had just grabbed them and now, after lunch, in the far corner of the practice field, handed them out: one for me, one for Kathy, one for Miriam, one for Gary, with one to keep for himself. Beneath the foil shrink-wrap lurked this occult apparatus of sexual penetration: to possess this object made the untested experience seem at once close and far off. At first I couldn't be entirely sure that heat didn't radiate from the package. All afternoon I kept it concealed in my jeans front pocket. It was fun to carry contraband (I was an old hand at smuggling cigarettes in and out of my locker), but I was conscious that in removing a Kleenex the condom could slip to the floor, whereupon, by mystic force, it would draw all eyes and I would have to explain. The principal would demand to know where I got it and what I planned to do with it; my parents naturally would be summoned, a complete nightmare. I was pretty sure no female teacher could discern its shape through my jeans pocket, but I didn't entirely put that past Mr. Ricks, the science teacher, a gruff, ham-faced he-man type, who surely had carried such items in his youth. At dismissal my friends and I met up. The two girls still had theirs. It had been fun, and this kind of shared experience made a group feel like a group. On the way home I flicked mine into a Dumpster. It wouldn't do for my mom to fetch it out of the laundry hamper. Later that afternoon, with a weight that fell from the day's failing light, it occurred to me that this had been a dead man's condom.

After school my friends and I occupied a booth in the greasy luncheonette a block from school. We chattered in the way boys and girls new to mixed company chatter; we became a pooled and ironic personality repudiating adult domination. We might be bad, but it would take a lot of bad to break the good-kid mold, more bad than any was apt to store up, beneficiaries, as we were, of decent parenting and middle-class safeguards and lives with margins for error. Over the course of a school year we spent hours gazing out the plate-glass window. The same passersby reappeared every day as though on a continuous loop. They were a cross-section of suburban humanity. For a few minutes we observed and commented upon our peers fresh from school. For the most part they got off lightly. Grown-ups were another matter. We had reached that age when youth not only notes adult flaw but looks for it aggressively, imagining flaw not even there. Adults own the world and make the rules, but youth has the capital that is its youth. In being not old it has what age can never regain. The prime years of beauty, strength, and sex were before us, like bank accounts that had not been touched, whereas the thirty- and forty- and fifty-year-olds, crunching outside in the stale snow, had largely depleted theirs. Our group personality conceded nothing to age. The worn but vigorous visage, that presumptive look of command, signified oppression. We disliked most the bustling example of hale middle age. Broken-down specimens, halt and lame, watery eye and unfastened jaw, simply appalled us. We couldn't have said why, but young as we were we keenly registered the stink of mortality, theirs to be sure but also our own, for the adolescent body has to throw off the corpse of its childhood. Kids have reason to be mindful of death; they begin to see that death can make unusual and unscheduled visitations. A presidential assassination structurally alters a youthful generation's sensibility. Fallout shelters admonish one daily that bombs can fall unannounced. The more you learn about past and present, the more you see the unburied dead left from previous wars. These include the walking dead. Numerous old folk in this predominantly Jewish suburb had been refugees: that one there with the cane and scowl is said to have survived the camps. The sight of him sends chills up your spine and makes you think of trick showers and villagers shot between snowdrifts.

Kenny, a totally different kid this year with dark down mustache starting to fill in, knew a lot about that side of the war and told about the heaps of stuff collected at Auschwitz—hair, eyeglasses, prosthetic limbs. He had done some project on what he called the Shoah as part of a history class; he had wanted to do it to mark his bar mitzvah. I remember being struck by the fact that he walked the halls with horrifying imagery, a whole winter landscape of death, available at instant recall. He pointed out several survivors who went to his temple. They spoke with a harsh German-sounding voice and crabbed at kids on the rare occasion they'd even speak to one. In the old neighborhood I'd been friends with the Radners. Mr. and Mrs. Radner had "got out," but my buddy Pete's uncles and aunts, cousins, and grandparents had all died in Poland. Pete's house had felt haunted (the ghosts of his extended family surely dwelt in that basement), and likewise it seemed as though the survivors' memories touched and haunted the town. This infused a tragic dimension to Brighton's bland atmosphere. Hitler would have gassed my classmates, their grandchildren. On every staircase there were dark-haired girls who could pass for Anne Frank.

FROM AN ADULT PERSPECTIVE the child year lasts no time at all. It is ephemerality itself, a dream forgotten the moment you awake. But for the child an hour of classroom seat work is an eternity multiplied by five, five, and four (for hours, days, weeks: a conservative estimate, allowing for vacations and sickness) and then nine (for months). The weight of time crushes the twelve-year-old, and it is the weight of time *times* tedium that assaults the mind, or assaulted my mind as I sat doing math problems and copying exercises. I must be learning something, but what?

Multiplication, for one. The tables helped only to a point; with odd three-digit numbers you just had to work through the details, and do it again and again, as though repetition would automate the process and not, as with me, dull the faculty you were trying to hone. Long division was the reverse action. Here, as with multiplication, you had to maintain strictly vertical columns but needed, also, in the case of word problems, to mind the difference between "divisor" and "dividend." A page of multiplication and long-division problems involving three- and four-digit numbers was my idea of hell. You had at least to attempt every problem before going home, and at the three-o'clock bell the teacher was in no hurry to leave. I hated these exercises: when in my life would I need to know the product of 307 and 679? Word problems made the procedure no more relevant: under what circumstances would I ever treat 5,781 square feet of floor space with 16.7 gallons of linseed oil? I'd steer around all such occasions. I'd do like my dad and hire professionals.

Sentence structure, for another. Today three pages of sentence diagrams. I tolerated this activity because I was good at it: good at it because I perceived and believed in the order it revealed. The more complex the sentence, the more pleasure in the exercise. I identified with the first-person singular. I liked my noun status and its infinitude of verbal options. Except when performing the task of negation, modifiers—adjectival and adverbial—were mere nuance. The story was in the noun and verb. Some noun and verb pairs were subordinate to others: the axis was the independent clause. The independent clause, however, might lose its footing amid an insurgency of subordinates. Sometimes we were given long faulty sentences to diagnose. There'd be disagreements between subject and verb, some obvious but others not; there'd be misplaced modifiers and fragments masquerading as sentences. Total breakdown put me in mind of a character I'd seen in a Saturday-afternoon TV movie: an aged cowboy having a stroke, sputtering in garbled and aphasic tongue before dropping dead in front of the saloon. Often the last problem involved a multiclausal proposition with no distinct center. It was fun but a little scary to see the dissolution of grammatical rule. I had an extra-sharp pencil for diagramming sentences and a dull one for long division, which I found interesting only when it generated an infinitely recurring remainder—a face in a hall of mirrors.

Math was not for me: my mind brought a principle of disorder onto its field of operation. Its system was unforgiving and I could not follow its paths. Geometry afforded a little more access, however, and I particularly liked the tools of the trade. The compass for school was not the same as the compass for hikes: a sharpened pivot soldered to an arm sleeved to hold a pencil stub. I had once seen a war veteran with one leg and one arm, and the compass reminded me of him. With this instrument you could create imaginary worlds out of perfect circles. Sometimes the pivot slipped and you produced an imperfect circle, a noncircle, rather, since it was either perfect or it didn't exist. I liked the geometry of curved space. But I enjoyed just playing around with the compass, creating series of concentric rings, perfections within perfection, worlds contained by a beneficent mind, alternate solar systems. Heavenly bodies—as they were called—rotated along an elliptical path. An ellipse is its own kind of perfection, unobtainable with a compass, as I found by trial, so I contented myself with the circle. My mind, I thought, was beneficent. It delighted in closed, clean, abstract utopian systems. For two years, in a dry aquarium, I had kept a pair of female mice and attended to their every need: fed and watered them, treated their eye infections, changed their cedar chips. When one of them died I'd replace it. But it was hard to judge genitalia with creatures as small as mice, and when the black-eyed mouse began to swell, it was clear babies were on the way. Meanwhile, the pink-eyed male had begun to lose weight and alternated between lethargy and hurling himself against the aquarium glass. One morning I found him wide-eyed and dead. The babies emerged a day later: little pink bodies that within the week were covered with white down. They were cute, but now the mother mouse had begun to exhibit seizures. A few days later I awoke to find the babies dead and (oh, how I resisted the thought) half-eaten. The mother died a short time later, and I was glad to be rid of such vermin.

French, for another. In study hall I copied new vocabulary and gazed at its foreign familiarity. I longed for the scenes in the first-year French book—Arc de Triomphe and Eiffel Tower and rue de Rivoli (not, as one of the not-cools suggested, Ravioli), racked *bouteilles* in the *cave cellier,* long loaves of bread in the *boulangerie.* The Eiffel Tower appeared again on my homeroom wall along with other posters of Europe donated by a Brighton travel agent: Big Ben, Leaning Tower of Pisa (not Pizza), Straits of Gibraltar, Markburg Castle on the Rhine. It was hard to believe that anything in Germany had survived the saturation bombing, yet Bonn was now our Free World friend. JFK had even gone to Berlin and, gazing across the Wall into the stony glare of Khrushchev, proclaimed, "I am a Berliner!" The *Weekly Reader* printed a story about the brave children of West Berlin who had lived through the blockade. How, in the space of a few short years, could an evil people like the Germans reform sufficiently to produce good children? They were all learning English now and hoped to establish pen-pal relations with us kids here. Dear Pen Pal, I'd begin, my name is Bill and I live in Rochester, New York, where my dad works for Eastman Kodak. We live in a new house on a green street, and I have an older brother, Tom. My great-grandparents emigrated from Germany long ago. My favorite TV show is *The Untouchables,* and my favorite group is the Kinks. My life is boring. I think about the Second World War all the time. I believe the Third World War will begin possibly at Check Point Charlie. How about you? Do you live near the Wall? Do people still try to escape? Does gunfire ring in the night? Was your neighborhood bombed in the war? Did your family hide Jews? Was your dad in SS? I've seen the reconnaissance photos: how is it Berlin can even exist? My handwriting, bad already, worsened with the effort to print clearly. You had to meet minimum penmanship standards to be in the program. I knew I'd never be a pen pal.

Boredom and discipline incubate humor. A kid becomes a wit, a wag, out of desperation. Our teacher, Miss Ralph, introduces the concepts of prefix and suffix. She provides definitions, then asks: "How, children, will you remember which is which?" "Easy," I volunteer. "*Suffix* is like *suffocation,* a way things can end." My classmates are nodding, yeah, that's good, a good way to remember! Miss Ralph shakes her head: suffocation is an unpleasant thought, and if you ever knew someone who died from suffocation, you'd think it not funny at all. ("Like when they hang people, Miss Ralph? Or when the diver runs out of oxygen?" I mouth these remarks but do not speak them.) And now she asks us to consider the prefix *mis.* What are some examples? "Mistake!" someone shouts. "Misfit!" snaps another. "Miss Ralph!" I chirp. There's that look on her face: not only *not* funny, but not worth the breath to reproach.

A GEOMETRY OF CURVED SPACE. This year the girls' hips could not be confused with boys' hips. For several months I marveled over this feature of female anatomy manifesting among girls I had known since third grade. Such curvature fascinated with suggestions pertaining to the structure of the universe. Hips curved for a practical reason, to house the gestation of babies, in submission to forces that would drag us all through the biology of reproduction. My sons, my daughters, will begin in that region of my classmate's body. But we were still children, weren't we? Reproduction was a long way off. Perhaps not in these halls, but somewhere on this earth, walks and breathes the girl I am fated to meet, marry, and join in parentage. Before that could happen there'd have to be college and a job; I'd need to complete the transformation into something resembling my father. We'd have to cease to be who we are for that to happen, but that is just fine since, day by day, at age thirteen, you cease to be who you are. Adulthood arrives only at the end of a very long process. But it can also set in on short notice. A high school girl, two years ahead of us, the sister of one of my classmates, was "going to have a baby," a phrase that allowed people to avoid the word *pregnant*. But she was not simply going; she had already gone, leaving before anyone was aware, and now lived in a special asylum for the scores of girls just like her. I visualized winter mountains, scenes from *The Sound of Music*, and a campus tended by nuns.

AT AGE THIRTEEN sexual fantasy is the defining reality of everyday life. No, it is not all in your mind. Every TV show, every song on the radio, encourages it.

Tall and tan and young and lovely.

Songs of the beach, songs about girls attired for the sun: you cannot know the torment you cause earnest young males in Snow Belt cities. Here, there are girls but not those girls. A pallid female in horn-rimmed glasses, coughing beneath a bulky sweater, blowing a reddened nose. A driven young woman whose eyes denounce indolence, hair bound vengefully back.

The one seated next to me has black wavy hair and waxlike skin. She wears braces with saliva-slick bands. All winter an ornery pimple comes and goes on her left cheek. But she has long arms and thighs; she meets your eye and doesn't stoop to disguise her height. Her hair gets longer by the month. In the morning she smells of citrus; after gym she effuses butterscotch. She is already tall and young; the beach will make her tan and lovely. She has another year in braces, but then her teeth will be white and straight. And dry. I'll forget all about the rubber bands.

We do French exercises together. She's smart, and her body exhales this nectar a person can practically taste. I like the French phrases we practice exchanging. I love her way with the word *la plage*. Say it: is that not the sound of waves breaking? I dig a French bikini.

The beach is a site of humiliation for weakling males. Guys with thin arms and spare tires. A tan alone won't conceal your deficiency. You need hard quads and phallic biceps not to get sand kicked in your face. With every opportunity not to be fat, every injunction not to be weak, you deserve sand kicked in your face. It was far easier for me to imagine receiving than sending sand. I knew I was somewhere in the middle, one of those guys slyly ascertaining his station relative to other males. A little reflection led you to see that guys kicked sand as a way of proclaiming, "I am not weak," when, in reality, they were uncertain, afraid of being perceived as weak, itself a position of weakness. Strength didn't have to resort to such tactics. No really splendid girl would admire sordid bullying. The Girl from Ipanema surely wouldn't. Girls have their own way of deciding your category, and the guys they approve can surprise you. They judge by mere look. They brook no appeal. But which was scorn, which mere neglect? She looks straight ahead, not at me. That is no help. The Girl from Ipanema looks at no one.

SO THIS YEAR IT'S TIME TO TALK ABOUT CAREERS. What do you want to be when you grow up? You had better start thinking because at twelve and thirteen you're more than half grown! This week is Career Fair. The featured guests during afternoon assembly include a doctor, an engineer, and an executive secretary. Doctor, first: "I am a 'specialist,'" he announces, "not someone you'll see very often in a waiting room," although on this occasion he has brought a rubber hammer to test somebody's reflexes. "You, sir!" A kid sitting in the first row now has to shuffle up onto the stage so that Dr. Klein can ping his knees. "Pretty good reflexes, don't you think!" asks the doctor, and when the applause dies down he tells us about his specialty, radiology: "the magic or shall I say the science of detecting pathology by means of X-rays!" He defines *pathology* and then asks us if we've seen those ads for X-ray glasses on the back page of comic books. "Well," he says, "I have the real thing!" Using an overhead projector he shows us several "exposures": the fracture line on a wrist ("How many of you kids have broken a bone? Wow! Hold your hands high . . ."), then a "benign cyst" in some lady's back, then a "carcinoma" in someone's spleen. "That is very rare," he assures us. The body has a secret inner life, quirks and flaws and illnesses no one suspects, and the impression he leaves, despite efforts to the contrary—despite assurances of the power of medicine to cure disease ("and what we can't cure now, wait a few years and we'll cure that too!")—is sooner or later this inner life gets you. Next the engineer, Mr. Simmons, who begins by saying, "At Eastman Kodak we make the film Dr. Klein uses to find your fracture!" He launches into a description of his work and in doing so employs terms like *logarithm*, a word I find almost as repellent as *cancer*, so for ten minutes I hear next to nothing. Then Mrs. Lipschitz, executive secretary, comes on to tell us how "men and women have always teamed together in the workplace!"

Another assembly: two paunchy town detectives have come to explain the dangers of marijuana and beer. After introducing the proper terms—*marijuana, beer, heroin*, and so on—they identify slang terms we're likely to encounter: *grass, reefer, pot, hootch, brewsky, horse*—which they pronounce with heavy quotation marks, as in: "Just last week we stopped a carload of kids who sold 'brewskies' from their trunk to an undercover agent—a Boy Scout from Troop 98!" A "toke" of "pot" leads inevitably to "a wild ride on that white horse!"; a glass of "suds" to alcoholism and the life of a bum. "What if you combine them?" I ask during the question-and-answer period, "Does that get you off the hook?" But these guys aren't humorists: the subject isn't funny; just ask the family of an addict if *they* think it's funny.

Not long after, in yet another assembly, we are issued a pamphlet entitled *We Can Agree* on rules governing curfews, smoking, drinking, dating, and premarital sex. (I had to look up *premarital*: I got it confounded with *premartial* and wondered, what was so bad about sexual relations before as opposed to during and after military service?) The message in short was don't do anything and be home by eight. The title didn't fool anybody: no one solicited our consent, no one agreed to be "we." It was exactly this sort of ploy, this exercise in pure dishonesty, that heightened a kid's ambition to break every rule in the pamphlet, and then some.

Kids naturally felt trapped in the township. No one at thirteen and fourteen could drive, but bicycles afforded some mobility and anyone could take the bus. Escape, escape! Temporary relief from suburban asphyxiation was easy: just board the bus and ride up Monroe Avenue to the heart of downtown. Parents didn't approve of this option: street crime flourished in byways off the main streets; girls might moon over slick city guys and boys come in contact with tough city girls. Moms and dads lived in fear of their kids coming home from experience transformed. The only thing worse was their not coming home. The lack of parental enthusiasm added to the appeal of downtown. Parents held a losing hand, and knew it. They could only say no for so long, and then insist that kids keep dimes to phone home on the hour. We were leaving and they could see it. No Berlin Wall impeded our movement.

"BOYS, IF YOU WANT TO BE ASTRONAUTS, you better get serious about math!" So opined Mr. Bini, the math teacher, to a class of boys and girls. Why, in the sixties, did grown-ups assume adolescent boys had no finer ambition than that of becoming astronauts? Girls, explained Mr. B, could never be astronauts because female anatomy didn't "mate" with the device invented for weightless urination. He sketched the diagram there on the board, precise and obscene. The thought of any such apparatus was troubling—What do they do? Attach the penis to a vacuum tube? I'd be happy to stay on earth with the girls. I associated astronauts with John Glenn's premature baldness and the public embarrassment of Virgil "Gus" Grissom ditching his capsule on live TV. As far as I could tell, the life of an astronaut involved overlong math problems and confinement to a vehicle apt to incinerate on reentry. Yet astronauts were national heroes, waging Cold War in space, and there was talk of Mars and moon landings. An obstetrician in the Soviet Union was still an obstetrician, but a Russian astronaut was called a cosmonaut. Put "cosmonaut" on the questionnaire when they ask you to list possible occupations, and see what sort of remark you draw. The astronaut was the man of the hour, and no disrespect could be tolerated.

Once again it's time for a special assembly. Three years before we had been brought to the auditorium to gaze at the big box television and see history in the making—the flight of John Glenn, the bald young man with a can-do attitude, a figure schoolkids were supposed to emulate. That was *Mercury-Atlas 6,* during Kennedy. There had been a couple of orbits since, but they weren't firsts, so who kept track? Besides, we had learned that televised history in the making could go wrong—no one forgets the abrupt appearance of one Jack Ruby. He owned a nightclub, an occupation very different from piloting space capsules. Put "nightclub owner" on the careers questionnaire, and see what kind of remark that draws. Today it's *Gemini 3.* We'll see if Gus Grissom has learned his lesson when it comes to securing his spacecraft's door.

There's a long delay, and anxiety builds in the reporter's voice as the camera pans an empty sea. Has someone's math error brought the fleet to the wrong coordinate, miles from splashdown? But now the crew has radioed their location, and they're all right. The camera has spotted the capsule; it is already surrounded by small craft, and helicopters hover. The hatch opens and the astronauts emerge. They wave, thumbs up. And now they're on the carrier deck. Heroes. Another day, another splashdown, A-OK. There's just enough time to get back to homeroom, copy the assignment, and get our stuff. I remember that day being far more intrigued by the idea of managing a nightclub than landing on the moon.

6

City

First the expressway cut the city's face. After the riot, housing projects vastly arose in place of the rundown immigrant homes gone up in flame. Office towers soon breached the skyline. Then hotel and convention center gentrified the waterfront: gone were the ghostly commercial buildings that hemmed the Genesee bank. No amount of renewal would completely remove such buildings, however, and in the shadow of soaring glass you could still find aged masonry structures, former hospitals, warehouses, and factories—here a Romanesque turret, there a Gothic belfry. Behind them stretched the old residential districts: battered files of wood-frame houses, streets named for European cities. Reared in a sixties subdivision served by the expressway's outer loop, I grew up determined to visit those places and learn their histories. Life in a second-rim bedroom community fostered, above all, an interest in urban lore. I would plumb the city's labyrinthine depth, pierce its lowest stratum.

Sometime before the demolition frenzy—I must have been ten or eleven—my father drove me down to a Front Street coin shop where a child could find affordable Civil War–era pennies. After I had made my purchase and we had stepped back to the curb, he suddenly made me turn my head and walk posthaste to the car. There was a public spectacle a half block away he didn't want me to view. It was years before I guessed the truth about the large-boned, brightly dressed women whose image he meant to exclude from my visual field. Among the rooming houses and saloons was a transvestite bar. Even after the massive razing Rochester harbored many open secrets, places to avoid if (like us) you were well-heeled and respectable. It had a nightlife—Salvatore's, for instance, supposed haunt of gangland assassins, or the Bamboo Club, which came as

Downtown. Courtesy Communications Bureau, City of Rochester.

close as law allowed to being a strip joint. One time a friend and I made a prank call to the club inquiring about items on the children's menu. To our delight we were told to "ask your little sister, ask your baby brother, but if you ever bother us again, we're callin' the police!" The city was like a foreign country a short ride away. It had excitements and pleasures that were bad for a person. It had disorder—crimes and fires nearly every night.

Urban renewal all but obliterated downtown's antique charm. With calm, keen, horrified interest I watched the wrecking ball bash to pieces the fond old landmarks. Most grievous demolition of all was that of the RKO Palace, a vision of glass and streaming light whose sherbet ripples had one entranced five blocks from the ticket booth. Given the choice, a kid always went to an evening showing. The electric splash of the illuminated marquee among the other brightly lit downtown businesses was like a freestanding hallucination. A downward-pointing neon arrow marked the entrance to a half-lighted stairway leading to a jazz club. A billboard flashed, and rotating panels changed the scene from one in which a rouged blonde smoked a Lucky Strike to another in which Topper Beer shimmered in a pilsner glass. Such expenditures made their appeal against a background of gaunt city buildings, dark or dully lit casement windows, and fire escapes laddering to acrophobic heights. I liked the glister, but it was the shadow of the city that lured with irresistible force.

MY PARENTS FAVORED highly choreographed downtown excursions. Besides movies, there were trips to the dentist and shopping crusades that had as their object acquisition of seasonal wardrobes. Our dentist was located in the Temple Building, which stands at the crossroads of Main Street, Franklin, and East Avenues. We'd go down for checkups in June and again during Christmas recess. Dr. Arnett, a shrimp-colored man in sage-green cap, had a suite on the eleventh floor at the end of a corridor occupied by other dentists and a psychiatrist. When opened, the door to his suite sounded a tone; upon entering, one was ensconced in a world of canned music and penetrating scents—fashion magazines, Lavoris, rubbing alcohol. Such eclectic sensation drew dreamlike coherence from the remote intermittent buzzing of a brush or drill. The elderly receptionist had a hand puppet, but I didn't respond to puppets. I didn't care to read *Highlights for Children.* Mostly I wanted to gaze out one window at the drab inner-city residential streets or another at the downtown buildings. In December it would snow, and the baffle of tall profiles sucked laden gusts abruptly around the parapets of a neighboring high-rise. The snow poured forth like a swarm of white bees.

After teeth cleaning we went to Sibley's department store. At Christmastime, two officers of the Salvation Army pumped handbells outside the vestibule. To proceed through the heavy brass and oak doors and find oneself among soft-lighted clothing racks and wooden display shelves was like entering a forest. The atmosphere smelled of perfume and money. A notions counter on the main floor held various objects that might fascinate a boy: gold- and silver-plated pen and pencil sets, pocketknives with spaces for monograms, beer mugs whose tops were molded into Prussian and Irish caricatures, the talking mugs—Schultz and Dooley—of a regional brewer's ad campaign. Until age ten my principal object was to reach the escalators and ascend to the toy department one level up. As a young child I had recurrent dreams about the toy department, losing myself in its red and yellow aisles. But as an older child I was more interested in slipping off to the cashier's window around the corner from the restrooms where I could trade dollar bills for silver dollars, some of them dating from the late 1800s and bearing the mint marks of far-off places like San Francisco, Carson City, and New Orleans. If my mother had a long list, we'd agree to meet by the cashier's window at an appointed time, and this gave me opportunity to explore at will. If you took the escalator all the way up, you rose past a floor of posh home furnishings to the Tower Restaurant. Children riding up to the Tower had to make a U-turn upon reaching the top or be promptly bounced by the maître d'. Going down the escalator I often ran late and was ready to skip the last few steps to meet my mother on the ground floor. But one time I absentmindedly rode down to the basement. Here, under the glare of fluorescent lighting, poor-looking women, white and brown and black, most with small children, searched through stacks of sale items while store employees picked up garments and shored up towers of shirts and pants. Our visit to Sibley's—winters or summers—wasn't complete until we had exited through the gourmet grocery redolent of crab and freshly baked breads. I'd head to the pastry case and try to leverage a purchase of éclairs. The grocery gave on to a multilevel garage reeking of exhaust fumes where customers after five were occasionally mugged.

My father bought his suits and hats at a men's store a block away and across the street. One entered McFarlin's through revolving doors of oak and brass. In an alcove past the leather-goods counter stood the bank of elevators. Above each door a half dial bore a single hand, and this curious instrument told where among six floors the car happened to be. While I waited for the car I watched the hand and let it play tricks with my mind, for not only was the clock's bottom half missing, but the hand went back in time as the car approached. When the wait was long I thought about testing the cartoon hypothesis that you can jerk the car from floor to floor simply by working the hand. When the door snapped open and people stepped in, a man the size of a jockey sang out, "What floor?" then sent the door sideways and popped the lever like an airman on a mission. At each landing he solemnly intoned the floor. "Second floor!" This was the formal-wear department, an entire world of dark flannel, white oxford, and black, brown, and cordovan shoes smelling of factory polish, where estimable men like my father bought their good clothes. Silk ties, single source of bright color, lay neatly on a glass counter like a catch of exotic fish. The head salesman, by profession an actor, moved and spoke as though onstage; the tailor, a short wavy-haired man with a thick accent—a central European refugee—emerged when summoned like a man who slept in a tree. My father stood to be measured; he wanted each leg measured separately, insisted there be no skimping in shoulder or seat. Always polite, he nevertheless tried the tailor's patience. The day would come when I'd be taken to this same floor for my first flannel trousers and sport jacket and my dad must exhibit the same concern over where cuffs and sleeves should be marked for alteration. These clothes, although oppressive to wear, were part of belonging to a group that was in the know and in control. Not everyone wore such clothes.

In summer, the suburbs gave off a scent of fresh paint and pines, varied by what flowers happened to be in bloom. The city by contrast had a smell of partially rotted things. Rather than repulsive the smell was intriguing; the very history of the place exhaled it. City buildings were constructed of old materials, wood, plaster, stone, so naturally they smelled like the bodies of old people. This was especially true of those by the river. Some of these structures had associations with my old people: here was an auto dealership where my grandfather once worked, here the studio where my great-grandmother painted china. Sometimes, after shopping or before a matinee, we went to lunch and, in the process, walked a couple blocks this way and that. Always we passed streets we were warned, more or less tacitly, not to walk up. An imaginary circle girded downtown Rochester, beyond which the streets belonged to people very different from us. A whole world of black people resided north of the New York Central mainline, which you crossed by passing beneath one of several railroad bridges. On the drive over to the city post office or railroad station I'd catch a glimpse of their small businesses: record store, barbecue, pool hall, wig shop. In the midst of a commercial block there'd be a storefront church. The schools, heavily wrapped in chain-link fence, had the look of factories and prisons. Here and there loomed a large brick union hall or former synagogue. On the old maps this ward appeared as a maze of tiny streets and alleys; just off the thoroughfare a stranger might lose his path. Perhaps because of the German street names, I'd have dreams of this part of town in which it figured as East Berlin, the Wall standing in place of the New York Central right-of-way.

The city museum had a children's summer program featuring weekly field trips. These ranged from nature trails and Indian portages to settlement history. Some of the trails took us about the Genesee River, which tumbles into a spectacular gorge north of downtown. The upper falls had been the site of flour mills, their brick remnants rising above us as we followed the path at the base of the falls and paused to hear the botanist identify flora that proliferated in this lush urban wilderness. Bodies were commonly fished from the Genesee, and I remember half listening to the guide while scanning the current for submerged human forms. I came back from such hikes with a pocketful of strangely shaped stones and tarnished coins. I liked souvenirs, the tokens of having been somewhere and felt something, but often the souvenir was all in the impress of a place upon one's mind. Surely, the most impressive of those museum outings was a tour of Underground Railroad stations. Frederick Douglass had made his home here, and the city had been active in the antislavery movement. Susan B. Anthony, Frederick's friend, lived down the block (we visited her house another week), while Harriet Tubman and Sojourner Truth were sometimes seen on State Street near the old Corinthian Theatre. After examining the Douglass sites, including his grave and the office from which he published the *North Star*, we were bused to several Greek Revival houses in the city and surrounding countryside (now the suburbs) where we were led down narrow staircases to ancient cellars that gave on to small, dank, low-ceilinged rooms. In such spaces runaway slaves had been quartered. Among the many strong old-house smells, I imagined I could smell the bodies of the slaves. The Underground Railroad, I came to see, didn't mean tracks laid under the earth and trams shuttling back and forth, as in a coal mine. Rather, it involved ducking and hiding, hustling through dark streets and across the nighttime countryside. At each "station" you were buried alive. To stand in such a room with your hand on its ceiling was like being in a grave, and returning up the stairs and out of the old house to the summer sunlight like coming back from the dead. I viewed the city differently after that tour. I was in on one of its secrets and had formed a sense of its heroic life.

In 1962 the city grandly unveiled Midtown Plaza, one of the country's first enclosed shopping malls. The central court featured a large, garish Clock of the Nations, with figurine dancers in peasant costume that danced on the hour. The twelve different nationalities were supposed to reflect Rochester's postwar outreach to the world. People gathered before the hour to watch. I had no interest in such entertainment, but I liked to study the crowd. Downtown always seemed to have a lot of European old people with root-vegetable faces and a keen-eyed look of permanent displacement. Often they'd be accompanied by middle-aged children or teen-aged grandchildren thoroughly naturalized to the American scene. Bands of teenage boys and girls patrolled the floor. Two or three years older than I, they smoked and smirked, and the boys and girls hung all over each other. The white artificial light and bland mood music gave the two-tiered cavernous enclosure a feel of unreality, as did the array of shops with their doors wide open. Feet shuffled and escalators moved processions of shoppers up and down. The place was supposed to be chic and utopian, a response to the shift of shoppers away from downtown. Two of the four downtown department stores as well as a local grocery chain were in on this venture, but small specialty shops occupied much of the space, some of them start-up boutiques given to pottery and soap and more or less destined to fail. Shopping as a kind of ecstasy was provided a stage in such a place, but you lost the sense of old downtown. Homeless people set up shop in the lower corners and all but owned certain restrooms. Above the mall were several floors of offices and the Top o' the Plaza Restaurant

where you could dine romantically on steak-house fare and pay a premium for the view.

INCREASINGLY, you could shop the suburbs for clothes. When the last
old-time movie palace closed, few traditional attractions remained. The
Eastman Theatre with its concert series was the only show in town, or
at least in central downtown, for us. Besides visits to the dentist, it was
the particular shop—jewelry or music or vacuum cleaner store—that
required a trip to the city, and more and more of these relocated. My parents seemed happy to be relieved of the chore of parking in the high-
rise garage, site now of nearly daily muggings and the occasional murder
of a suburbanite, and hiking two or three blocks to a destination. Going
downtown had always been a production, as my father felt obliged to put
on a sport jacket if not a tie. At the suburban plazas you could park and
shop and be home in half the time, and you didn't have to change out of
your flannel shirt and old shoes. As my parents found reasons to avoid
downtown, I found reasons to go, and the bus system provided easy and
pleasurable access. The bus took streets parallel to the expressway, and its
stop-and-go progress gave me a chance to mark the change wrought by
its extension. Generally I'd go with a friend, but I was happy to go alone.

My first solo errand took place late in the summer of 1964, my destination the Democratic Party campaign headquarters. Lyndon Johnson, the
vice president become president, was running on what seemed a benevolent platform, and although the family traditionally voted Republican, my
parents' horror of Barry Goldwater opened the door for me to consider
a Democratic Party affiliation. The Republicans were old and vengeful,
and I liked the idea of the Great Society. The ladies minding the table
were Jewish and African American and very maternal; they spoke to
me as though they'd come in with the express purpose of greeting and
educating a twelve-year-old suburban boy, son of a Kodak manager—for
surely they could see at a glance what I was. They loaded me with bumper
stickers and lapel buttons and insisted I fill my pocket with mints. "And
remember, dear, Democrats fight for everyone." I took on faith their warm
affirmations and wished deeply if vaguely to join in the real work of pro-
gressive change, whatever that might be.

Up Joseph Avenue in the Seventh Ward was a shop where you could buy records of the blues singers the English bands listened to. This was the music behind the music. In *Rave,* a British magazine that sold out within a day or two of its monthly appearance on local newsstands, I had read about the Memphis and Chicago blues scenes from which these bands drew inspiration. No regular record store carried such albums. A clerk at the suburban plaza, frankly contemptuous of his own store's timid inventory, urged me to check out the black shop and provided directions. I rode by myself, transferring at Midtown Plaza to the North Clinton and Joseph Avenue bus occupied mostly by middle-aged black women dressed in white work uniforms returning from the suburbs. One or two eyed me curiously; as I stepped off the bus, I felt as though I had crossed a state line. Coming up to this part of town, I realized at the time, could make a good story, but it wouldn't do to wander and explore. At the small record shop, nothing but blues, jazz, and R&B, I bought two albums, a Jimmy Reed and a Howlin' Wolf. These joined a collection that included early Rolling Stones, Beatles, Yardbirds, Pretty Things, Miles Davis, Junior Walker and the All Stars, James Brown, Van Morrison, and Van Cliburn. I listened to Jimmy Reed ("Bright Lights, Big City") and dreamed about the smoky cellar clubs in London and the free spirits—long-haired men and tank-topped women—who frequented them. I thought of these people as having broken out of a world oppressed by drab work and polite monotony. The music facilitated the escape. The really good music was not popular and could almost never be. Anyone who knew anything had become an expert by doing the legwork, going to out-of-the-way record shops, reading British magazines, placing special orders.

Mitch was my music friend. He lived in a subdivision a half mile from mine, and we collaborated in locating odd currents of rock music and pop culture. We went to the early Beatles movies together. He collected comic books, the weirder the better. He wanted to be a jazz musician but lacked musical talent—could do a few licks of blues harmonica and that was it. So he concentrated on drawing comic strips. His favorite subject was not-yet-famous British blues groups doing gigs in cellar clubs. He would ask my help in building plots. I think both of us suspected that, after writing songs and doing gigs that maybe led to a recording contract and maybe didn't, our stoic rockers plunged into a world of sexual indulgence, but we were still a few years from imagining that world sufficiently to generate true-to-life details. So the strips remained incomplete. Rochester in those days seldom got star performers, but often a lesser act, like Eric Burdon and the Animals, came in to play the hockey rink and all-purpose event site known as the War Memorial. Mitch and I were driven downtown on a Thursday evening to what would be our first rock concert. We had good seats, above and behind the sea of girls who screamed as though the Beatles themselves had come to town. At one point, just before the interlude of "House of the Rising Sun," Eric Burdon took off his jacket and flung it to the girls, who leaped like piranhas. It was a spirited performance. I'd attend many concerts in years to come far inferior.

I introduced Mitch to the record shop on Joseph Avenue. Mitch, in turn, by means of a complicated set of bus-line transfers, brought me to a guitar shop on some northern rim of city I didn't even know existed. In the cramped basement of a nondescript house, electric and acoustic guitars stood on display along with drum sets, tambourines, electric organs, and harmonicas. Posters promoting shows of local bands plastered the walls. The bands were small time but already had caught the attitude: no one could make the members dress alike, smile for the camera, or even look in one direction. As rockers they did as they pleased. The long-haired salesclerk knew we weren't there to buy much beyond sheet music or a harmonica and made no effort to conceal his annoyance as we strummed the Gibson Melody Maker. What would it take to get my fingers to play this thing, I wondered, and what realm of pure will might I enter if only I could play it well? But I knew from years of piano lessons that all the practice in the world doesn't make a musician.

For a while I went downtown with Miriam, a tall Jewish girl I knew from French class who lived in an apartment with her mother (her father had died a few years earlier). One of my first female friends, she hovered somewhere between sister and girlfriend, there being no urgency on either side to settle the issue. I rode my bike to her apartment house across from the junior high, and then we stepped over to the bus stop. Within fifteen minutes we'd head up Monroe Avenue past the Jewish delis and clothing stores of Cobb's Hill, then down the long slope past Temple B'nai B'rith into the city proper. Congested late-morning traffic slowed the journey, but that made no difference to us. We passed the branch YMCA and then the Monroe Theatre where I'd seen all the Bond movies to date. We got to the intersection of Clinton and Main and then hit the back streets. Miriam liked to browse resale shops, so we'd go to the secondhand clothing store where people just beginning to be known as hippies shopped for clothes. Then we headed over to the used bookstore where, about this time, I bought copies of *Songs of Innocence and Experience* and *Paris Spleen* with French and English versions on facing pages. Miriam and I walked the rows of used magazines, pausing to consider the nudist-colony pictorials, women, men, and children, lumpy and slender, in the state of nature. "Look!" exclaimed Miriam once, pointing to a page of adolescent boys. "There's you!"

One time after milk shakes at the White Tower on East Main, we decided to head over to the Powers Building, a spooky edifice on the west side of the river with an extravagant mansard-roofed turret. On the ground floor was an arcade of specialty businesses—a Catholic paraphernalia shop, a Tarot and exotic playing-cards emporium, a military-surplus store, a leather-goods outlet run by a guy who made motorcycle jackets to order and had a room set aside for the S and M crowd (I heard about that much later). Miriam and I walked over to the Powers Building with the fixed purpose of taking the staircase to the turret, and the first flight up was easy—second floor occupied by lawyers and local union offices. Third floor, sparsely occupied, held the same. Fourth was deserted. Cobwebs hung from corners and plaster leaked from walls, while the corridors and stairways were like sets from horror films. We climbed to the fifth and then paused before a staircase of worn and broken steps. The high, narrow hall windows were patched. There was a pervading smell of ancient plaster and now and again a whiff of dry urine. The sight of an old winter coat and whiskey bottle in a hallway recess suggested these floors had residents. There was no telling who might come screaming down the stairs. We had imagined getting to the top and looking out over the city as though we owned it. Instead, we felt eerily immured, a horrifying but electric sensation. We shared, for the moment, an intimacy borne of terror. Then somewhere between panic and euphoria we tumbled back down, abandoning the adventure's consummate moment.

We caught the return bus at the corner of South Avenue and Main, a block east of the river, in front of an old magazine shop that had recently become an adult bookstore. While waiting for the bus we kept our eye on the heavy green wooden doors, left over from the days when the large decrepit building had been an opera house, and watched men enter and leave, toting their purchases in flat brown bags. We noticed that customers coming singly were furtive and tended toward middle age, whereas groups of two or three, generally young men from nearby construction sites, were boisterous. These men were not respectable; those in jacket and tie seemed especially depraved. Often the traffic in and out of the store was heavy, and the customers at such times were less individually noticeable. I wanted to go in and have a look and on impulse one day when I wasn't with Miriam tagged along with a group of guys in baseball uniforms who seemed more like curiosity seekers than customers. The door was wide open, and as one of a crowd I descended the steps and walked past the sign forbidding persons under twenty-one to enter. Then came the eyeful: racks of magazines wrapped in plastic, exposed orifice and bizarre coupling, nothing held back. It was dizzying to see such practices so brazenly, baldly published, wickedness unabashed and triumphant. The store was full of men on their lunch hour; they made as much eye contact as guys in a crowded restroom. Suddenly, an obese, long-haired bearded man, the clerk on duty, came up to me and asked, "How old are *you*?" I turned on my heel and headed for the door. The powerful imagery stayed with me: Kodachrome, I could see, knew no bounds. For a long time I had dreams of going back to the store, but they always turned nightmare as on nearer inspection I saw that these magazines really depicted the bodies of dead people.

RETURNING TO WHITEWOOD LANE, a twenty-minute walk from the nearest bus stop, I had little to say about my adventures. I provided a narrative strictly true with zero reference to my enormous need to see and know beyond my parents' ken. I'd say something congruent with the suburban home I had come to look upon as a way station. After watching a drunk collapse on a sidewalk, after hearing two girls on the bus extol the pleasures of sex on cocaine, it was hard to join my parents in our carpeted living room and engage in small talk. I couldn't begin to convey the distressed, exhilarated state of the teenager for whom the childhood home has become a phantasm. The city had powers to entice and repulse, and there were satisfactions afforded by its blatant ugliness. It excluded nothing. It held the possibility, indeed the certainty, of death, and the heart raced in its imagined proximity. Home was a fiction of good order and swept space, the bland half life of one's elders, fully secure private interiors, an inexhaustible supply of food and fresh clothes. You could close the door and flip a switch and the world outside would vanish. By design this well-lighted, insulated house cast a long shadow.

THE SUMMER AFTER I TURNED SIXTEEN I went to work at Star Market, a grocery just inside the city limits where my mother had shopped for years. The store was managed by a not yet middle-aged but perpetually irritable Italian American, Mr. Tony, and my coworkers, with the exception of the older women who worked the cash registers during the eight-to-four shift, were city kids, some of them Italian and nearly all Roman Catholic. The day I first reported for work was also the start date for several other clerks, so Tony took us all back to the storeroom, where, among the empty crates and with the stink of raw meat wafting from the butcher shop, he read us the riot act. I was amazed that this man, so obsequious to my mom, spouted such obscenity behind closed doors, as though that alone, combined with a lot of shouting, would get the attention of an adolescent boy. He didn't "want no fucking fooling around! Youse guys gotta listen here like you gonna listen to your sergeant in the army! I'm not taking no shit from you or you or you!" When he was through he swaggered and patted his hair, pleased with his performance.

The guys were companionable on the job, but I'd never see them elsewhere, whereas the girls were interested in after-work dates, mostly stopping off for Cokes and pizza, and usually they'd do the asking. I sought in them the tough city girls of suburban lore, but they didn't really conform to type, being in reality pleasant and average. Midway through summer a girl named Lisa assumed cashier duties on the four-to-nine shift. She was a slender girl with long brown hair, soft green eyes, and a slightly down-turned mouth made fuller by the metal jacket that wrapped both upper and lower teeth. She read a lot, particularly fantasy, and we would talk books. Because of her hair I faked an interest in the *Hobbit*. References she made to someone named Ronnie (she spoke as though everyone knew Ronnie) led me to believe she had a boyfriend, but during break one day we agreed to see each other on Wednesday evening when neither of us worked. I'd put on khaki slacks and an oxford shirt and thus appear in something other than work clothes. Like most of the cashiers at Star Market she lived in one of the southeast city neighborhoods just over the border from my township; her family's large, boxy house had a full front porch and prosperous glow. She came to the door right away (the porch echoed with footsteps—hardly any need for a doorbell) but accompanied by a dark long-haired, heavy-set girl introduced as Sharon. This was pure disappointment, as I figured at once that Lisa didn't think of this as a date, but as we walked down the steps I took heart at the explanation that Sharon needed a ride uptown and that would be our first order of business.

The address—Cuba Place—was obscure, but Lisa and Sharon said they knew the way. This immediately became doubtful as, simply getting out of Lisa's neighborhood, they exhibited an annoying habit of issuing commands like "Turn right—no! Go straight!" just as we entered an intersection, and five minutes from Lisa's house—after weaving through a neighborhood shortcut to a city thoroughfare—I was directed to take an on-ramp that spiraled sharply and blindly upward to an interchange known as the Can of Worms because of its complicated crossing and merging, all at sixty-five miles an hour. With Lisa and Sharon shouting over the radio that Lisa had set at a blaring volume (neither wore seat belts, the one in front perpetually squirming to yak at the one behind), I took the on-ramp and merged before I thought to look; checking the rearview I saw to my horror heavy, high-speed traffic stacked on my bumper. The rest of the evening was destined to be similarly out of control. Where exactly were we going? We had become part of an evening procession speeding north- and then westward along the city's edge, a river flowing into imminent summer night, and I had the sensation of being dragged along with my hands on the wheel in a car with two girls neither of whom was much better than a stranger. I tried to relax and enjoy the adventure, but there was something frantic and compulsive to the steady stream of traffic and nothing to inspire confidence in the judgment of my companions. "Here!" Sharon shouted from the backseat, indicating the Hudson Avenue exit, and all the suburban reflexes I had worked so long to suppress came alive, for we were now on our way to a section of city where, whatever welcome might be tendered Italian American girls from Southeast Rochester, white boys from Brighton had no place. And then it occurred to me that, driving my father's car into the core of the inner city, a male with two young females, I might be obliged to serve in the capacity of protector.

Where in fact were we going? I knew by now I had accepted this errand with lethal passivity, assuming a role in someone else's plot. The answer that didn't explain was "Dameon's." He lived on a street of two-and-a-half-story wood-frame houses, most of them run down with a lot of refuse in the yards. These houses were broken into flats, and they looked so much alike that even the girls had to peer closely to note street numbers in the thickening twilight while I made a second pass down the street. Creeping along at five miles an hour, I managed to suppress a wave of panic and was about to insist that we leave *now* when Sharon noticed the two black males approaching from our rear and said, "Wait—I'll ask these guys here." To my astonishment they politely indicated a house three doors down and continued on their way. Sharon wanted to be dropped off (do I allow this as male protector of a girl with the sense of a small child?), and as I idled the car she said, "You guys park and meet me there." She exited the vehicle, slamming the door, and I recalled at once that she had slammed the door on her way in; such practice, annoying anytime and anywhere, might on this street attract dangerous attention. Leaving the car was not part of the bargain. The street in any case was parked up. I had all but determined we'd wait in the car (I had the path back to the expressway mapped in my mind as though traced in red at the Triple A) when Lisa said, "Wait—there's an alley, you can park there, everybody parks there. The cops never check, they never come up this way." And so the option of making a clean getaway without Sharon—an interloper into this supposed date—was lost.

Parking my father's blue Caprice in the litter-strewn alley seemed the height of folly; when I told Lisa we were staying no longer than five minutes she said, "Sure—whatever you say. It shouldn't take long." The alley was two doors down from Dameon's, and as we passed a porch of older men we were loudly and ironically but not, so I thought, belligerently greeted: "Evening there, pretty young white lady! And evening there, young man!"

The front door to Dameon's house was wedged open, and we started up the central staircase in a wash of cooking smells emanating from different corners. We reached the first landing; behind a door on the floor above I could hear voices of two or more men who seemed to quarrel but then burst out laughing. Still on our way up, Lisa suddenly remembered that Dameon had moved from his sister's to a basement apartment, so back we went and out and around to the far side. Here a set of concrete steps led downward. Down we proceeded—far down indeed, for the basement seemed unusually deep, to a metal door, against which two of Lisa's delicate knuckles rapped.

Sharon came to the door, minus some article of clothing—the sweater she had been wearing over what I now saw was a low-cut top, as though in the interval she had become the wife. She brought us through the cramped kitchen smelling vaguely of gas to a windowless room thick with incense and lit with candles and black lights. There, cross-legged on the floor, as it were in state, sat a person who had to be Dameon, the inscrutable. He couldn't have been taller than five feet five with a rather slight frame. He had an oval, feminine face and shoulder-length straightened hair. He wore a loose-hanging outfit that reminded me of my aunt Margaret's pantsuits but with African motifs. He—or was it she? I was by no means certain, for the first minutes we were there, that this person was male, although when he angled his head I noticed a mustache sparely crowning the upper lip. I figured he was black from the fact that he lived in this neighborhood, but his face was pale in the black light and his hair flashed red when he rotated his chin. Green side up, a stack of bills lay by his knee. He seemed to be wearing blue-tinted glasses, but all color in that place remained speculative. I was introduced as "this guy here, our friend who drove us up," as though that designation guaranteed safe passage, at which Dameon adjusted his sublimely disinterested gaze approximately in my direction with the evident conviction that there was nothing to see. Dameon presented the aspect of a totally occluded consciousness in which you hardly existed even in theory—less than naked: *not there*. His walls were adorned with scimitars and tapestries and under the cloud of incense I felt somewhere in Asia Minor. Bass-heavy funk flowed from the corners of the room. Beneath the sandalwood lurked an earthen, humid, penetrating odor that combined the stench of a butcher shop with that of a clogged toilet. The longer I sat on what I suspected to be a rather moist carpet, the more aware I became of the odor. It was, as a person knows instinctively, the smell of death, most likely produced by mice that had died in the wall, but at the time I visualized evening news stories in which bodies were recovered from houses like this. After about five minutes, during which the four of us sat as though absorbed in silent prayer, Sharon caught my eye and smiled with what seemed grotesque calculation while Dameon spoke to Lisa in whispered falsetto: "Here, no more after this."

Having pocketed a vial she glanced at me sheepishly and said, "Let's go."

As we stood up Sharon remarked, "Cobra will give me a ride, so just go have fun."

We moved through the kitchen and up the stairs, and my biggest anxiety eased when we got to the alley and the Caprice was intact and we had a clear shot out of those streets back to the expressway. When ten minutes into the return trip Lisa asked, "Can you just take me home?" I had the impression she had spoken that question five minutes earlier. Not much of a date, but as an unsuspecting courier I had seen a part of the world. I had penetrated at last to the bottom of my city if only to see it as a tourist. As we approached her house Lisa, for reasons best known to herself, said, "Don't get out," and then kissed me hard on the mouth, full lips with metal just behind imparting a coinlike taste.

Ten minutes later I parked the Caprice and mounted the steps to the kitchen. My parents had just fixed bourbon highballs and were entertaining Mrs. Smiley, a neighborhood friend. Did I want to be the fourth in bridge? They dealt me a hand.

7

Urban Paths

Asuburban teen exploring the city, I was well aware that certain byways had furnished the scenes of my parents' youth. If I were passing in their vicinity—up or down Lake Avenue, say—I'd feel the proximity of quiet streets where people dead for thirty years strolled and spoke and went about their business. The old neighborhoods had been like villages: snug rows of upright houses with three generations under one roof, church and schoolhouse just up the block, grocery and tavern down on the corner. Children and old people went everywhere on foot. Sidewalks remained open through the long snowy winters, and cousins dropped by. In spring the city erupted in leaf and flower. Then, even modest streets acquired a parklike elegance, large elm and blossoming lilac adorning the postage-stamp yard. On Memorial Day, flags and bunting proliferated on cornice and streetlamp. An observant child in my parents' time might note, among the various contingents in the Main Street parade, the half-dozen wizened veterans, black and white, of the GAR. Downtown, in the old photographs, is a setting of big parades. Well-heeled pedestrians revel in a dated glamour, and the streets are full of stylish cars. Young and unmarried, each of my parents knew how to make a grand appearance. There was always something to do—matinees and shopping by day, dining and entertainment far into the night. Concerts at the Eastman School, where my aunt Margaret studied organ, supporting herself by playing piano in a movie theater on Gibbs Street, featured the world's most prominent virtuosi. You might want to avoid the seedy blocks on either side of the river but otherwise come and go as you please.

I grew up hearing about this erstwhile city peopled by family and friends long deceased. The ghosts of my mother's reminiscence populated

Snowplow on Clifford Avenue. Courtesy Communications Bureau, City of Rochester.

my early mental life. It was hard to know where her memory left off and mine commenced. During meals, before bed, in the seams of a day scheduled around household tasks, she could always open a door to past life. She could just as quickly close the door. Apropos of who knows what in the living day she would begin her story, "When I was seven . . ." She told short, easy-moving anecdotes, tributaries, I would later surmise, of a large and turbulent current that never entirely came into view. Her stories possessed the vividness of dreams, an occult charm not explained by their ostensible content. There was the ice cream her mother made for her seventh birthday. The touring car her father brought home one warm summer evening. The stormy afternoon her grandfather called her to the third-floor landing to see that it was raining on one side of the house but not the other. There were the tales of young womanhood—parties and yachting excursions and adventures connected with her clerical job at Kodak Office on State Street. As she told and later retold those stories it was hard not to feel that I preexisted in that far time, for wasn't I, before I was I, already a part of her life and destiny? And now the shadow of the Great Depression fell over the narrative. There was the sight of her grandmother sitting at the dining table tallying her stock losses. The dowdy

Model A that replaced the touring car. The hungry men at the back steps looking for work or food.

When I was a child her stories evoked a distant past, but as a teenager I noticed even recent events assumed, in her telling, a certain antiquity, as though time in its brief as in its longer passages effected a fatal estrangement. Perhaps that explained why she favored details: what people were wearing, what they said, under what conditions of light and shade. Brief as the story might be she will not hurry the plot. Usually, plot doesn't count for much—what matters is that after forty, sixty, eighty years, here she is remembering a moment that took place when she was seven, fourteen, twenty-one, can close her eyes and see it "just like it happened yesterday." Time, which washes all things away, is powerless to weaken memory's hold on certain objects—beloved faces, the house where life was whole and free. My mother recalls what it was like to think, dream, and remember at an early age. She spoke fluently before her second birthday, and her powers of memory were already active. She grew up the youngest of three daughters, and her siblings often accused her of recalling events that preceded her birth. If the accusations are true, it only proves that she herself has always been a deep listener. Her stories are centered in the remote, lost world of childhood: the three-story residence on Birr Street in the then fashionable Tenth Ward where she lived with her mother, father, and two sisters, as well as their live-in black servant, Lydia. Her father, "Dada," my grandfather Culp, entrepreneur, actor, singer, songwriter, and yachtsman, wore the ermine of a local celebrity. Her mother, Flora, descended from a large German clan whose success in the horticulture industry had given their name, Ellwanger, social prominence. Rochester, by virtue of their achievements, had come to be known as "the Flower City." (I remember thinking all at once in my twenties: Flora, horticulture—the name an exact fit.) My grandparents lived the life of parvenus in a city that lacked old wealth. The neighborhood was wooded and landscaped, and there were parks developed on land donated by the Ellwanger family. Down on Lake Avenue, outside this sheltered enclave, the girls could catch the streetcar south to downtown or north to Ontario Beach.

As a child eager to know my connections I was intrigued by the female character of that house. It contrasted with our own household, where males held a three-to-one edge and the boys lacked a sister's counsel in learning the ways of young women. As the object of nurtured memory, my mother's girlhood home possessed an unhurried air, as though young and old the women moved to their own mysterious calendar. The little stories my mother tells, all but a few, take as their focus some pleasurable novelty that affirms the bonds of family and friends. Life is a series of happy surprises that leave one unchanged. The days brim with a quiet joy that night preserves against the morrow's coming. The world thus invoked resists time, and so vivid are her recollections that as a child I could imagine making my way to a downtown corner across the river to catch the Lake Avenue streetcar (defunct for years) and ride it up to Birr Street. There, the child my mother had been would stand on a porch impatient to greet her lost sibling. Together we'd let the day elapse, then look to the west as the sun set in a sky framed by elms and the gables of neighboring houses. The world in that dream settled into an eternity of pink sky and yellow leaf.

As an older listener I could hear in her stories an understated sorrow, an unappeased anger. At thirteen my mother lost her own mother to pneumonia. A few years earlier, to my grandfather's dismay, Flora had joined the Church of Christ, Scientist, and in her last illness stuck by her creed. "She was never sick," my mother recalls. "That Saturday I had gone off to watch a circus set up in Edgerton Park, and when I came home I saw that she had come down with a cold. The next day she lay all day on her back, and the day after that she died. Dada took me along to pick out a casket. He sent me off before the funeral to get my hair cut. I sat in the barber's chair and looked at my face in the mirror, thinking, 'I've just lost my mother.' I can still see myself in that hard leather chair. The week after that I took the tenth-grade Regents algebra exam and made an A. I don't know how I ever survived."

This was the second wife my grandfather had buried, and he would preserve ever afterward a contempt of faith-based doctrines—to his businessman's temper, Sunday-morning Episcopal service addressed every conceivable need. But Flora, cousin Anne would tell me years later, had really died "of a broken heart," for George had already deserted her before departing for the West Coast and a year's employment with the Bank of

Italy, and after his return their marriage was merely charade. With Flora's death my great-grandmother ruled the household. When I was a teenager my favorite story—favored because nostalgia didn't impose—told how, the following year, my mother had been forced by Grandmother Franke to share her bedroom with an elderly cousin in the final stage of cancer and to provide impromptu hospice care. My mother's grief over losing her mother came out in that story as it did nowhere else, perhaps because it allowed her to vent a deep-seated resentment of her exalted grandmother, the brilliant and occasionally generous figure who fully usurped the mother's place. Tipsy with bourbon, speaking to me alone on this subject at the edge of holiday gatherings, Aunt Margaret, oldest of the three sisters, would dwell on their grandmother's severity, whereas my mother, Marion—"Mooma's little lamb"—typically emphasized her sweetness.

The other story I greatly prized I didn't hear until nearly twenty. It concerned the time my mother attended a movie at the Capital Theatre and the man seated next to her exposed himself (or so, by delicate implication, she gave me to understand). She was wearing high heels and, planting one heel just above the toe of the man's shoe, pressed down with all her weight. Stifling a scream, the man fled. The youngest sibling in a family of overbearing personalities, my mother was no pushover. As needed, she could draw herself into a citadel and ready her defenses. Her resilience had always been obvious, but I admired this capacity for militancy.

One day, the lady who lived next door on Whitewood Lane, a doctor's wife fifteen years my mother's junior, presented her with notebook and pen and urged her to get those stories, "an untold history," in writing. Months and then years passed, and the notebook remained blank. To tell a story was not the same as writing it.

What, under sufficient inducement, might she have put on those pages? How would she have managed the plot? What large wise statements, at her narrative's conclusion, might she have made?

The house would have stood at the center of the writing. She'd have had to describe its ample interiors: how you go up the steps, cross the front porch, and enter the hallway, whereupon you proceed past the staircase into the parlor. On the left is the music wing. Straight ahead, an arched doorway gives on to the dining room where every night the table is set with a whole array of plates, forks, and serving vessels. One dresses for dinner in this house. The kitchen lies at the very back, and passing the stove you come to steps leading to the cellar, itself worth an inspection. When your eyes adjust to the cavernous dark you see the coal furnace in the far corner; in the series of cell-like side rooms there is space for Pau-Pau, Franke's second husband, to pursue hobbies. Make cider, for instance: here is the press, there the bottling apparatus, and when people upstairs hear a pop beneath the floorboards they know that one of his bottles has blown its cap. From the kitchen you mount the steep back stairs to the second and third floors where each member of the household has a bedroom door and beyond it a plush box of solitude. Once at the top—it was here that Lydia had rooms before she left the family to marry an undertaker and live in the historically black neighborhood on the city's southwest side—you descend the open center staircase to the front hall. On the landing between the first and second floors, light cascades in prismatic shafts through a stained-glass window. If you go out the front door and look to the west, you see a house that is this one's twin, its asymmetrical features reversed as though a mirror image.

The house enfolded the large family. It brought them together at mealtime. It accommodated their guests—the girlhood friends of the sisters, the matronly friends of their mother and grandmother, their father's chums who came for musical evenings, their step-grandfather's cronies. The house afforded space to be alone, and at times, when you were there by yourself, it welled with palpable emptiness. I am pretty sure that, in death as in life, my grandmother Flora was there, assuming the nearly tangible absence of one who stepped out but is expected any moment—the impression unfading after five and ten and fifteen years. Might not the sisters console themselves with the thought that she came in through the side door and has yet to emerge, in this lapse of time, from one of the house's many interior rooms? In dying she had vanished behind a wall. To be sad in this house was to be comforted by her person's lasting impress.

My mother's girlhood friends lived in similarly complicated houses. Some of them likewise had ghost family members. Always in back there were fruit trees and vegetable gardens and secret paths traversing property lines. Out front, sidewalks extended in every direction under the unbroken canopy of the elms. The streets had green center medians. You had to be wary of the bearded stranger toting his scavengings in a cloth bag, but even he inspired little fear. Stationed about the neighborhood were elderly relatives in straw hats—men in suspenders, women in black dresses. But there was a multitude of young people, and banding together they could easily slip the elders' watch. If you went one block east you came to a park; three blocks north there was another park big enough to contain a pond on which you could skate in winter. Or you might congregate with friends at someone's house where there was room for anyone who should join your company. Two blocks west the houses narrowed and the lot size shrank, and three blocks farther you came to a north-south rail line where Birr Street terminated. To the south and west on public land you might still find remnants of what was once a quarter-mile horse track. The neighborhood constituted its own little world within the city. Downtown was never far away.

The sisters grew up. The middle girl, my aunt Jane, married into a wealthy family whose money had been made in real estate and automobile dealerships. Then Margaret married a Cornell entomologist and Great War vet twelve years her senior. My mother was left with the house and the old folks as the Great Depression lent its gloom to the household's underlying sorrow. Increasingly, my mother would feel the need to flee this house of primal sympathies. The elders fell ill and the neighborhood declined. My mother was in her late twenties when, one afternoon, she returned home to find Pau-Pau sick with agitation. Some boys had entered the backyard and hurled a volley of stones at the house, shattering the stained-glass window on the second-floor landing.

EIGHT BLOCKS NORTH OF BIRR STREET you come to Flower City Park, another tree-lined residential street, middle rather than upper middle class, and it was here that my father grew up. He was five years older than my mother, and they could both inhabit this circumscribed world and only meet in adulthood. As a small child trying to comprehend my parents' story—puzzled they weren't always my parents, were once strangers to each other, and once small children themselves—it was easier to think of myself as the dormant indweller of my mother's girlhood than the spectral companion of my father's youth. It was not merely because children understand the material connection with the mother before the genetic tie with the father. It had for me as much to do with the fact that my dad was less frequently a storyteller than my mother. I had plenty of scenes from my mom's childhood to contemplate, but the one clear image of my father's concerned the time—he was about eight— an automobile knocked him down and ran right over him. The vehicle, little more than a motorized wagon, sat well above the pavement, and my father was able to lie flat within the track of the wheels and thus avoid injury. Never again, in situations answerable to prudential reflex, would he ever prove so incautious, to hear him tell it. His childhood, so far as I could make out, reduced to schoolwork and chores and responsibilities for his younger siblings for whom he existed as father surrogate. (There was something Abraham Lincoln–like in this precocious and sorrowful responsibility, a parallel enforced by the fact that his birthday is February 12.) His father had a rheumatic heart and died in his fifties. His mother had illnesses, including a brain tumor, but was said to retain, through all her trials, humor and grace. Her name was Elsie, which I associated with the Borden cow. When I was an adult I would learn that my father's two sisters could be difficult and that his younger brother required direction. And no wonder: the second of the two brain surgeries had left their mother paralyzed on the left side. She required constant care. At fourteen my aunt Bina, assigned the task of serving breakfast, never knew whether her mother would accept the meal or hurl the tray with accusations that her daughter was trying to poison her. I learned about that from cousin Sandy only in middle age. But I would also hear of my father's abiding patience and tenderness through all his mother's moods. After his father's death he alone arranged for her care. He alone put his brother through college. Of these chapters he scarcely spoke a word. Late in life he did relate an additional childhood incident—about the time in Nova Scotia when the river current made off with his boat, insufficiently secured to the dock. All afternoon he searched but couldn't find it, and that night dreamed it had come ashore in a small cove he had never seen or even knew existed. The next morning he searched for the cove, found it, and recovered the boat. It was a page out of Wordsworth.

In the life of my father the mechanical engineer, this was the one concession to mystical intelligence I'd hear him make.

After the move to Whitewood Lane we might occasionally, on a Sunday drive, visit Walden Road, which held together nicely despite the expressway at its perimeter. But if we happened to be on the northwest side, there was never any detour to inspect the Birr Street or Flower City Park neighborhoods. We would only infrequently venture into that part of town, far from where we lived in the southeast suburbs. The one regular errand that way was Thanksgiving at Aunt Bina and Uncle Ott's Knickerbocker Avenue home, just two blocks north of Flower City Park where the Decker brothers and sisters had grown up. Aunt Mary and Uncle Frank drove up from Hornell. Bina and Ott's house featured the verticality of the old city houses, two full floors plus an attic, as well as a finished basement where Uncle Ott had a wet bar with a splendid collection of illuminated beer signs. The cousins could sit on the bar stools and make believe they were reprobates at some dark tavern in a tough neighborhood by the river. We would eat Thanksgiving dinner, the children seated at a card table, and then go to the neighborhood bowling alley and roll a game or two, very jolly and down to earth. Everyone would have a good time, yet, after we had driven back through the city, across the river, and south on the expressway until we came to the familiar exit ramp, and from there home to our horizontal residence with its new-house sounds and smells, my parents visibly began to relax, having retraced their exodus from the old neighborhood and its disquieting associations. It was fine to see family, wonderful to reaffirm sibling bonds, and fun to indulge in a bit of nostalgia, but having done all that, it was good to reassert the distance you had established between your origins and this life you had chosen and made for yourself. My dad poured himself a bourbon highball and told a little about his early years as a Kodak engineer.

There were other nights when he talked about remote family origins—his mother's Scots Canadian ancestry that could be traced to a Viking settlement on the northeast coast of Scotland, and his father's Dutch lineage, connecting us with a shadowy figure whose descendants had drifted from the Hudson Valley into central and western New York. My father spoke of the notoriety of this person, a lawyer who sailed with the settlers from Amsterdam and later dared quarrel with Peter Stuyvesant, founder of New Netherland. But such people were so far removed as to seem unreal.

FROM INFANCY, it seems, I knew the story line. Slowly, as the suburbs grew, the city became poor. One after another the neighborhoods "declined," meaning people couldn't afford the upkeep of aging houses and sold them to investors who lived in Florida. A single house became two or more flats. Dutch elm disease reduced the shade, and July sun blistered the house paint. Aluminum facades disfigured the downtown storefronts. In the sixties many old structures, decayed or not, made way for expressway and modernist high-rise. The wrecking ball was an accustomed sight. Its work laid bare the interiors of grandmotherly buildings—closets, bedrooms, bathrooms several flights up. Vast lots appeared, and the snow of several winters might drift and discolor about the rubble before the grand envisioned project—scaled down—went forward. All about downtown Rochester you saw the outlines of a vanished affluence.

By age fifteen I scorned it—despised the city in the way one hates what one deeply and involuntarily loves. Rochester, I deemed, wasn't a place you'd choose to be if you had options: the name itself a premeditated ugliness, certainly not a beautiful name like Santa Barbara, Pompano Beach, or Philadelphia. It lacked the merit of being unique, as every state in the Snow Belt claimed some dumpy, industrial midsize city called Rochester—Vermont, Pennsylvania, Ohio, Michigan, Minnesota. You might as well live in Warsaw or Kiev. The snow fell all winter long from gray, steaming skies, blanketing the cramped, interminable blocks of wood-frame houses. Short-tempered residents snapped at each other in the flat-voweled accent. Half the cars on the road were rusting hulks. The local papers forever chronicled the assassination of two-bit wise guys in downtown alleys. The place was totally impossible.

The suburbs were worse. The smug set, moneyed folk younger than my parents, lived entirely for the ski slope and golf course. There was nothing for young people to do but groom for such diversions and experiment with vice. The suburban cul-de-sac was a scene sequestered (with what to a teen seemed malice aforethought) from places of genuine interest and merit, and it seemed to me, growing up in this setting, that life got on miraculously without a pulse. It was bad enough to live in western New York, far from New York City and California, but to reside in the Rochester suburbs meant you were really out of it. On summer evenings before I could drive, I'd walk the streets, noting the blue mesmerizing beam radiating from interchangeable living rooms. Through with the work and errands of a day, the residents were content to observe life, such life, that is, as appeared on TV, having lost the capacity to live, or so I dismissively thought. When middle-aged people got together, they'd engage in the predictable patter concerning where they had been and what they had done and what mutual friends had been doing, and then they'd get on the subject of lost city worlds. Those worlds seemed far richer than the one they inhabited now.

The suburbs held an elegiac memory. The adults talked of old times as though youth for them had been spent in the golden age. You'd get the impression that only they had known how to live. Back then they'd gather in the parlor and sing to someone's piano accompaniment, or they'd hike six blocks to the ice-skating rink. They didn't just sit. And fun could be wholesome. There weren't all these drugs and premarital sex. They talked about how they'd enjoyed their good times despite hardships today's youth couldn't conceive much less survive. Today's young people listen to noise and live from "shindig" to "rock" concert. (You heard the quotation marks in their voicing of certain words.) But old times were past and there was no going back, and really you didn't want to. The world had lost character but nevertheless improved. The advances in medicine were stunning. Still, the world had become poorer, cruder, harsher—had coarsened in basic tone. With every imaginable advantage people just were not happy. Life had become complicated. Gathering before dinner on the backyard patio the old people, silent as they sipped their drinks, seemed weirdly displaced, émigrés beset by a cumulative fatigue. As night fell the sky to the west, toward the city, held a dull, urban glow.

DURING THE SUMMERS I WAS TEN AND ELEVEN, I sometimes tagged along with my mom on Thursday mornings when she went to her hairdresser, a Lebanese who kept a shop above a liquor store on the city's southeast side. I hated the shop with its oily fragrance and smell of grilled hair, not to mention the sight of old and middle-aged women turbaned in hair dryers. They'd smile and coo at the nice young man accompanying his momma. Nodding politely, I excused myself and strolled down to the corner grocery, where I'd extract a cream soda from the cooler stocked with soft drinks and beer. After purchasing it and popping the cap, I lingered by the newsstand, gazing at the girls who adorned the covers of the men's magazines. I'd learn from the *National Enquirer* about the boy who beeped Morse code in his sleep or the Klansmen aliens had turned into Negroes. That done, I'd have at least a half hour to walk down Park Avenue's leafy corridor. Huge houses, of stone and wood, lined this street. Once the homes of affluent single families, they had mostly been divided into flats. College students and young professionals lived in this neighborhood. It was the center of the local arts community, and the ground floor of some houses had been converted into coffee shops and galleries. I might wander to the gates of Park Avenue Hospital, where I'd had abdominal surgery at so young an age my only memories were of shadows on a dimly lighted yellow wall. Then I'd head north to Alexander Street where my grandfather Culp lived in a residential hotel. He still worked, so there was never any question of dropping in for a visit. Or that's how it was one summer. The following summer he couldn't be visited because he had died just before school let out. Three or four blocks farther were rows of fine old houses humbled by the length of inner loop that had annihilated the sector's west side. On one of those streets, Gardiner Park, Grandfather and Grandmother Ellwanger had lived for many years. I wanted to go up and look at those houses, but to do so would have taken me four or five blocks beyond the bounds set on my roving.

That family branch interested me. Except for my Canadian grandmother, this was my ancestry's most recent foreign infusion. My mother could recall her grandparents' accented English. They were gentle adults tolerant of children (they had eleven of their own), and Grandfather William, né Wilhelm, was so conscientious that he washed the nickels he'd dispense to his granddaughters. They had arrived as children in the 1840s, Maria from the lower Rhine, Wilhelm from Württemberg, and met as teenagers in the large German settlement that had gathered in and about Rochester. They had lived on Joseph Avenue when it was the center of the German and German Jewish communities. The fact that they were German troubled me, as World War II cast a huge shadow and *genocide* had entered my reading vocabulary, but I could form no real association between Nazis and these people who had come from a Germany that didn't quite exist to farm and lead a pious Lutheran life. There was nothing to suggest they were anything but good, harmless, intelligent, loving people who had migrated to America—or so I imagined—because they foresaw what was about to happen and wanted no part of it. You could have German ancestry and be a good American—look at Eisenhower, who led the campaign that took Hitler down. My Ellwanger great-grandparents eventually moved to Rosedale Terrace, a neighborhood that acquired a Jewish flavor as the preferred destination of well-to-do Jews leaving the streets north of downtown. They lived together peacefully, I surmised, former Europeans become hardworking, prosperous Americans.

Rosedale Terrace, like Gardiner Park, was just out of range of where I could walk during my mother's forty-minute appointment. Besides, I would have had to traverse streets where I was sure to be accosted by a pack of boys on undersized bicycles chanting, "Hey, kid, hey, kid, what you doin' here, kid?" threatening all manner of confinement and torture. I avoided such encounters by walking in the opposite direction, down Westminster Road past the old city homes and the Friends' Meeting House, to East Avenue, where I could take my ease on the grounds of Saint Paul's Episcopal Church. A power and a peace emanated from the church at midweek when the congregation wasn't there and the streets were busy with workaday traffic. On Sundays the church mood extended up and down East Avenue where the Methodists and Greek Orthodox likewise maintained large neo-Gothic compounds. But on Wednesday, with the noise of the world at midmorning pitch, Saint Paul's offered palpable asylum, and I could sit on the grass beneath the stained-glass windows, listening to the organist, Mr. Craighead, run through scales in the empty church. The gurgle of treble notes put me in mind of the water of life. I might have entered through the front or side portal, but that would have involved committing myself to an emotion I wanted to touch but not enter, at least while I needed to be conscious of the clock and the rigid requirement that I rejoin my mom at eleven fifteen and no later. It was an emotion I had first felt during Good Friday service around age ten when the strangeness of worshiping on a weekday combined with the beauty of the spring afternoon led me to see that the world didn't stop for crucifixions. Rather they were ordinary events, and every moment of every day Jesus found himself nailed to the cross in some miserable, neglected urban corner. This had been a disturbing but exhilarating discovery. Easter suddenly meant something. That year, as usual, Father Cadigan led the congregation outside the church on Easter morning, and when all were gathered he released a dove to the spring sky. The sky on that day seemed a vessel created expressly for the purpose of distilling heavenly light.

Another time the front page of the *Enquirer* featured a girl of eleven who had been punished with a cigarette lighter. The grainy photograph purported to document burns to the cheek, upper arm, and torso. Momentarily, I gave in to the fascination of this bizarre behavior (my eye searched the caption for some clue as to what the girl had done to deserve such treatment), but I had to turn away. I had trouble getting the image out of my mind, and for the next two weeks averted my eyes whenever I'd pass a newsstand. The very smell of newspaper and magazine pulp stank of the world of adult cruelty, stupidity, and corruption. There were crime magazines with depictions of sensational grossness and, on the rack just above, the smirking naked girls. Although I probably knew better, I pictured the burned child living in the apartment above the store. She had to live somewhere, and Rochester was hardly exempt from crime. Just that spring, off Penfield near the old Walden Road neighborhood, the body of a teenage girl had been recovered, and some middle-aged man had been arraigned for murder and rape. My parents abruptly switched the channel when the Pamela Moss story aired. Too late! I had learned to look upon the world with abhorrence. In whose neighborhood, behind what closed doors, did such practices take place?

Rochester, city and suburb, was one vast crime scene in my momentarily fevered imagination. Many times in the course of a day I was sure to encounter criminals (past, present, and future), and whereas some very much looked "the type," others masqueraded as perfectly good citizens. But it wasn't news of the Mafia hit that bothered me (the dismembered corpse of a rival boss discovered in the trunk of a car parked by the sausage factory—so grotesque as to be almost funny) but the dawning knowledge of domestic violence and sexual crime, the horrible things adults did to child and female bodies. What, I wondered, so broke down inside a person as to permit the perpetration of such deeds?

THERE WERE OTHER, stranger, sections of the city I'd also get to know. Various errands sent me various places.

This new job consisted of hanging plastic bags stuffed with samples and coupons on doorknobs. The products ranged from laundry soap and fabric softener to air freshener, body soap, toothpaste, and gum, but they all had pungent fragrances chiefly designed to mask human odor. My boss was the son of a couple with whom my parents were old friends. He'd made various attempts at self-employment, and this was his latest thing. The hours were supposed to be flexible, although you were required to report mornings at 7:30 to a warehouse on Lyell Avenue, west of the river, in a stretch of old city where commerce and residence mingled in common dilapidation. I parked the car on the street and walked past a pizzeria and a tavern. In the precocious heat of a July morning the smell of last night's pizza and beer hung in the air like vomit.

There were maybe seven of us, and they included, besides a teenage girl and two college boys, people who qualified as adults: two not very steady Italian-looking older men and a vigorous black woman in her thirties. We were issued boxes of samples and neighborhood assignments. It took two or three trips from the warehouse to the car, and Evelyn wanted to see what neighborhoods I was assigned. She had opinions about neighborhoods. She complained of always being dispatched to the black sections, but once, when she saw that I was about to depart to Avenue D, in the heart of the Seventh Ward, she snatched the little map from my hand and marched to the office, muttering, "White boy go into some of them buildings and never come out!" So we exchanged and I worked the blocks in and about Normandy Avenue. Like a mail carrier delivering parcels in an evil hour, a person working this job mounted the porch of two-and-a-half-story houses—most of them busted into duplexes—never knowing what was on the other side of the door. Ideally, you wouldn't find out: you'd hang the bag and get back to the sidewalk, no one hearing your footsteps, which couldn't have been louder if you weighed three hundred pounds. But it could happen that, even before you had stepped to the porch, a dog would snarl and lunge at the door, or get between the curtain and front window to bark and thrash. Or the bag would slip from the knob before you could get away. Or someone would open the door while you were in the act of fastening it. She, and almost as frequently he, would say, who are you? Or, what's this? Or, can I have a few more, please? Working the middle-class black neighborhoods could get awkward for a white teen, particularly if he disturbed someone who had just gone to bed after a night shift. There was a look that said, what now are you asking me to bear? One of my fellow employees, a young man named Tony who attended community college, claimed that a lady dressed in a negligee opened the door and asked for a personal demonstration of the product, a jar of moisturizing cream. "Being Italian" (a phrase that began many of his sentences), he of course obliged. "Strange," he remarked, looking at me cockeyed, his cheekbones vibrating with silent laughter, "this hasn't happened to you."

Another time I was sent to Greece, the suburb west of the city neighborhoods where my parents grew up. This was unknown territory, as I'd never had reason to set foot there. The address was suburban nondescript, but when I reached the site I saw three large apartment complexes to perambulate. They were of recent construction, built chiefly of cinder block, and featured a top-heavy mansard roof enclosing third-story windows. There would be no pleasure working this location; the day would be spent entombed in the half light of stuffy halls, breathing the cooking odors of a multitude of kitchens, and having to explain myself over and over to every man, woman, and child whose threshold I'd darken. Here you could not simply hang the bag and walk, taking refuge in public easements. Setting off one dog meant setting off all dogs, upstairs and down. But in one building there was no possibility of my being heard by the occupants of a corner apartment where a man and a woman berated each other while a child whimpered and *The Price Is Right* babbled, with buzzers and bells, in the background. Out of control the adult voice—male or female—is a frightening thing, and as I hung the bag I could feel the door shake with the man's rage. I was grateful for the more ordinary bickering of siblings or a mom hollering at a kid. This too generally meant you could hang the bag and get away. Old people tended to set the TV volume high, and this was also a help.

The next day—another hot morning with no prospect of relief as the rising sun incubated fumes in city Dumpsters—I was sent to another group of apartment houses a block away from the first, same basic construction but less new. You could see cracks in the outer wall where the foundation had settled, and in the halls some of the globe lights had been vandalized. Walls in and out bore half-erased graffiti, *Jes* and *MariJo* and illegible words of partially formed letters, like dream writing. Half-dead insects lay beneath the fluorescent lamps by the fire doors, and cockroaches hunkered into water-stained carpets beside the Coke machines. In one building there was an odor of burned wood and insulation: sure enough, the far end was cordoned off as the charred remains of a unit were in process of being dismantled. At eight thirty in the morning the complex lay steeped in yesterday's heat. About an hour into working this site I decided I just couldn't stand it. On one floor a pack of children, three toddlers and two grubby girls who served in loco parentis, surrounded me, chanting, "who are you? who are you? what's your name? who are you?" then whooped down the hall, detaching the bags I had just hung. My heart raced, and I made my way to the end of the hall and opened the fire door to sunlight and air, hot humid stuff that stank of the Dumpsters but at least was not boxed and fermenting in a dark, squalid hall. Going back to the car to restock the mailbag, I was aware that I myself smelled of detergent samples—I could taste the scent on my lips and felt it sting my eyes as I mopped sweat. It added to my self-consciousness as the doubting apostle of soap.

I decided to get through an additional building and break for lunch. I descended the stairs to the basement, and here again every other light fixture lacked a bulb or was vandalized. I gulped for air. On both sides the row of doors flexed and wavered, and the hall seemed to narrow. I began to suspect the detergent scent, under my skin and in my bloodstream, had hallucinogenic properties. Then out of nowhere an impossibly fat yellow-haired woman accompanied by her scrawny, unwashed daughter materialized ten paces down the hall. They were coming my way, and I had to contrive somehow to pass them. By now I was not hanging bags; it was enough to plot my escape from this hallway where the walls were rapidly closing in and I was about to be consumed by the approaching wall of flesh. Just when I thought I would collide with this twosome, a space of about six inches opened between the girl and the wall. I got by, breathing the acrid sweet-sweat odor, noting the girl had scabs in her scalp. Her eyes, looking upward at me, registered something alien.

I got out of that building, left the remaining sample boxes open at the parking lot's curb, drove home before the noon rush, and phoned in my resignation.

Why had I been working this job anyway? My dad had questioned whether the pay even covered the gas it took to travel to remote sites. He had wanted me to do the math, but until now I had been too lazy; to do so would have compelled applications for other jobs, more effort yet. I was jealous of Tom, who did real work in the service department at Heinrich Motors. I was the job loser in more ways than one. There was enough family money that I didn't have to be decorating doorknobs, bagging groceries, or mowing lawns. But of course even with three times the money, you worked a job, because family tradition said you must work, no matter how much money has been made, because there never really is any money, only the illusion thereof.

So work I must, but for a day at least all I wanted to think about was the space our money had bought—spacious rooms, space between bodies, green space between quiet habitations, soaped flesh and fresh clothes. Such was ecstasy! Such was true wealth! All this I fairly craved, and all this the suburb, claustrophobic otherwise, abundantly delivered. Such cleanliness wasn't acquired on the cheap. It didn't come in a bag hung on a doorknob. Rather, it was the structural feature of a whole way of life. The next morning I arose early to go out to the club with my mom. My parents had encouraged me to play golf for the same reason they had enrolled me in ballroom dancing class. The country club and golf course were not consistent with the person I thought I wanted to be, but the green solace of contoured grounds rimmed with woodland provided relief, and I took comfort in the thought that our affluence meant I wouldn't have to live in a tenement, although someday I might do so voluntarily. In the afternoon I could sit in my room with curtains drawn, reading. For the rest of the summer I might earn money mowing lawns in early twilight.

TWO SUMMERS LATER I breached the most restricted and mysterious part of the city. Between sophomore and junior years I planned ahead and applied successfully for a position in the substitute janitorial corps at Kodak Park. College boys, typically sons of the managerial class, worked night shift from June to August filling in for regulars taking vacation time, so every week you were sent to a new building to work with a different crew. You'd hear perhaps a little about the man whose place you were supposed to fill. He was off on some lake fishing or fixing his mother-in-law's roof. You were always "the kid," sometimes "the college kid," and generally the object of scathing criticism in your handling of a mop, but at no point was allusion made to the likelihood you were the son of a Kodak engineer. It was nothing you yourself would mention. Dad worked days, arriving at his office just before eight, navigating the industrial yards in the glare of summer daylight, while I, punching in at eleven, floated among the deserted offices and laboratories of night.

Crews worked in loose proximity to one another, spreading out among different rooms and floors. At break conversation was sparse. You often had the sensation of being alone in this paradise of high voltage and toxic waste, giant vats, mammoth tubing, half-ton insomniac computers processing queues of endless data, oscillators, separators, red and green blinking lights, steel doors marked DO NOT ENTER, acres of desktops and workstations, long Formica lunchrooms, steely antiseptic corridors and stairwells, all under the spooky half light of after-hours illumination. When venturing forth from a cleaning station, I made it a point to map my progress, for it was easy to get lost among the maze of interconnected passages. Tunnels and causeways made for wrong turns, and attempts at taking a shortcut could put you in another location entirely. Buildings ran together; they had numbers rather than names. I waited to hear that I'd been assigned to 31, my dad's building, but it never happened. On the strength of a deep filial emotion, sometimes I'd entertain a proprietary fondness for Kodak Park, but recollection of its role as the area's big polluter and probability that the plant aided and abetted the Vietnam War muddied the sentiment. I spent most of the summer in Research and Development, and every so often, where signs warned of electrical hazard, wondered whether this had been the scene of Dr. Bright's death. After many years I could still visualize Chris's dad and half imagined him, test tube in hand, in the dark behind some counter. Could not a vast industrial park solemnly dedicated to material process have its complement of ghosts? With day jobs I never had such thoughts but rather daydreamed about female coworkers. The hallucinatory quality of my Kodak experience could be unsettling but was nothing to worry about—it naturally arose from the hour and the setting.

One night as I dry-mopped a partitioned workstation I heard a voice: "Come with me."

The man wore a white lab coat and resembled a young version of Dr. Abraham Van Helsing in the Tod Browning *Dracula*. "Leave your cleaning things here. We just want your eyes."

I had been told by another college worker that some of the R & D men were geniuses who woke in the middle of the night and rushed to the lab half dressed. This was my first encounter with daytime staff, and I resented this man's intrusion at an hour when the building belonged to the janitorial crew. He led me down a corridor and through a set of swinging double doors to a counter with stools, on two of which lounged his slightly younger assistants, one with a pelt of dark, wavy hair, the other with a pink, prematurely bald dome fringed with red curls. Both wore a sly, bemused look, like teens engaged in a practical joke. On the counter lay three glossy eight-by-eleven photographs of tumblers, each with a cola-like liquid. A fourth glossy depicted a bare-breasted pinup model.

The bald one spoke: "One is Coke, one Pepsi, one RC. Which is which? Don't think, just say."

"Why are you asking me?"

"Please answer quickly."

The only difference from one photo to another lay in the camera angle. This was my first thought. I sensed a bluff and decided to call it.

"Same cola, different angles."

"No. Three colas," the bald one said. "Not funny. Answer the question."

"A mix of colas, then."

"No. See if this clears your head."

One of them turned the pinup face downward, while another drew from below a tumbler half full of cola, or what appeared to be such. Obligingly, I took a sip, and only then recognized my incaution. This was a plant devoted to lethal chemicals. My hand stank of industrial cleanser, and the smell mixed with the taste of flat cola on my palate.

"What am I supposed to be seeing?"

"Color photography. Which color for which brand?"

Too many minutes had elapsed since I had been recruited for this experiment. I was distressed by the thought that crewmates might be looking for me. The sly look had returned to the guy with the pelt.

"Is this for an ad campaign or something? Do you do that here?"

"No," Van Helsing said. "Pure science."

The longer I looked, the more I thought I could see difference in the shades of amber.

"Okay," I said, pointing. "Pepsi, Coke, RC." Immediately, I felt used—someone had placed bets on how I'd respond, and that person had won.

The bald guy escorted me back to my cleaning site. "You are so wrong it's almost a pleasure," he smirked, adding, "We can't possibly employ you in this department. But thanks for your help." He presented his hand. For the next hour I awaited symptoms of poisoning. Later I learned from my boss that those guys were just jackass assistants who sometimes spent the night monitoring a procedure.

Notwithstanding the role I filled as the butt of an occasional joke, I prized what I looked upon as my initiation into the ancient order of workers of the night, a peerage that included short-order cooks and prostitutes. Some of my fellow workers made sufficient impression that I still remember their names. Mick Trudeau, my first supervisor, an owl-eyed French Canadian, arrived, like the owl, in complete silence. Barely monosyllabic, he conveyed by a series of head-tilting gestures his opinion of a job. Freddie Como, a man in his fifties, shocked with a face that had been damaged by caustics or fire, and I formed an idea that this accident had occurred by day on one of the production lines. Cruel fate had banished him to the night shift. Marvin Stokes and Willie Grim, coworkers in one of the research centers, had a technique for every operation, whether it involved broom, mop, or rag. They'd demonstrate and then watch until satisfied I'd never master it. If their partner, Mr. Toller, were there, they wouldn't have to waste time coaching me. In saying as much they were not being particularly unfriendly. In my presence they addressed each other as Mister and would have insisted I call them Mr. Stokes and Mr. Grim had I not picked up on the protocol. Only Wendell, the sixty-year-old shift foreman, addressed them by first name. Mr. Grim and Mr. Stokes were deacons in a north-side missionary church, and it was easy to imagine them performing in that role. Mr. Toller, their fellow deacon, was visiting family in North Carolina, getting in some fishing and guest preaching. Choreographic in movement, they had the whole seven-hour sequence timed, and once when I was about to get a head start on an office, Mr. Stokes looked at his watch and said, "Wait." They were silent at work and silent at breaks, but every so often erupted in esoteric laughter.

I liked that they didn't want to talk. That meant you had the long night free for private meditation. Mr. Stokes and Mr. Grim were far better company than Wayne, an Apostles of God "emissary" or something who repeatedly attempted to draw me out on what "the college kids are up to." He wanted the inside scoop on the sex and drug scene and angled for graphic details to confirm his sense of our utter depravity. He lost interest when, in retaliation, I discoursed on academic subjects. One coworker, Boswell, I came to admire. He had very long hair that he managed to pin up under a ball cap and worked at night to support a start-up organic farm west of the city. He too quoted scripture but from an edition that must have been highlighted for countercultural purposes. But no one got into extended religious or political discussions. The foremen were not shouters. Everyone I worked with kept his voice low, as though not to disturb the somnolent city outside the gates.

I'd get home after seven, just as my dad was about to leave, and eat a light breakfast. Then I'd carry all that industrial nighttime imagery up to my bedroom, where I'd learn to sleep through morning birdsong and sunlight piled against the feeble dam of my curtains. There in that bedroom I experienced the familiar sleepy sensation of regarding the world beyond as something I had wholly dreamed into being. But I knew very well I hadn't. Kodak retained the mystique that it held in early childhood; it counted still as the great providential structure of our lives. I was not aware of the flurry of antitrust suits that had begun to challenge the company's supremacy in the field of photographic supply, prelude to Kodak's precipitous and astonishing decline.

I WOULD RETURN to my suburban bedroom after two near-romantic misadventures that never, on reflection, held any but one possible outcome. Misadventures: call them, rather, side steps or traps along the paths of escape. Or such at least was my young man's view.

We worked in adjacent departments at J. C. Penney's—women's and men's clothes. We'd have lunch together at the plaza sandwich shop. Paige had auburn ringlet hair, and the bones in her face and arms were long. She lived with her mother over a garage on the grounds of a mansion in the shadow of Cobb's Hill, not far from Rosedale Terrace. They had moved there from Long Island for the mother's job, and Paige spoke with a downstate accent—in Rochester she passed for Brooklyn. She had been involved with someone in Garden City, but they had split up. The evening I went to visit her she met me at the door. Her face was flushed; she announced right away that her mom was not expected until late. I could see that, at the touch of my hand, her clothes would drop in a heap. But I was guided by inhibition. I said yes to the offer of iced tea. We talked about work and school and sex, and ultimately got on the subject of God. I told her the god I acknowledged wasn't personal, and she said a bit tartly she wasn't surprised. I left about ten, and in the void between eleven and midnight was dogged by the thought of having missed an opportunity, but that was simply male chemical reflex. Whatever the source of my hesitation, I was right to have trusted it. A month later she told me at lunch she might be pregnant. She had given notice and was returning to Garden City to patch things up with her fiancé. Then late one evening six weeks later the telephone rang: she was back in Rochester, there was no fiancé, she had had an abortion and was looking for work. Paige talked for an hour, telling me, at intervals, I was such a good listener. But I declined to see her. True to the suburbs, I dreaded an accidental involvement in lives I perceived as unrelated to mine. I would keep the space between us clean.

Then, home for spring break my sophomore year, I sat next to a girl in the church auditorium. Her name was Mina. The lecture was entitled "Jesus: The War Protestor." Unlike most people you'd sit next to in a church setting, Mina wanted to chat. She had a legal pad in her lap and wrote while she conversed as though a part of her brain were taking dictation. She had brown wavy hair and sky-blue eyes that were just like one of my cousin's. She had commenced to tell me something just as the lecture began and said she'd get back to it, yet after the lecture announced that she needed to go. Could I meet her for coffee tomorrow? Yes. We met in the student union at a small local college whose spring break was later than mine. I sat at a table and waited for her class to get out. She was heavier than girls I was used to dating, but her body language repudiated apology. She floated rather than walked. A senior, she was at least two years older than I. She sat down with her books: a copy of *Crime and Punishment* and an anthology called *Naked Poetry*. She was an English major and aspiring writer.

"What did you think of the lecture—kind of lame?"

She herself preferred frontal assaults—not lectures, not prayer. "I don't like a lot of bullshit." She was raised, she said, in an atmosphere of bullshit, all of it very polite, good manners masking her parents' insistence on controlling the details of every little thing. "But they can't control me." She had attended political demonstrations and written a lot of Maoist poetry. Now she was writing a novel called *Breaking Away*. She cultivated exotic plants and wanted me to come to her apartment for tea. She lived pretty far from the college, she said, across the river up on Lake Avenue, but that's where she and her former roommate had found a cool city place. Her parents preferred that she reside in the suburbs or, failing that, on the artsy, expensive side of town, but that would involve taking their money and she wanted to live on her own, mostly. Besides, she enjoyed being far off campus in one of the old neighborhoods.

I was told to park by the curb right out front. I drove up Lake Avenue, and sure enough, a half block north of Birr Street, there was the apartment house. It was a three-story brick structure the color of dried blood (her suggestion). Paint peeled from the building's wood trim.

The whole place was a hippie colony as you could see by the murals in the foyer—peace signs, bare buttocks, cannabis leaves—and hear in the music (Jefferson Airplane, already a bit dated) one resident effectively pumped through the vents. The hallway had odors: marijuana, tomato paste, damp woodwork, ancient dust. Mina's apartment was on the ground floor. There were plants stuck everywhere and cannabis under black light. She had made tea, and presented copies of two poems she wanted me to read. One concerned Walden Pond, which she had visited the summer before: the last lines (or all I ever remembered of them) were "my fond / Hope buried in the mud of Walden Pond": a couplet, not so Maoist after all, I thought. The other was about the war. But this (she picked up and waved a manuscript) is what puts bread on the table: an erotic novel-in-progress that you write according to formula, really one big uncensored fantasy. Takes about two weeks. This was her second. "I might read you a passage or two," she announced with just the slightest suggestion of solemnity, "but not yet. I like having intellectual friendships that are also sexual friendships."

She said this as we stood by her stove waiting for the water to return to a boil. Her bed, a mattress on the floor in a narrow nook off the kitchen, visible from where I stood, had a pronounced center hollow. Beside it lay a stack of legal pads with a single pen on top.

No—I don't think so. This shabby apartment was right on the edge of my mom's old neighborhood. To be polite I asked to see the poems again. I found things to admire. Then I thanked her for the tea.

"Coffee next week, maybe?"

Not only will I leave this city but go so far away that to return will seem like journeying to a foreign land.

8

Crossings

In September 1664, Jan de Decker sailed up the Hudson with a cargo of powder and forty slaves recently arrived in New Amsterdam from Barbados. His errand, beyond turning a profit, was to meet with the English at Orange to discuss the surrender of Dutch territory to British rule. By all appearance he had abandoned his country to pursue his own fortune. His descendants, small farmers and village artisans, multiplied and fanned westward from the Hudson Valley through the Southern Tier and Finger Lakes region of New York State, intermarrying with the English and French.

Three hundred and four years later, never suspecting that anyone in my line had engaged in such traffic, I worked with my peers to clean up the waterfront of Peekskill, New York. We made an apt crew: Frank, Paul, Ben, and myself: shoulder to shoulder, two white and two black. We were the "Can-Do's," a group of volunteers from Saint Peter's, the boarding school I attended as a result of my brother's brush with the law. My parents had wished to remove him from his circle of quasi-delinquents. They'd given me a choice: go with Tom or attend Brighton High, living at home as an only child. Sibling allegiance and family unity allowed no room for hesitation: I chose to go. I might have gone anywhere to escape the boredom of another suburban school year, but to me at that age the Hudson Valley with its mists and crumpled landforms seemed an enchanted if melancholy country. Just north of Peekskill, upriver from Bear Mountain Bridge, the navy stashed a fleet of destroyers left over from World War II. In rainy weather their profiles might pass for a ghost squadron commanded by Hendrick Hudson.

Footbridge. Courtesy of the author.

In ill-fitting gloves we gleaned a mixed refuse: broken bottles, government forms, torn clothes, a mysterious green ash. We avoided the fish that gave the shoreline its distinctive odor. They lay everywhere, in varied stages of decomposition, with staring, desiccated eye, like lost souls. Out on the water, freighters shuttled back and forth between Albany and New York City. Behind us, on the elevated right-of-way, New York Central freight and passenger trains rolled north and south. Train and ship horns wailed into far longitudinal distances. Peekskill itself saw little commerce, and dull brick factories lay in ruin about the shore. Only the nuclear power plant at Indian Point, south of town, offered a promise of revival. For now this stretch of Hudson shore existed as an unpatrolled waste, a space for dying and discarded things, the sluggish wave depositing an oily detritus. I made no complaint. I liked this dreary beach set amid dead wharves on a notoriously polluted river. "Suzanne takes you down to her place by the river" sang in my head. The far shore lay in full sun, and as the clouds broke I entertained visions of caravels swinging out of the sky to take us away. There was no mistaking the futility of this enterprise: within a week our effort would be erased. But it offered the grit of a hands-on activism, put us in touch with a world we knew we would have to address—the true nasty condition of things our parents and most of our teachers had lied about. For youth there is tonic in seeing the world *ugly*, as it is.

SAINT PETER'S SCHOOL sat on a hill just east of town off Main Street. The campus combined two former summer residences. One had belonged to Henry Ward Beecher, minister and abolitionist, and Boscobel, the neo-Gothic "cottage" that served as our headmaster's house, had been the scene of a famous nineteenth-century sex scandal. At the time I knew no more of Beecher's alleged adulteries than I did of Jan de Decker's trade in human flesh. We learned that Boscobel had been a station on the Underground Railroad and that an opening in the hillside behind the house gave access to a tunnel. You felt the presence of ghosts on the grounds as well as in the house. During my sophomore year I was one of six students living in the small second-floor rooms that had been the servants' quarters. We came and went by back stairs and raided the large kitchen for leftovers, hors d'oeuvres, and pastries served to trustees during their periodic visits. From windows that looked north a cold light came into our room. There were autumn moments of pure abstract sadness. Rain fell in torrents while "Eleanor Rigby" played on the radio.

Faculty and students took their meals in the large Tudor dining hall that had once been Beecher's riding stable. On the way to dinner Boscobel residents often fell in with Father Swafford, the headmaster, a kind, white-haired, motherly man, and sometimes Mr. Worth, English master and imagist poet, emerged from his cottage to take up the slack. We'd have grace before meals and announcements after the main course. Once a month the dining hall was converted into a dance floor, and girls from Saint Mary's School, on the north end of town, would arrive in a yellow bus for an evening of mixed company. For a little while my freshman year I chose Activity B, viewing a western or war movie chosen solely on the basis of being long—three hours or more—so as to provide distraction.

But for all its hazards Activity A, meeting and mingling with adolescent girls, was the preferable choice.

It was not an elite school. A few of the boys were sons of wealthy families, and one especially dissolute youth was heir to a detergent fortune. Perhaps the majority were well-adjusted or adjustable middle-class boys, but quite a number made the place seem like a salvage yard for wrecked teens. There were the lumpy, the pimple lipped, the pasty haired; there were the fair of face with haunted eyes who had drunk prematurely from poisoned wells. The truly wild rarely lasted a year, a second incident involving drink or unexcused absence leading to expulsion. But you had to want to be expelled, as suspension and extra chores were nearly always negotiable options. Those kids regarded as normal had found ways of masking their own habitual infractions, or else their generally untroublesome behavior had purchased faculty connivance. Surely, some of the teachers knew that Frank and I were frequently up until three in the morning at the classroom building writing papers, taking to the fire escape for cigarette breaks. They could have intercepted us Sunday afternoons when we left campus without permission to meet girls at Saint Mary's or tracked us Saturday night to the wood at the hill's crown where we kept beer in a leaf pile. Guys who lived totally within the box defined by the rules were as messed up in their own way as the compulsive renegades.

A younger brother is less conspicuous than his sibling. Upon our arrival at Saint Peter's, Tom had to forge a place for himself in the junior class, while I, a freshman, joined mine as a charter member. He meshed with his fellows and I rarely saw him. His presence offered a measure of protection, and the fact that he got on with his peers rendered me unremarkable. Not that I escaped everyone's notice. One afternoon that first September, I was walking back from the shopping plaza across from campus when I heard a click! click! and felt a stinging sensation in my ear. I turned to see a black kid my age rapidly walking away with something under his armpit. I put my hand to my ear and expelled an object—a copper BB—lodged in the cartilage. As blood poured from the wound I saw seven or eight older boys, in blazer and flannels, taking down the kid with the gun, while two or three others led me, light-headed, up the hill to the infirmary. The boys in a crisis closed ranks, and past brawls with local toughs formed much of the campus folklore. Guys at the school you had to watch were those a year older than you but in your own grade, as they were apt to take out their academic frustrations on younger classmates. Within a week of arrival I bonded with my roommates, Paul and Frank, and we formed a triad that repelled bullies, the dread label "queer," and scapegoating generally. Our friendship was our fortress.

Year in and year out we arose at seven, did morning chores, ate breakfast, attended chapel, went to class, ate lunch, returned to class, took to the practice field or gym, showered, did afternoon chores, ate dinner, attended study hall, went to bed. The instruction was competent and occasionally rigorous. The faculty consisted mostly of young men taking a year or two off between degrees, although three of the language masters were refugees who had found a foothold in this Rust Belt exile. In addition to the headmaster there was always a second priest on the faculty to hold chapel and teach religion. Father Welch, the teaching priest for two of my years, lived in an A-frame house at the edge of campus and preached the pure selfless love of the gospels. The most vivid of classroom memories are ever unpleasant, and so it was at Saint Peter's. A boy with a stutter being told repeatedly that he must work through the catch in his vocal apparatus. A pink-bald historian's monthlong lecture on German monasticism, delivered in sadistic monotone, while the cherry tree outside the window burst into bloom. I recall my head pitching forward as I dozed in first-hour physics, never for more than a second but long enough, in the view of the retired General Electric chemist who drove from Armonk five days a week for the pure joy of "inspiring tomorrow's leaders," to demonstrate the law of gravity. We had our own names for the teachers and, in some classes, our own agenda. When I graduated, I could read *Le petit prince.* I had made the acquaintance of the Brontës and Dickens, Hawthorne and Faulkner, Joyce and Eliot. I had an idea of what the Bible said and in what books and how True Doctrine interpreted it. And I knew that second opinions existed.

In after years my mother would ask if sending me off at age thirteen had been a good idea. She was haunted by memories of saying good-bye to my brother and me at the campus gate that first September and making the long trip back to Rochester without us. And almost as bad was the thought of us boarding the train at the huge decrepit Victorian railroad station on Central Avenue to return to school after Thanksgiving. As to whether going off was a good thing, putting aside the fact that such questions can't be answered—the alternative, staying home and attending the local high school, hadn't been tested—I always said yes. Saint Peter's was claustrophobically small, isolated from the depressed blue-collar city for all our efforts at outreach. Confined as it was, it gave on to new worlds and experiences I couldn't have had in the Rochester suburbs or in those parts of the city with which I could be safely familiar. After Saturday-morning chores you were free to leave campus until Sunday evening if someone's parent signed you out, and since Paul lived just down the road in Dobbs Ferry I would often go home with him for the weekend. Frank would sometimes come with us, but he didn't feel comfortable with Paul's dad, a severe Austrian immigrant who looked upon interracial friendship as strange. Paul's mom, a warm, maternal woman who told ribald jokes, adopted all of his friends as a matter of course. She would have welcomed the whole world to the cramped and messy three-bedroom home that smelled of cat and pipe tobacco. A teenager could flop at Paul's place, enjoy the meals and affection his mom freely lavished upon youth, and rest assured that beer at that house was bought by the case and not monitored. But the real opportunity in spending the weekend at Paul's involved getting up Sunday morning and catching the train to Grand Central Station.

Manhattan, to someone from western New York, is like London to youth raised in the Yorkshire Dales. No other place could be so fully real, exhilarating and sensationally dangerous. The eros that powers the world lies beneath the pavement like a radioactive ore. The air is charged, and everything vibrates with the density of an ongoing human procession. Streets and avenues and the infinitude of high buildings channel the current; around every corner one meets an incoming sea. People's bodies are electric—brown, black, and white bodies, cloaked and broken down, lithe and scarcely covered. It got so I could tell native from tourist at a glance. Even the white people from Manhattan held themselves and spoke distinctively as though it made an ethnic difference not to grow up in the suburbs on meat loaf. The very smell of the city stretched one's capacity to register sensation, for you met, all at once, everything from the stench of the alley to the coffee and roast chestnuts and chutneys of street vendors to the sweat and lavender and bubble gum wafting off the group at a bus stop. So full was the tide of impressions that you had to acquire skills in navigating your way and get over the novelty of circuslike streets if you didn't want hustlers accosting you. To stand at the south end of Central Park was to find oneself at the center of the universe. Just inside its southwest corner I experienced for the first time hearing all around me, in exchanges generated by dozens of conversations, language other than English. In penetrating to the heart of Manhattan in October 1965, I realized a cherished boyhood wish. My first actual trip to the city had been that summer when the family drove downstate to look at the campus and then south another forty miles to attend the World's Fair. But the fair was in Queens, and while technically that put us in New York City, it was not the city of Times Square and Central Park and the Empire State Building. My strongest memories of the World's Fair are of intense heat, a pervading smell of Belgian waffles, and the sight of three people, a young man, an old man, and a teenage girl, at three different points in our visit, stepping out from the crowd to double over and vomit, right there on the sidewalk. I might on that basis have connected New York City with the idea of excess, but I hadn't yet seen much of the world, and there was too much of the city still to know before removing it from a life's itinerary.

THE BB SHOOTING was never a big deal: fully recovered within the hour, I dismissed the incident as random. After all (so I thought) I had made a black friend, and together with Paul we had begun to spend Sundays down in the city, where contact with brown and black worlds seemed an inevitable human fate.

Paul's mom would drop us off at the Dobbs Ferry station around ten. We'd board the train, which reeked of cigarette and newspaper, and sit back as it bumped from station to station in lower Westchester before entering the vast plain of apartment buildings in the Bronx and Harlem. Simply crossing the border into the northern borough gave cause for elation, and I lost myself in eager study of block after block of drab brick tenement. By eleven we were hiking up from Grand Central Station. We grabbed lunch at a greasy spoon off Times Square. Then we headed to the park and mostly walked around or sat and observed—listened to people speak the French, Spanish, and English of the islands, conversed with folk who approached to talk politics and then ask for coin.

New York City became for me a collage of familiar sights. There was a school somewhere on the Upper West Side where the fencing team would go for competitions, and the way there brought us down Lenox Avenue, crossing to the west on 125th, straight through Harlem. This for sure was far from my origins, and I took in isolated street scenes as though my mind were a camera: people in doorways, groups on street corners, a lone man in a long winter coat making his way down the avenue and into a side street; a woman having a shouting conversation with an unseen interlocutor; taverns and pawnshops, grocery and liquor stores, all with dense armored curtain; Nation of Islam, Apollo Theatre, burned tenement, and stripped car. Some of the buildings had slogans written on them calling for power, now, and for black people to unite and kill whitey. Once, during intermission, I asked the coach for five minutes' leave to get some air. He said sure, but don't go north of 105th or east of Columbus. I walked six blocks to that exact corner, contemplated what he had designated as the boundary line, and crossed north. It was a Saturday afternoon in February. A copper light settled onto the roofs; there were few people in sight and none, now, was white. I gazed up the forbidden avenue, nothing but large, dark stone apartment houses encased in a cage of fire escapes. I dared myself two blocks farther before deciding I had ventured far enough. But I wanted a souvenir of this expedition and stepped into a corner drugstore. "A pack of Chesterfields, please." The clerk, a broad-shouldered man in his twenties, eyeing me as though I'd arrived from the moon, slapped down the pack and said "fifty-five" in a West Indian accent. I paid with a one, pocketed the cigarettes and change, and turned back.

One evening a group from the school went down to Lincoln Center to see *Carmen* with Leontyne Price in the lead role. I'd always liked this opera's music, but there was no comparing the pleasure derived from a scratchy recording with the electrification of a loud live performance. The story concerns exploited women who roll cigarettes for a living. Rightly considered, *Carmen* serves as a lesson in class, and I was vaguely aware that here was a portrait of poor people's lives. But such awareness only enhanced the evening's most vivid impression, that of the opera hall's red plush opulence. In this enclosed and artificial world you met the glitter of the concertgoer—women decked out in shards of glass, immaculate men resembling John Lindsay springing for refreshments that would have emptied my wallet of a year's allowance. Another door to this expanding universe was the high, narrow portal of Saint John the Divine, where the glee club joined choral groups from other area Episcopal schools for Christmas and Easter services. Beneath the great vaulted ceiling the thundering surge of pipe organ, trumpet, timpani, and bell totally annihilated a teen singer's voice, lost at once in Gothic space—vague, vast, dark, and thick with incense. The boy choirs eyed the adjacent girl choirs and, church or no church, thought about the fragrant female body under the blue and white robe. From loft to nave people here were far more diverse than at Saint Paul's Church in Rochester: black, brown, and casually dressed worshipers all had a place. The drive down and back up Amsterdam Avenue figured in the trips to Saint John's. I pondered the relationship between a church and the world that surrounded it. In the way a person can detect new meaning in the words he has heard all his life, I recall being struck, one morning, during regular weekday chapel at the school, by reference to the poor and the multitude. I saw now not the ragged extras in the Bible movies of the era but people you would see any day on the blocks approaching the cathedral. New sights, new sounds had jolted me out of my perpetual daze.

In trips to Central Park I paid increasing attention to groups holding placards. Some huddled to decry instances of local discrimination, not always intelligible to tourists. From sophomore year forward there were larger and more vocal bodies, black and white standing together, protesting the Vietnam War. The grisly photos that "Vietnam" invokes for anyone born before 1960 had begun to make a weekly appearance in *Time* and *Life* magazines. Three of the younger faculty members took a group of us down to the park to take part in a demonstration. To the populist chords of acoustic guitar, the vision of Justice that had enlisted youth in the struggle for civil rights now rallied a fervent opposition to this war. Although I had grown up in a Republican family that wanted to believe the country went to war honorably and only when other options failed, from the time I gave any thought to this war I saw that it served no good purpose.

Peculiar emotions accompanied a young person's recognition that the Vietnam War was wrong. I had known from middle childhood that adults made bad decisions and that powerful men were willing to stake the whole world on a single play. The war exemplified this arrogance and stupidity. Its prolongation revealed a tolerance of carnage disturbing to see in one's elders. Their trite justifications made it clear that youth not only had the right but also the duty to judge for itself. The war provided ground for a generational break far exceeding the normal separation of adolescent child from balding parent. To discern the older generation's authority as nonbinding made for a collective euphoria. In your soul you seconded what the speaker at the rally, what the vocalist at the rock concert, publicly declared: that the war is over because we say it is.

Yet only radical longhairs were taken in by the histrionics of protest. And a genuine sadness underlay the theater of youth assertion. In this awakening I shed a belief instilled in nearly everyone brought up in middle-class homes following World War II: that the United States would go to war only in a just cause and prevail not only or even principally by virtue of superior fire. Young people were angry with the remote men who had engineered this shadow usurpation. There was something childish in their laughable equivocation—their wish to use the terms *conflict* and *military action,* their refusal to call the war *war.* Perhaps this contributed more than anything else to the change in the way youth perceived the legitimacy of the paternal regime. The white dad of the late 1950s had presented a benignly military aspect, genially presiding over a peacetime prosperity, a boxy affluence of contented wives, carefree children, and jaunty days scored by Leroy Anderson. This deeply beloved, industrious mannequin, farsighted and unseeing, beneficent of motive but obtuse to the claims of others, had always fixated on the security of his world's borders. He was obsessed with national and neighborhood boundaries: having lived through Pearl Harbor, his nightmare was the surprise attack. His domino theory required the Soviets and Red Chinese to plot destruction of our landlocked cities. He could never be sure that blacks and Asians weren't on the communist take. With the Vietnam War these fixations had become psychotic. By the midsixties the father's justness, benevolence, and sanity had vanished in what seemed an Abrahamic mania to sacrifice Isaac. This patriarch with his strict partitions, his despotic sense of other people's duty, was the problem. Young people had to theorize and occupy an alternative world alongside his. Abandoned, his world would crumple and fade away.

The sensation, at age sixteen, was that of crossing a threshold but from the perspective of passengers sitting with their backs to the train's forward movement. The cars paused at interesting stations, one in particular, hardly more than a siding, above a meadow filled with young people gathered for a concert. Nearby stood blocks of row houses where everything was free; beyond the houses an estuary met the ocean. Anyone hereabouts would take you in, and anything that was someone's was everyone's. A new wisdom that was an old wisdom was making the rounds. The times compelled you to rethink everything, which naturally led to the rejection of much that older people valued, beginning with the careers and houses we had been brought up to desire. There was more to life than boxes, labels, and endless anxiety. The world was full of fascinating people you'd been trained to ignore or avoid. On the contrary, you were born to mix. Sit with these over here; they've actually lived in the park several weeks. The cuts on his face are from a fall or a fight or a scrum with the police, hard to tell which. They'll heal with time. He looks like Jesus, but the hair is what you call dreadlocks. Bring something to share? They'll show you how to look beneath the garbage for the donuts. Here is life, an untried experiment. Get out of the habit of calling home. We are not put on earth to live up to someone's expectation. If you don't live in the present moment, there isn't much point in drawing breath. Go boldly if blindly into life today, since you can't foresee where you'll find yourself tomorrow.

Like a radio tuned between signals, my ear received multiple messages; my mind became a guest book in which all sorts of visitors left comments. Paul and I sat cross-legged at the house of his dropout friend. Each of us had a pair of Rheingold longnecks and was getting through the first one fast. Travis wanted to play a record just out by a new LA group, the Doors. "You haven't heard anything quite like this," he said, then proceeded to play "Break on Through to the Other Side." The beer did its work, but we didn't need beer to be persuaded this was the new music. Jim Morrison spoke cryptically, but the truth required only a few choice words. In the concert over in New Rochelle, Richie Havens was preacherly; at the disco in Yonkers, Country Joe and the Fish offered satire. The words and weird disharmonies spoke with oracular power, warping the world and imparting an anxious enchantment. Not long after, with Frank and two nomadic girls in someone's dirty apartment, I toked on the reefer as it circulated from the left while more of the new music, "Purple Haze" and "Time Has Come Today," relayed the now familiar theme.

1968: my junior year, the end of the world. In the gloom of a Hudson Valley February, boys a year away from registering with the Selective Service absorbed images of the Tet Offensive—a punishing of American hubris so complete that even a war protester felt chilled. Three soldiers defending shattered fortifications, each gazing in a different direction. A firefight on a narrow city street. Corpses by the blackened wall of the US Embassy. A pistol firing point-blank into the temple of a captive Vietcong. Refugees on a rural road littered with bodies, the sky behind them aflame. Dead and half-dead peasant bodies seared of their clothing, hair, and skin. (And again the recognition: Kodachrome knows no bounds; cameras exist to publicize folly, vice, hypocrisy, violence, death.) Then March: during Easter vacation President Johnson goes on TV to announce that he won't seek a second term. April: Father Swafford interrupts chapel to tell us that Martin Luther King Jr. has been assassinated. Finally, June, end of the school year: word breaks on the eleven o'clock news that Bobby Kennedy has been shot. In the morning we learn that he too is dead.

Two weeks later I took down the RFK-for-President poster from my bedroom wall. I had fallen asleep reading *Siddhartha*. In a dream I found myself in a cavernous enclosure, rather like a crypt but unkempt: Saint John the Divine but also Grand Central Station. I had missed the train. Across the concourse a five-year-old Jimi Hendrix started to play a single note on an electric guitar. Everything—walls, pews, passersby—reverberated with that note, and all things solid, including my hands and face, began to undulate. I understood that the note was a flame and that it had taken hold of everything within its radius. Smoke billowed from under the floor. All other sound joined this note in a rising crescendo—the one that concludes "A Day in the Life" on the *Sergeant Pepper* album. This was the funeral in my brain, and by an act of will I pulled myself free as though that dream were a pool of glue flowing from my fissured skull. Falling back, I dreamed again, although this time of a large clear river moving through rushes, and of a smaller river, equally pure, running alongside and joining it farther ahead. Invisible people, I now understood, were alive and well on the other side. I dipped my hand in the water, and a coat of ash fell from my skin. Sunlight dazzled the far shore. I awoke with the conviction that I had seen another world.

FOR MY FATHER AND ME the war had become a matter of heated discussion. Our exchange followed a script read by fathers and sons in kitchens and living rooms across the country. I had seen the world, some of it, anyway, and had concluded that it was only too easy to live on a winding suburban lane and believe the war existed to some purpose. From my parents' window the view was plain. The World War II generation had bled to hold the line on totalitarianism, and now, on a larger stage but in a more limited war, it was the sons' turn. As the war dragged on my father's opinion altered: John Kennedy had gotten us into Vietnam, but, once in, see it through! That another Kennedy, the pretend senator of New York State, elected courtesy of New York City Democrats, should aspire to the presidency to get us *out* of Vietnam was absurd. Meanwhile, my brother had turned eighteen, and a boy from the old neighborhood had been killed in action. To my father, Canada wasn't an alternative. But he had come to see the war as a blunder and at least acknowledged the mess on our hands. Frailties had begun to appear in his step. I didn't want to do battle with him.

I didn't want to battle my parents over their views. Whatever I said made little difference. Like artifacts drawn from a time capsule, their attitudes had no place in the world I was coming to know. In fairness to them I bore in mind their honorable early privations. They had seen it all: war, want. They had earned enough money to disregard trouble that didn't involve them directly. They rarely ventured from the home ground and cherished the thought that my brother and I, having traveled about, would return to its formidable shelter. To me their life was a steady narcosis. I had escaped intellectually, or so I imagined, and had begun to theorize my parents as creatures of set demographic trends. To grasp the arbitrary nature of things freed you from laws of necessity. It freed you to reject old men; it prepared you to enter a new society blind to color and class. But as a child of their house I was conscious of certain ligations, bonds of love and indemnity exerting a strong gravitational pull. I fantasized, hesitated, and plotted, but balked at the genuine leap. Sooner or later that moment would come. It was never a question of repudiating my parents but establishing cognitive distance.

I couldn't have guessed how long that would take. I had no idea that centuries shape the most casual of human relations. Ten generations separated me from Jan de Decker. Years would pass before I'd read that name in a dusty tome at the college library—see its shameful mention in a half-page footnote. *My* name. I would understand then that I'd spent my life in houses he continued to haunt.

BY JUNIOR YEAR Frank and I had developed a genuine friendship. As freshman our tie mostly partook of the military alliances kids form when they are thrown together in a new situation. But in sophomore year our relations proceeded on mutual sympathy, a shared sense of humor, and patterns of conversation that restored perspective, now his, now mine. I prized his friendship. We partnered together in community projects, and I liked what I thought it said about me to have a black friend. Such contact represented a step away from the white suburban origin. But despite this strain of narcissism—the flattering reflection that the world is rebuilt on such bonds as I have the grace to form—something like friendship for its own sake ultimately governed our relations. Each knew the other's weaknesses, understood and respected what was strong in the other, and could offer the refuge of companionable silence. Paul and I were probably Frank's only real friends. Everyone liked Frank, but he seemed isolated, probably because he didn't hang out with the other black kids. Occupying a corner of the school's new dormitory, they mostly hailed from Harlem and Bedford-Stuyvesant and looked upon Frank as someone who had defected to the world of white ways. His light complexion was an added issue. Junior year he'd have an ugly falling out with Ben, a kid in the class ahead of us who maintained affable relations with whites but who had seized upon an intellectual militancy he insisted Frank share. Ben championed Malcolm X and had even discovered Frantz Fanon. Pressed by Ben, Frank devoured *The Wretched of the Earth* and for half a week barely spoke to anyone. Ben had wanted Frank to wear a black and green armband during the bishop's annual visit to perform the Eucharist and bless the campus, and Frank refused. For years I resisted remembering their exchange outside chapel that February night—words I was not meant to hear:

"Just want to suck white dick, nigger, and you know it!"

"You the one sucking dick! You the one know about that!"

"Black girl shut you out with that milk in your face!"

"Black girl shut you out with that hippo snout!"

"Gonna wear fay tie and whore yourself some cash!"

"Yeah, and you gonna die in some rat-house black toilet!"

Frank understood the white fascination with the disputes that tore black people apart. The one time he commented on the subject he did so with a tone suggesting that it was only congenital white stupidity that required such explanations: he was southern and they were northern, he was middle class and they were not. People aren't friends by virtue of race. Naturally, we couldn't begin to say what makes or breaks a friendship across the country's class and color divides, but for the moment companionship alone sufficed. Frank and I now spent most of our weekends together since Paul, girl crazy, was dating an Israeli exchange student in Dobbs Ferry. All the next week, he'd regale us with details of fugitive sex and search our expression for signs of envy. For those without recourse there were girls to visit at our sister school, Saint Mary's, but Frank felt stifled in this social possibility. Each time the schools hosted a dance he would be paired with one of the handful of black girls. It took a while, but finally I realized why this so offended him.

I passed some weekends with Frank at the apartment of his guardian in Hartford. Her name was Theodora, a dark-haired, heavy-set, unmarried white woman in her forties. She worked for one of the insurance companies, but her life's true calling was civil rights activism and she had gotten to know Frank's family while on a voter-registration drive in the South. She had known, and marched with, Martin Luther King Jr. Frank's parents were divorced and both held full-time jobs, father an optician, mother a teacher. Both wanted Frank out of the South, and Theodora's connections in the Episcopal Church led to his enrollment at the school. Frank went right along with this plan. Somewhat passive, he usually, but not always, did as he was asked. When he wasn't trying to come off as hip, he exhibited the manner of an old-time librarian. He once told me that, at the height of the agitation, when Birmingham city fathers loosed dogs and fire hoses on demonstrators, he had thrown a brick through the back window of a police car. Although I never thought to disbelieve him, I could never quite picture it. As the self-consciously well-meaning middle-class white, I tried to be sensitive if also a little wary. Even among friendly black people, I surmised, centuries of oppression had nurtured a reflex that responded to subtle as well as flagrant provocation, transforming the person into a bomb, and deep in Frank I sensed the bomb's presence. But he exerted control over its detonation. Our friendship, I was sure, had moved beyond complications of race.

Theodora would pick us up accompanied by her friend Ward, a gregarious fellow who must have been in his midfifties. He had a full head of dyed hair. He and Theodora had met as partisans of a cause. Professionally, he worked in regional theater and spoke openly of his companion, Delano. One rainy evening in November '68, Ward insisted that we stop at a bar just outside Peekskill, where he proceeded to order Manhattans for the three "men," while Theodora, the designated driver, would have to content herself with a Shirley Temple. The elixir was delicious and strong—I closed my eyes and felt the barstool lift a hundred feet in the air. So there I was: an underage drinker of hard liquor, having one of the best times of my young life in the company of an ultraliberal "old maid," a wisecracking, self-styled "commie homosexual," and my black fraternal twin. The talk consisted of cynical assessments of what to expect of Richard M. Nixon, the president-elect, and I admired the elders' attitude: they would fight on. Ward sang a verse of "Solidarity Forever!" He told us about the great Paul Robeson and the Peekskill goons who had tried to kill him. After drinks and sandwiches we got back in the car like any other nuclear family and began the ninety-minute drive to Theodora's condominium on Asylum Avenue.

Theodora regarded us as adults a year away from conscription. Her liquor cabinet was open to anyone who could drink in moderation. Hartford wasn't New York City; in fact, it reminded me of Rochester, only more interesting because the capital of a New England state. One evening in early spring we ate dinner with Theodora and then decided to take the bus downtown on the chance we'd fall into some excitement. Had we thought about it we wouldn't have been able to list many options besides walking around, for the drinking age in Connecticut was twenty-one and so to pretend we were eighteen got us nowhere. Once arrived in the city center we looked about for a movie worth seeing. Not many theaters in evidence, and we weren't in the mood for a family feature. An art cinema, intriguingly seedy, caught our eye, and on impulse we bought two tickets and took our seats in the small trash-strewn auditorium. A German-language film with English and Spanish subtitles opened with a shower scene in which one electrically platinum blonde joined another, whereupon they spontaneously and graphically discovered a mutual attraction. These women were a revelation: grotesquely Caucasian, ugly mutants from another planet! This was not something I cared to see, and after about twenty minutes—at my insistence—we left. A half block from the cinema a short bloodless man with transparent mustache approached us. He had seen us leave and wondered if maybe we wanted to try the real thing. Profoundly repelled, we walked on rigidly for three blocks as though the man were a dog that would follow us if we but glanced behind.

THERE WOULD BE TIME for the real thing—every real thing. College was around the corner, and we lived in the near prospect of being among young men and women crossing into something like independent adult life, borne on a generational wave that obscured for the moment every social origin. We just had to get through the final term and put up with routines we had outgrown, like a blazer you put on one morning to find that it's short in the sleeve. By April college choices had narrowed. It looked like Frank would enroll at the University of Hartford, while I would attend Denison in Ohio. The apocalyptic mood of the previous spring had subsided. Nixon was removing affairs of state to an infinitely remote plane, and the opposition vacillated between despair and revolutionary fantasy. The future—personal and collective—was opaque, but Frank and I obeyed an impulse to relax. We had done well in our senior studies, and as a way of rewarding ourselves and concluding our high school years with a memorable epilogue, we laid plans for a trip to Bermuda.

The idea was most likely Theodora's. It would have been like her to dream up an adventure for young people as a way of urging them into the world. She acted vigorously as travel agent, identifying flights, a hotel on the beach, interesting day trips, even a business that rented motor scooters. Her pleasure in this was entirely vicarious. I was to meet Frank at JFK, and we would make the journey by ourselves. Frank and I had visions of riding our motor scooters on the road above the beach. We could scent the clean surf; we could see lovely females of every racial mixture and hear them speak in island accents. In her neat handwriting Theodora wrote my parents with all the particulars: dates, flight times, hotel, phone numbers, including that of the US Embassy. Graduation passed. Frank had returned to Hartford; it was June and time to make reservations and almost too late to apply for a passport. I knew my parents hadn't shared my enthusiasm, but I was thunderstruck when, one evening, my father called me down to the kitchen to announce that the trip was off. The tone betrayed a pent-up anxiety. It proclaimed that the idea had gone on long enough.

But a part of me had been expecting this. The scene unfolded like a déjà vu.

It just wasn't safe, my father explained, for Frank and me to travel together in a place where there had long been animosity between white master and black populace. Hamilton had experienced its own riots. On the back streets a young white tourist would be a marked man. There was a history to the world and my position in it about which I knew next to nil. Could I not see that my being white made Frank unsafe, that Frank's being black compromised me? I countered that change has to start somewhere; that Frank and I had traveled together in New York and Connecticut, places if anything less safe than Bermuda; that we had furnished proof of reliable judgment, each having lived nearly eighteen years virtually trouble free. But my father was immovable. We would be in way over our heads; we could find ourselves in an unruly crowd, and terrible things could happen fast. He insisted that it would cost far more than Theodora had figured. And he maintained that you could get yourself killed at low speeds on a motor scooter if you hit a curb. Not, I rejoined, if you wear a helmet. Sure would be a hell of a lot safer than going to Vietnam! But the discussion had descended to trivialities and drawn in other issues. In substance it had ended.

I was left with the task of phoning Frank to tell him my dad had vetoed the trip. This was the hardest thing I had ever been asked to do— plunge a sword in the heart of my very best friend. The sorrow, looking back, is that I did it with only token protest, did it that very evening, did it without running the blade immediately into my own. I hadn't yet learned that there are moments in life for which there can be no atonement. Frank and I spoke; it was a short conversation. He would think, but have the tact not to say, that racism lay at the root of this. He would not force me to say—what I think even then I believed—that whereas my father intellec- tually recognized the injustice of racial prejudice, he regarded the world as treacherous, as who wouldn't in 1969, and feared for the safety of his younger son. We kept the tone pleasant and closed by agreeing that we'd meet again. (And we did, a year later: we got together in Hartford, drove to Dobbs Ferry to visit Paul, now a complete pothead with little to say, hung out at Theodora's and laughed about old times, said good-bye and see you again—and then Frank moved to Paris, ending all contact.) I spent the summer bagging groceries, packing for college, and watching televi- sion—Rowan and Martin were in their prime, and this was the summer of Chappaquiddick and the moon walk. All to be followed by Manson, the closer.

From day to day I'd stay on the narrowest of neutral ground in con- versation with my father, tuning him out. A considerate man, he justly intuited my deep-seated anger but couldn't begin to fathom my horror of being entombed in this life. At night I read in my hot bedroom as though return to square one lay at the end of all experience. So much I couldn't yet see: my life in fact was in total flux, and there wasn't a door in the whole house and the world beyond that didn't stand wide open.

9

Girl at the Lake

B ut by some miracle I did get away. The chance came in defiance of
laws that decreed I should have only long and dead summers. It took
the form of a petite letter penned in a modest schoolgirl hand.

"Would you like to spend a week with me at my place on the lake?"

The fact that the girl was all but unknown only made this idea the
more intriguing. Katrina, known as Kit, had attended Saint Mary's. We
had both been involved in a volunteer program removing trash from
inner-city lots. She was little more than a casual acquaintance, a bright
face across the room in a large company whose collective life dominated
one-to-one contact. Prompted thus to contemplate someone to whom I
had never given second thoughts, I really had no clue who she was. I
recollected rather emaciated good looks and an air of confiding naïveté.
She had filled the role of everyone's kid sister. I could always expect
surprise invitations from girls I found unattractive, but this definitely
wasn't the case. Her unsuspected notice was flattering. Two hundred
miles away, knowing little of my summer situation, she had imagined
a scene and assigned me a part. I puzzled over the strange girl-mind
on which I had clearly made an impression and wondered how she'd
obtained my address. With absolutely nothing to go on, I fantasized her
romantic reveries.

Accompanying the invitation was a note from her mom guaranteeing
meals and adult supervision. Thus equipped, I negotiated use of a car. My
parents had spoiled my grand summer plan, so I entered the discussion
with leverage. I had never embarked on a five-hour drive, but neither, to
their knowledge, had I ever exhibited poor road judgment. My dad could
hardly say no. Well, he could have but didn't.

Noon Lake. Courtesy of the author.

I took I-81 south to State Highway 17, exiting at a small town in the Southern Tier and traveling the final hour on county roads. I had studied the map and pondered this patch as a great unknown. I had always looked at maps so: curious about what I should find in odd cartographic corners. This fascination would eventually lead to salt stretches of desert Southwest and touristless pockets of Rust Belt Europe, but those experiences belonged to the future. A hundred miles south of Rochester nothing could seem dramatically unfamiliar—a peculiar cast to the sky, perhaps, over undulating country between ridged uplands. Much of it was for sale, and here and there ground had been cleared for what billboards celebrated as future communities, promoted as though they were feature-length films.

I drove fifteen minutes without passing another vehicle or seeing an occupied farmhouse, yet a highway sign at a crossroad indicated New York City was but a hundred miles away. A left turn, according to a billboard, put you on the road to Jerry Lewis's favorite resort. His goofy caricature seemed out of place in the somber semiwildness of this crenellated landform, the road winding up and out of sight in the forested middle distance. All my life it seemed I had traveled such roads, traversing voids between upstate cities, a backseat passenger on family trips, or riding shotgun with my brother. From the driver's seat these rural views looked much the same, but because I was now entirely on my own I had the sensation of crossing enchanted thresholds. The six days about to unfold would in fact be nothing like normal, not even in a vacation sense. Revisiting this experience is like recalling frames of an Alfred Hitchcock or space-alien movie: the part of the story where normal bends into weird. Years would pass before I could fathom the precise aberration of what I was about to observe—a broken family, a mother's solipsism, a father's unspeakable villainy. The land deepened between horizons, and in the distance I saw the far side of a valley bathed in vapor. Beneath the vapor stretched the lake, serene sparkling views of which lay like a reward for the traveler's patience: a blue mirror lengthening as the road began its descent toward the shore. I passed a colony of summerhouses and the familiar scene of a middle-aged mom with teenage kids unloading a wood-paneled station wagon. Kit's place stood two miles below this settlement. Guests had to watch for the hard-to-spot turnoff ("Everybody misses it the first time!"), but I found it simply by monitoring the odometer. Approaching the long, brown clapboard structure I panicked at the notion that I'd totally invented the idea of Kit. Would I know her from her sister if she had one?

The question was moot. Kit hopped off the porch and directed me to park in a shady recess along the side. She wore stylishly scant denim shorts and a yellow top that fitted her boyish torso. Her hands and ankles were long and delicate. As her face emerged from light-brown hair that had a habit of shifting forward, she bore an expression that seemed to refer to shared if entirely imaginary understandings. She was prettier than I had remembered, blue eyes and lightly tanned skin and a cluster of small pimples on the side of her jaw. I'd had no relationship with this girl beyond one memorable conversation on the era's set themes—war, music, the mendacious character of adult society and our generation's need to leave it behind. But it was exhilarating to think that we might have had a past, had circumstance favored, or that our souls conducted a secret correspondence.

She greeted with a hug and escorted me past a stack of firewood to the house, a rambling structure whose screen door slammed with a two-note pop. I breathed the scents of forest and wood smoke and heard in the distance the intermittent croak of what I knew from Adirondack vacations was a water pump. I entertained sensations from early childhood and remembered that I should telephone home to confirm safe arrival. I did so, dutifully, using the black wall-mounted rotary just inside the door, then felt free, euphorically, to commence adventure in the remaining daylight hours. As Kit led the way through the low-ceilinged house I noted approvingly pine-paneled walls and a room beyond of slouch-slung chairs set beside large bright windows—no doubt affording views of the lake. Just off the kitchen, Kit opened a narrow door: here stood a room occupied by a captain's bed on which she placed my overnight bag. Closing the door against the two cats, as yet invisible, she guided me into the living room.

An adult male sprawled in a chair in the far corner where two large windows nearly touched. The lake in fact stood in full view, a blue, reflective, agitated surface. Against the bright horizontal background it took a moment for my eyes to adjust. Kit, I saw, was about to introduce me to her dad, who grasped a beer can while reading a section—neither front page nor sports—of the paper. But she abridged the ceremony and referred us to one another in a rushed and garbled undertone, as if fundamentally at odds with such rituals, and then led the way back out of the room, tugging me with a glance. I noticed that she called her dad by a name. "Ken," I thought I'd heard her say, yet it sounded more like "Kern" or "Can." I knew that in some very liberal households kids and adults were on first-name basis, but then Kit, as we retreated, tossed out the phrase, "Tell Mom we went for a walk." I tried to remember references to a divorce, but all I recalled were "my mom" and "my dad" occurring as separate phrases. Over the next day I took stock of Can, whose name I would see printed on an *Art News* subscription label as "Khan Higgins": a long face that served as an example of "lantern jaw," a look I first interpreted as groggy but later discerned to be that of a man who refrains from eye contact. When he glanced sideways I saw that his hair streamed backward in a ponytail, the first such instance I'd seen on a middle-aged man. His sideways glance recurred, a sort of tic. He hadn't offered to shake hands—had conveyed the warning, don't even try. From a forty-year distance Khan wears the face of an aging rock star, but I couldn't of course have observed that then, when the rock stars were young. Slipping through a narrow side door, Kit led me down a path to the lake.

Waves lapped the rock beach, and a distant outboard motor droned. Kit identified the houses of neighbors, reciting the names and approximate ages of parents, children, dogs, and cats, with a smirk that proclaimed the utter meaninglessness of such data. She got me talking about my own summer, asking follow-up questions about boring details in what seemed an attempt to stay off topic. She seized my arm as we walked side by side and wrapped it down around her hip, impressing a citrus scent on my denim shirt. Just out of the neighbors' view, she retrieved a joint and kitchen match from her hip pocket and declared, "We're going to smoke this." I wanted to keep my head intact—the world I had entered seemed already a bit stoned—so when she passed the joint, I faked the toke. Already talkative, she now grew voluble. It was her mom's idea that she invite a friend. It was her idea that it be someone not from the city. Her dad was coming from Binghamton on Wednesday, and she'd stay with him through August—that is, if she didn't catch the Greyhound to Rochester! She was glad I was there. It had been a rough summer. She had written a lot of poetry and wanted to read me two of her favorites. Drawing out a tightly folded sheet, she proceeded to speak phrases devoid of syntax: staring eyes and stapled lips and deaths where you don't really die. A doorless room, a haunted house, a perfect lily in a cracked vase. She showed me the ruled yellow sheet with words set down in tiny hand and nearly invisible pencil.

When we got back from our walk, Kit's mom had returned. She looked much like Kit but with twice the body weight, made-up face, and chemical hair. A stack of legal-size folders lay on the counter. They bore the words *Peerless Properties* over a coat of arms embossed in gold: so, she was a real estate agent. Supper awaited on the pine table. "We're having cold tongue," she announced. "Ever have tongue? It's a lot like corned beef."

"I had corned beef for lunch," Khan observed, as if to say he could stand some variety. His accent was definitely downstate. Beer in hand, he gravitated to the table, and it was clear from his movement that, whatever the menu, his appetite would not be finicky. His relation to this household puzzled me.

As did this household's table talk, which kept catching me off-guard.

"Milk or more beer?" asked Kit's mom. "The water unfortunately tastes like soap. How was your trip down?" She asked me to call her Sue Ann. "I had a lovely note from your mother. She must be a special lady."

"Did you go out in the boat," Khan put in, more statement than question.

"Yes, we did," Kit replied. We had not and the lie hung in the air, pulsing with enigmatic life.

"Kit's not a strong swimmer," Khan spoke in my direction. Then, turning back to her, "Did you wear the life jacket?"

"No. I like death to be an option."

"I've taken lifesaving," I remarked, hearing my voice as the teenage cutup on a situation comedy, thinking this supper could definitely use levity. "I learned mouth-to-mouth. We practiced on dummies."

Khan wasn't in the mood. "Kit's only part dummy. If it comes to that, you let her drown."

In deference to Khan, alpha male of this wood, the rest of supper passed without talk.

After supper, twenty yards offshore in the aluminum rowboat, in the prompt twilight of a late July evening, I asked, "Who's Khan? Your stepdad?"

"He's my mom's friend. Guy friend. I think they're breaking up."

"Is he like an actor or sculptor? With the hair and weird name."

"No, he's a broker. He used to build sets for TV. You know, studio sets. Actually, he doesn't work."

"He isn't real friendly," I protested. "But I like your mom."

"He's pretty cool."

"He treats you like a dad. Or a dictator."

Kit looked down. Her toe played with the life jacket on the boat floor.

When we got back Khan was gone. Kit's mom sat examining *TV Guide.* WABC was about to show *Son of Dracula,* so we settled onto the sofa to watch. The cats came in and stretched out on the pine floor. By the end of the movie we were all half asleep and just managed to stumble the few paces to bed. I dozed a while but then my mind milled. I lay awake a good three hours and heard Khan come in after two.

I EXPERIENCED A NIGHT OF VENGEFUL DREAMS. I had been treated roughly and had watched Kit receive the equivalent of a slap in the face. I despised Khan and hated the position he'd put me in, with no grounds to object or intervene except as a male protecting a female. How does a seventeen-year-old stand up to a man more than twice his age? Would Kit even want that? I sensed there was something between them—had been or would be—and that a knowledge of erotic refinement had darkened her mind. No, I could not then think "erotic refinement." I had simply an intuition of something wrong, a deep if aggravated intimacy in their relations. I deplored Khan with a fine indignation and formed an image of his coarse face at Kit's soft throat. A week or so later, after I'd returned from the trip, I developed a contempt for the mom who seemed to arrange her life to excuse herself from protecting her daughter, sacrificing Kit to retain a boyfriend. My own parents were overprotective, but that on balance was the better way. I wanted middle-aged people to look and act middle-aged. I didn't want them imposing on people young enough to be their own kids. In her change purse Kit kept a photo of her dad, a bald man in a business suit whom it was easy to imagine in the morose moods his daughter ascribed to him. My sympathies, my identification, were with him. This wasn't a novel or movie, and by the end of the visit I didn't expect to get to the core of a household's secret life. But I sensed within hours that it had a secret life. I probably couldn't rescue Kit who in any case didn't ask to be rescued. Or at least she was not asking me.

I awoke to a cat meditatively inhaling the air above my eyelash while the other picked a fight with my toe. Sunlight poured onto my pillow as from an open spigot. It was seven fifteen, but I could see at once that there'd be no more sleep in this east-facing room.

Coffee on the warmer and the *Binghamton Monitor*, already perused, folded neatly on the table. Kit's mom got up at four and left at five.

I got through the *New Yorker* July issue before Kit emerged at ten till noon. Tousle haired and warm from her bed, she came into the kitchen and gave me a hug. She had awakened with an angry pimple on her chin, universal liability for anyone our age, but after last night I registered details. "Do you still want breakfast?"

BY NOON THE SKY WAS OVERCAST. The day had a sedate quality, as though evening had set in early. When we left the house, sometime after two (Khan hadn't surfaced, but I felt his torpid presence back there in the house), storms had begun to appear in the distance south of the lake. Kit wanted to go out in the boat. "Is that okay?" I asked, with reflex deference to Khan's displeasure, which consciously I wished to defy. "Anything's okay," Kit asserted, as though my question came from an alien custom. The boat glided between rowing, water plants scraped bottom, and I tried to see beneath the lake's surface. About five years earlier, Kit explained, before her parents split up, a storm hurled a bunch of dead trees into the water. Their branches reached up and sometimes caught at the sides of the boat. There's a stretch of lake—over there (Kit pointed)—where you don't want to row, where tree hands show when the water level drops. A girl she had known every summer for years fell out of a boat at night and drowned. They found her white body snagged among the limbs of a large algae-coated tree. There was something in Kit's telling of this story that made it seem made up—true as parable, perhaps, but not as fact. She claimed to have written twelve poems on this subject. Now she wanted to drift out farther where there were no phantom underwater shadows. A river current moves like a god through the lake's deep center, she remarked, keeping it cold, clear, clean. We were almost, she said, at the edge of that current. Sit on the floor, she enjoined, and then moved carefully down from the bow to be kissed. She did not seem at home in this act, as though she were abstractly playing out ideas. She wore a low-cut top, and her freckled chest looked small and white and vulnerable. As she looked to the shore I could see her house, distant but on direct line.

We had nearly a week of improvised activity. She seemed desperately pleased to have me about, but we struggled to mold the substance of this time. During the first two days we toured the neighborhood. We hiked up and down the old lake road, dodging the occasional dump truck. We walked along a dusty lane beyond the row of summerhouse construction sites to the ruin of a small railroad station then followed the weed-choked rails to an abandoned house. Kit wanted to take me inside, but we were stopped at the door—or at the void where a door had been—by an evil smell and the organ hum of flies. We made the rounds of the local dark sites: the rumpled cemetery with rust-bound gate and fading Dutch names, a dilapidated carriage house where, as she said, "that famous poet, you know, the one who hanged himself," spent an autumnal summer, and a spot in the diminished wood where discolored water issued from the ground and one of the neighbors—"no one knew who"—posted a pentagram to mark the spot as a witch shrine. Her friend Faye, she said, was kind of a witch; I would meet her in a couple days. We got in the car and drove with the vague idea that these unpaved lanes would give on to a length of sylvan concealment where we could park and talk, but none such materialized. She'd pour forth a sort of automated chatter and then go silent. I guessed she had scenes in her head she intently wished to bring to life—scenes that awaited an exact circumstance that might never come about.

In the course of several disjointed conversations the family history emerged. The mother, dad, two older sisters, and Kit had lived in White Plains until the divorce, thereafter in Albany, and the middle sister briefly attended NYU but now lived in the East Village where she worked as an artist's model. "Let's get up tomorrow and visit her!" Kit suggested and could not conceive that I'd have to ask my dad's permission to drive to the city, permission I knew full well he wouldn't grant. Her mom and dad weren't on speaking terms. She was fifteen before she understood the problem: her mom liked men, and didn't want to be with just one. She, Kit, was okay with this; she herself was kind of the same way, and felt anything but sorry for her dad who fumed and schemed and claimed everything for himself. In hearing this I formed an image of a household in which a bomb had detonated. "My dad's a hard case," she added darkly, "someone only a daughter could love. You don't want to be here when he comes."

A TYPICAL EXCHANGE with Kit might open like this.

"Did you ever notice that Cindy has barf breath?"

Cindy had been a compatriot in Youth Action Kleenup Squad, tall and shapely with enviably straight, long strawberry hair.

"No. I was never able to get that close."

"She's bulimic."

Kit had to define the word. She smirked—not too obnoxiously—in her knowledge of both the medical condition and the specific case. Much shorter than I, she seemed to enjoy catching my eye with the look of an older child.

"She used to puke after lunch in the girl's room. Greasy fries and stuff. Did it without making the *ralph* sound. Come out of the stall like she'd taken a pee, then ask for gum."

I was slow. "Why would she do that?"

"To not be Libby." Libby was an overweight girl whose dress affected Janis Joplin. "The fries were nasty. I barfed once on experiment, but the stuff went up my nose."

I had to say something. "Yeah, I puked through the nose at football practice last year. Seven thirty and they had us doing sprints. Frosted flakes, orange juice, sour milk."

"Oh, yuk. Guys have it easy."

"The coaches are stupid."

"My swim coach was a lesbian, but she acted like we were lepers. Like if you couldn't swim the English Channel you were hardly worth coaching. But she'd pat our fannies if we won or came in second." She caught my eye. "It wasn't like she was feeling us up! For once I'd like to have a guy coach."

"I wouldn't want a female coach."

"It's not like they'd ever coach football!"

We had been walking the aisles of a general store that had adapted to the summer-vacation community. Here, beside the Slim Jims, was a section of clothes: mass-produced jean jackets with peace signs embossed on the shoulder, straw hats with *Flower Power* printed on the ribbon. I watched as the granddad who ran the place stink-eyed a black middle-aged man accompanied by a ten-year-old daughter. Kit meanwhile was examining vitamins.

"Oh, there's Daryl," she remarked, and ducked behind a stack of motor oil. Daryl sported boot-heel sideburns and a tight, transparent powder-blue shirt. He paid for his cigarettes and quart of beer. Later she explained: "We were on a date, once, and he slapped me."

We talked by the lake and in the car and in her bedroom with Donovan on the record player. We engaged in the perennial activity of young people, identifying ways in which we'd lived some common generational theme. Her life was a distorted mirror of my own. My parents were undivorced, and my family remained TV Land whole. I hadn't seen a therapist, hadn't attempted suicide, knew about and admired kids with propensities for nervous breakdowns, but hadn't detected symptoms in myself. I had a very small cache of tolerable narration. I was the boring, storyless norm and Kit, like most of the kids truly worth knowing, the fascinating, traumatized variant. As ever with my contemporaries, I was the listener and only spoke fluently on the subject of future plans: leave the East, head to California and afterward Europe, live in big cities close to the action, taking the pulse of real events. Kit's sentiments were the same, and except for her plan to stay in the East our facile aspirations agreed. What had we to look forward to? Realistically, anything and everything, but what mostly met our eye were unreal prospects of college and career in a world set to explode maybe ten years out. The future enticed and intimidated anyone standing at the verge of adulthood, but for kids like Kit and me—from either end of the range of upper-middle-class life—there was no compelling hurry to decide anything. We were both newly no longer kids; we recalled childhood as though it were last year's summer memory. The stories we told all had reference to what a mom thought or a dad did or what had occurred in a parent's absence. Our stories adverted to relentless change. Normal and otherwise, childhood stories were all about change. In places like this resort community, the past we had known on an old street in a real neighborhood—before moving to the inevitable subdivision—lingered on. Yet even in sleepy vacation land, incessant construction was bent on erasing evidence of past life. A transitional local topography had formed the basis of everyone's childhood.

Throughout the visit Kit maintained a physical contiguity, one that she'd seek with any male come to visit, I was sure. She wanted to sit thigh to thigh; she was cold and wanted an arm wrapped around her. That a girl might willfully achieve proximity to the gawky adolescent male body still seemed like an astonishing development. Two weeks earlier I had attended the annual union picnic with my fellow Star Market employees at a Lake Ontario beachfront park. Tony, the store manager, arrived in rare holiday mood. In his hearselike Olds station wagon, along with hamburgers, hot dogs, buns, and potato salad, he had packed several cases of Genny Cream Ale. The teenage checkers and stock boys had access to the ale, and the girls—not very inhibited under normal circumstances— became publicly affectionate. The prettiest wanted to sit on my lap and kiss with stunningly open mouth. All the guys were attracted to her, and one of my fellow workers, a rather introverted kid who at age seventeen had set his sights on dental school, pretended to be her boyfriend with such canine persistence that she grudgingly came to accept his claim, but in her present state she was ready to stage a revolt and the attention she lavished on me—I realized—was entirely for his benefit. When her demonstration was over a girl who truly wanted to be my girlfriend took her place, but such fun came at the expense of good order. I wanted to go home but was still impaired (I would not have said drunk). Somewhere around six, as the mosquitoes came out, I left with a case of ale in the trunk and a heightened awareness that, for the first time, I was driving under the influence. But I drove, so I thought, like a model citizen: pedantically minding the speed limit, stopping at yellow lights.

I was back at that picnic in a dream the third night at Kit's. A dark fog had swept off the lake, and it was too late to go home. Kit appeared and led the way to a cabin. We sat down on the bed, and she took to my arms as though I were a bicycle. She knew the machine, from gears and brakes to the subtleties of balance and uphill acceleration. She wanted to take this one for a spin and then return it to the rack by the side of other bicycles identically equipped. There was something destined about this moment, something sweet and warm and affectionate, but at the close it all seemed to have proceeded abstractly with little prospect of repetition. But then it would be hard to repeat an experience in which nothing essentially had happened.

OUR WEEK, it turned out, did have an agenda. On the third evening Kit made two calls. One was to someone named Ram, the other to Faye, the witch. Ram lived in an apartment in the village's large nineteenth-century commercial block. We drove there after supper. Kit dashed up the stairs and came down in five minutes with six hits of LSD. That would be tomorrow's diversion. ("But maybe I'll just take them all now," she joked, and, to my horror as we sat in my dad's Chevrolet, directly across from the village police station, put all six in her mouth. Then, unable to bluff with a straight face, she spat them out and dissolved in laughter. She dried them out on her shirt—the blue dye ran a little—and then put them back in the plastic bag.) And the day after that we'd visit Faye.

For me this would be the first time, but I wasn't going to tell her that. I had smoked opiated hash but had never swallowed a pill. The two tiny cobalt-colored tablets nested in the palm of her hand. It was eleven in the morning: her friend told her that we'd crash a little past midnight. The world began to slip its frame around two, and then, toward three, the lake turned violet and purple, with all the light in the world alternately cohering and going to pieces across its wide surface. It all seemed very postnuke, supposing a person to survive, or to die and still retain consciousness. We walked along the shore, entering this forest of chemical psychosis, and our exchanges diminished from sentences to phrases, phrases to words to mere tones of voice. We sat on a bench. I closed my eyes and heard voices—voices of all the kids I had known for the past ten years, my father, mother, brother, deceased grandfather, saying just whatever it was in them to say on any given day. Then opening my eyes I saw the waves slapping and gurgling along the rock shore, and heard the wind make the leaves sing in the line of poplars that screened the shore path. I closed my eyes, and water and wind once again assumed the character of human sound. I would not have wanted to drive a car, but I knew that; would not have wanted to go out in the boat, would not have wanted physical contact with Kit or anyone else, though I did not want to be alone. But I knew these things, and nothing astonished me more than the fact that I could be so out of my head yet so coolly and rationally observe this state that I'd entered and wouldn't exit until sometime tonight or tomorrow. For an eternity Kit rocked back and forth and sang like a solitary child.

In the course of a day spent mostly outside, Kit picked up a sting on the left cheekbone (at one point the sky seemed to rain yellow jackets), and she awoke next day to a furious bruise. She treated it with antihistamines and by evening the swelling had eased. But that afternoon, at the little grocery attached to the gas station just up the road, her lesion attracted attention: as Kit paid for butter and eggs a lanky youth with starter mustache strolled up to my face and with no preamble asked: "What did you do, buddy, haul off and smack her?" Could I have done such a thing? I answered with a look meant to say: I spit on your question. But what struck me was not so much the loathsome imputation as the guy's tone of voice. This wasn't a display of chivalry. His manner had been confiding, not adversarial. If my answer had been yes, I think he might have shaken my hand. Never in my life could I strike a woman— I would die first, of that I was sure. My father had modeled an ideal of masculine tenderness. But there were moments over the past twenty-four hours I couldn't recall. Did someone unseen attack Kit, punch her face, throw her to the ground? Had I failed somehow to protect her?

ABSENT FOR TWO DAYS in New York City, Khan had faded as an object of animosity, but in the steadying light of this acid-day-after, there he was again in his chair, sipping a beer and reading. This time it was *Penthouse.* When Kit and I appeared in the room he made no attempt to conceal it, as anyone with a normal shame reflex should have done, but continued to flip through the pages as though such amusement had an open place in a house shared with teenagers. A half hour later Khan left on some errand. Kit's mom was off showing property, and Kit herself was in the shower, which you could hear through the house because the old pipes groaned. I sat in Khan's chair and had a look at his stash: an issue of *Playboy* I'd already seen, a freakish pictorial entitled *Big Boobs 'n' Butts,* and the *Penthouse.* I flipped to the Girl of the Month. Generally, I imagined the models in these magazines as comfortably older than I—well into their twenties with plenty of opportunities to have been seduced, corrupted, coarsened. They were surely invulnerable to the gaze of male teens. This girl was different: as young as twelve, no older than fourteen. She had dark hair, a heart-shaped face, and semideveloped breasts, absurdly exposed in foldout display. (I thought of the girl with the cigarette burns: either they had healed or the photographer had contrived to conceal them.) She was identified simply as Baby Breeze, a girl who came and went at her ease, a favorite of the London gentlemen's clubs. I closed the magazine and put it back down as though I had touched a leprous limb.

THE STAY, Kit assured me, would not be complete without a visit to her friend Faye. From Kit's description I had trouble imagining Faye: she was a little older, had been "out" a few years (out of school, away from home), held a job with the township water department, and had a range of rather specialized interests: show dogs, Yoga, and handguns. Twenty years later I would have appreciated Faye, but at the time she was a complete rune. She lived out in the country, but that was the norm since there wasn't much town, and her one-story century-old farmhouse sat on a rise above a ravine. "Wait till you see the ravine!" Kit exclaimed, as though it harbored extra helpings of forbidden ice cream. During the drive over to Faye's, Kit seemed infatuated with the prospect, and this gave me to anticipate keen and esoteric pleasures.

As we pulled up the gravel drive, a lank woman dressed in jeans stepped out on the porch accompanied by two fluffball dogs. No longer a kid, neither did she seem the responsible adult—she was our elder, significantly, though not by much. She had black wavy hair severely tied back and covered with a blue kerchief. Her pale skin was freckled in a way that told you this was her summer face. Her green eyes took in the world with a hesitation that skeptically seized the near object—or one near object, namely, myself. Anyone Kit chose to drag about certainly deserved exacting scrutiny, but at the time I felt distinctly unwelcome. Nor did I feel any less so after she had kenneled the dogs and brought us inside and seated us amid an assortment of second-hand furniture draped in corduroy. The room was airless and smelled of dog. As though meeting the obligations of a Spartan hospitality, Faye proceeded to wash three cups into which she poured a flavorless iced green tea. She sorted through a box of albums, selected one by Herb Albert and the Tijuana Brass, and started it at oppressive volume on the sputtering hi-fi. "Theme from *The Dating Game*" was the first track, and the girls laughed as over a private joke. Then she and Kit settled into a chattering, acerbic conversation concerning Alex and Ram, Oscar and Phil, on and on, and just when I thought I had it down that Phil and Oscar were show dogs, the one was revealed to be a sister's boyfriend and the other a waiter at a local resort whom the sister's boyfriend "liked." It was about that time I detected an undertone of anger, one that intensified as the topic bridged to Edwin, Ferris, Myra, and Dick, a litany of swindles and betrayed confidence. "So it's true the cops were out here?" Kit blurted. Faye's face instantaneously hardened and Kit blanched. The topic shifted to the local band that borrowed and wrecked Faye's Ford pickup, another grievance, then circled back to Dan, "that asshole," and at one point Kit, comparing personalities who figured in this rogue's gallery of their collaborative spoken wrath, dismissed Khan as "harmless," a "Quaalude sponge." Right about then I must have evinced interest: first Faye and then Kit looked me dead in the eye. As though on cue I studied the walls, fitted out with "personality posters" of the era: Albert Einstein like Granddad Hippie, Annie Oakley with fancy six-gun, Bette Davis in epic endurance of the world's unregenerate stupidity. Having entered this world of inbred relation I was compelled to eavesdrop on conversation outsiders weren't supposed to understand. My status was that of serviceable decoy in social storage phase. My eyes needed space to wander. Behind me on a large sawhorse table lay evidence of artistry—newspapers and magazines cut into pieces and images spliced together. As I craned my neck I could see pieces of Nixon's visage, or was that Brezhnev? To turn and gander would have seemed rude. It was while sizing up this cluttered room, hearing the dogs whine and yap out on the porch, that I was startled to hear Kit say, "Please, can't we just shoot a few rounds?" With an intake of breath that made her eyes widen with a strange combination of annoyance and exhilaration, Faye said, "Okay."

Faye led us past the table where I could see the results of her handiwork: composite faces of world leaders—Nixon's eyes, Brezhnev's mouth, Mao's forehead—like botched reconstructive surgeries. There were several of these, clippings glued to cardboard, and Faye selected two and handed them to Kit. Drawing a key from a chain attached to her belt loop, she unlocked a door to what once might have been a pantry and stepped into a room that you could tell from the threshold was hot with stale air. Must be cold and dead smelling in winter, I reflected, as Faye came out with two revolvers she identified as "police-issue .38s." She pressed on me a big orange box of ammo with the comment, ironic in tone, like all five of her lifetime comments to me, "Think you can hold the fire?" The box radiated a new sensation. Firearms didn't exactly sort with our generation's utopian sentiments, yet anything in that era might acquire, on short notice, a warped cult chic. We exited the house through a back door that gave on to a small wooden porch, descended the steps, and crossed a backyard with a garden boxed in chicken wire. Between trees that marked the backyard's edge a path descended into the earth, and the moment we reached the shade you could feel a fresh coolness welling from below. That was a relief after sitting in Faye's stuffy house, yet the air betrayed a slight septic odor. The ravine really wasn't very deep. As a topographical feature it was a fairly average gully.

Yet this ravine, which I had envisioned as an erotic grotto with hanging cannabis gardens, concealed a private pistol range. We situated ourselves at the firing station, and then Faye hopped over the nearly dry creek bed to post the "world leaders," as she called them, on the crude target board nailed to a wooden frame.

I sat on the bench, an old clapboard propped on rocks, while the girls, having loaded, commenced to fire. I am remembering this through the haze of that week's steadily accumulated weirdness, natural and induced, but according to memory they fired in silence until Kit, warmed to the task, proclaimed:

"This is for Oscar!" Blam!

Faye rejoined:

"This is for Ram!" Blam!

"This is for Alex!" Blam!

"This is for Phil!" Blam!

They went through a few more names and then paused, looked at me, and smirked. Faye read something like alarm in my face and then laughed. Kit, I could see, was a vessel dominated by this strong personality. I did not truly think, starting with me, they'd take up joy-killing as that afternoon's diversion, but in this company I was odd man out. From somewhere on her person Faye drew out a small clip-loading piece and handed it to Kit. "This is the new baby. Hides in your bra" (both girls were braless). Kit looked it over and then slid the gun down into one of her tight front pockets where, far from concealed, it showed like a steel erection. "Not there, sister!" Faye protested. "Let's get back to work."

Faye scraped aside what was left of the assassinated leaders and tacked up regular targets. Now it was my turn with one of the police .38s, and in this patch of wood not far from where Leatherstocking performed similar rites, I sighted the bull's-eye. I knew from Y Camp how to breathe and squeeze the trigger; I knew that you learned from the first round how to control the jerk. Taking my time, I emptied the six chambers. Then Faye retrieved the target to see how well I had shot. She held it up to the one shaft of light that penetrated the ravine's canopy: the black center remained intact. Noting my disappointment, Faye displayed it before her chest and counted five perforations. "I'd say you got your gal."

It was time to go. Back in the house Kit asked Faye, "Do I get to take the little gun home?"

"Unh-unh."

"Please?"

"Unh-unh."

"Please? I'm asking you nicely . . ."

"Bring me a note from your shrink!"

Faye patted the top of Kit's head, stroked her ear, and we left.

SUNDAY NIGHT we watched the late news: out in California there'd been murder and mayhem. First a movie star and her rich friends, then a grocery store owner and his wife. Slain in their solid, affluent homes: shot, stabbed, butchered to death! Words written in blood on the door: *pig, war.* In the way the mind entertains unrealities for fractions of seconds I envisioned Faye and Kit on some rampage. Something had taken a turn, or perhaps events merely confirmed the country's psychopathic condition. My memory of Kit and this visit would be everlastingly tied to Charles Manson and family, even though it would be some time before his image came to dominate this phase of '60s youth culture. After all, Woodstock was about to take place not a hundred miles to the east.

WITH FIVE DAYS OF TALK, some of it revelatory, much of it aimless, there remained the enigma of Khan. I had formulated a theory. Khan was by nature a slob and freeloader, a career sensualist whose jaded tastes cultivated outlaw delights. He was a generational outsider who aped the attitudes of young people so as to come on to girls young enough to be the daughters of his dissipated youth. Like Genghis Khan he was a marauder, but a cowardly one who preyed on the weak. It was amazing he didn't teach art or poetry at some private academy. Girls, but also boys, commonly became acquainted with this type at some stage in their schooling. Khan was a deep-water creature. I would have liked to have seen his head and hands confined to the stocks on some old village green.

There was only one bathroom in the house, across the living room in the bedroom suite where Kit and Sue Anne had separate but adjoining rooms. I awoke after four to the sound of heavy rain and could hear Sue Anne in the kitchen. Other nights I had avoided ingesting liquids before bed so I could hold off until well after Sue Anne left and then slip outside. But last night around ten we decided to kill a quart bottle of Schlitz. The instant I heard Sue Anne start the car I got up and in near-perfect silence moved across the living room but halted just as I approached the suite. I heard a voice, Kit's, sleepily murmuring, telling a story, minutely detailed, punctuated by little moans. I quickly retreated, glad the rain came on just then in a pelting heave that covered the creak of the floor. I went outside and returned drenched. My intuition had been correct. But I really hadn't a guess as to what they were doing.

On the eve of departure, acting on, what, a sense of responsibility? I ventured the question:

"Khan's a pervert, isn't he?"

"He's just a sad person. He's got a really great mind. He was rude to you, and he's like that with everyone. But he's sweet to me."

"I heard you talking to him, reading or something."

"So? It's not like he makes me. I like reading to him. I'll read to you too. I do what I want."

"Don't let him touch you."

"Are you kidding? It would be nice if he did! He won't touch any-one"—here she smirked—"except himself. That's why my mom's kicking him out. With him it's just words. I read to him, that's all, and write crazy poems only he'd like. My mom can't do that."

So I had pierced this mystery but was left with the sense that it remained unsolved. I was not up to the task of facing the question: Why would she participate in such sordid pleasures? Why didn't she just live with her dad? Why couldn't all things be normal?

THAT LAST MORNING Kit got up early so we could walk along the lake, barely visible for the layer of fog. The angry pimple was back. Her mom, home that day, appeared with Instamatic before we left the porch. If my shambling teenage frame didn't ruin the photo, Kit's pimple assuredly did.

We had spent the week in generic reminiscence. We had talked about friends who had crashed and burned. Our discussions of the near future induced symptoms of motion sickness. We had no idea what our lives held.

It had been, we agreed, a meaningful visit. And we promised to write.

I couldn't know then, but from time to time in the years ahead I might expect to hear a little of Kit's subsequent life, a piece here and a piece there. Those fragments would blend with reports of other girls I had known in my teens and early twenties. How she had attended NYU, dropped out and toured the West with some guy, surfaced in LA, got busted for mari-juana, lived a year in the Netherlands, returned and enrolled in a state university. Married and divorced, taught elementary school, remarried. Adopted a child from Korea the year her son left for college. Became a community activist. Beat breast cancer. Her life at third hand might fuse inextricably with what I heard at third hand of other acquaintances, but the gist would be, like many another, she had survived her '60s and '70s youth. Summer was nearly gone, so I wasn't surprised not to receive the promised letter. It couldn't have surprised her that she never heard from me.

THEN, TWO YEARS LATER, at a large party in someone's off-campus apartment, I was shoved toward a girl a year ahead of me, the two of us having been identified as upstate New Yorkers, and the ever-unlikely but somehow inevitable happenstance occurred: two strangers knew the same person from long ago and far away—or what, in the headlong acceleration of young adult life, seems as much. She was from Binghamton, and Katrina had been her wait-staff cohort. "Yeah," she drawled in the flat upstate accent over her plastic tumbler of beer, "that stuff that came out about her dad was really something. Bald bastard screwed them all."

10

False Positions

Bound to my parents by love and money, I knew that forces beyond our control had set us adrift. Generational difference had made us inhabitants of two distinct planets. Viewed from a proper lunar distance theirs was a beautiful, cloud-wrapped orb. It seemed only natural to gravitate home from the varied trajectories of young adult life. I could come home in body, sprawl on the bed, turn on my grandfather's ancient TV (but to no effect, now, as the picture tube was dead), and feel both in and out of time. I could hear the clock tick. I read the signs of parental frailty: my dad's bad hip, my mom's tachycardia. But I didn't want to think about my parents. I longed for a place of my own where girls could spend the night.

Whitewood Lane was alien ground to a son in transition. Best to keep a low profile. Not to be drawn into neighborly chitchat, I'd wait until dark and then move about. Look at the size of these houses, I'd think, resolved to own nothing. Homes up and down Whitewood Lane seemed vastly overbuilt. There were too many vehicles, lawnmowers, leaf blowers, machinery of interminable upkeep. The scent of fertilizer, pesticide laced, seeped from every garage. There were too many bikes and plastic toys and spoiled little brats of a new generation. The houses were large but strangely small, reflecting the smug Lilliput mind for which the plush house was the whole world.

So I'd get in the car and drive. The drinking age was still eighteen: at seventeen I might cruise at will until the lights of a tavern caught my eye. I'd park the car and order a beer and see what sort of friends I could make. At first I'd go to a very safe bar across the street from the shopping plaza. Lodged in a small satellite mall that housed a pet store and optician's shop,

Neighbor, Indian Spring Lane. Courtesy Brighton Municipal Historian Collection.

this place affected an "Irish pub" ambience, but the music was simply white noisy blues band for a mass market. The clientele consisted of young sleepy salespeople from Sears and J. C. Penney. Unaccustomed to professional garb, the guys loosened their ties and tousled their hair; a shopgirl signified she was off duty by releasing the top two buttons of her blouse. I knew these kids, a year or two older than I, and sometimes a girl would come by to flirt, but not seriously. She could see that I was underage, but they'd all recently turned eighteen and weren't about to blow my cover. One girl grew up on Indian Spring Lane and had rebelled: instead of going to Vassar, as planned, she moved in with her boyfriend and took a job in a specialty grocery just inside the city limits. She was studying Eastern religions part-time in the college at Brockport, living, she said, in the eternity of each new day. Her boyfriend's friend worked at the plaza record shop, and she'd come to the bar with him. I could tell she was sizing him up as fresh boyfriend material. For some people the world abounded in boy- and girlfriend possibilities, and every time they turned around they'd lock with a new pair of eyes. But this was not my experience.

Not that I wouldn't have liked that experience. There was a face I longed for, an image from the album art of the day: a girl with large doe-like eyes bathed in the dews of erotic bliss, long cascade of light-brown hair, lips parted in ethereal, or was it visceral, utterance. An off-the-shoulder blouse covered a body hot to the touch. Assuming you could touch it, but you'd have to die and go to heaven, the heaven of bodies and not souls, the only heaven, at that age, worth contemplating.

There were a couple of other bars. One, near the rail yard in East Rochester, had the reputation of a place where no one was carded and you could connect with village party girls, but the instant I walked through the door I knew I had made a wrong turn. Middle-aged men talked and hawed in loud beery voices, and the music was Lawrence Welk. The eyes of the beefy bartender said, "*You* ain't eighteen." I all but apologized to the cigarette machine as I made my exit. Another suburban bar was attached to a bowling alley. One bartender was legally blind and would listen attentively as you placed your order. He'd immediately detect a guy's attempt to deepen his voice and indignantly refuse service. When in doubt he'd say things like, "You know you're on your honor, kid!" and "You know you could get me fired!" It wasn't worth getting him fired or even agitated. The only girls you'd see in there were league players in their twenties. They'd come as a group and weren't looking to meet anyone like me.

And still another, just off Cobb's Hill. I had first visited this one with Lisa from Star Market. I think it was called the Hilltop and was known as the doper's lounge. Nothing fancy about this place: dull-looking bar on the right as you walked in, battered tables on a scruffy wooden floor, old brick walls with ancient mortar smear, testament to an antique sloppy workmanship, acid rock pulsing from elevated speakers. The place put me a little on edge. It did so when I braved my first tentative underage entry but even more so the summer following as I was legal now but still felt tied to the fake ID. The bartender, a dead ringer for David Crosby, had shoulder-length hair and sweat stains extending practically to his waist. Nearly every guy there had that look: very long hair, handlebar mustache, broad shoulder, and big gut. The girls had long straight hair but were as noticeably thin as the guys were fat. The place could get crowded, so you really noticed the bodies. But at times it could also be quite empty. If that was the case, I might order a beer and sit in a booth, cramped and right-angled as a church pew, and let my mind wander over the neon signs and bare-shouldered girls. Nina and Renée, two of the regulars, socialized freely. They were very nice looking but so speedy and beelike you were glad when they moved on.

One night I had taken a small corner table when I was joined by a guy who at first glance bore a striking resemblance to myself: six feet tall, medium build, long brown hair, beardless face, small-lens photo-gray glasses. "Ain't you Jerry Sundown?" he asked. Seeing that I wasn't, he said, "Oh, well," and sat down as though this were nothing to hold against me. He extended his hand in Black Power fashion. "Barry Sandal. Sorry. You look a lot like Jerry." I could tell already his *ain't* was affectation. He looked like me only a year or two older. He was nervous, or else ever in the process of small physical and psychological adjustment, and within two minutes I'd pegged him as a knuckle cracker. Still, I couldn't get over the degree to which I saw in that face only a slight distortion of my own. He looked like me and I looked like Jerry: there were three of us, then, who could pass for one another in the Hilltop's smoky ambience. "You live around here?" he was quick to ask, and I answered by saying I worked pretty close. Then came talk of mutual acquaintances, a guy who had worked at Star but was fired, a girl who trained two days and then quit. He spoke of the live bands I had missed by coming only on week-nights. That led to talk of music generally and a discovery we hated the exact same bands. They fell into two categories: those that specialized in songs with fairy-tale lyrics, and those that featured a thin white voice attempting to wail the blues. (You wanted to hear the Isley Brothers, not John Lennon, sing "Twist and Shout.") Aversion formed our initial bond. From there we readily agreed that Rochester's music scene was second rate and you really needed to be in New York City. We had begun to drift toward the subject of schools, an awkward topic for me inasmuch as private school suggested privilege. I was ready to claim I'd been sent downstate after having been caught with a pint of scotch. From there I might talk about New York adventures. But then two girls stepped from the haze and sat at our table: one was Gretch, Barry's girl, and the other her friend Nance. They were both cute. They had brown hair no longer than Barry's or mine. In the barroom's deep aquarium light, we all four looked alike.

We had a round of beers while the girls prattled about some guy who had tried to pick them up. This allegedly took place at the Department of Motor Vehicles. At first the guy followed them on foot and then in a rattle-trap pickup truck with bags of stinking garbage. Clark, Nance's boyfriend, rescued them in a bigger truck, the one he drove for the tire store. He'd been their superhero. The girls laughed and laughed, and I could see that the story was a joke at Clark's expense. Barry cracked a set of knuckles (he would do this as though performing a ritual, like telling beads) and then stood. "Ladies and gentlemen. Got some herb for your discriminat-ing palate." He said this with the showman air he'd exhibited when he first sat down. As we made for the door I took the rear: here was my cue to part ways. But no, I was to be the guest of honor; Barry's place was just two blocks up. Tomorrow, I proposed, I could come then, but tonight I'm supposed to get the car back. So tomorrow night was confirmed but not, I sensed, with conviction.

But at least I'd keep my end of the agreement. Entering the Hilltop I thought it best to take a table and wait to be seen rather than go in eagerly scanning. Sure enough, no one was there at the appointed time or even ten minutes later. The kids were flakes just as I'd suspected. But then someone patted my shoulder, and standing before me with her hand on my head was Nance. She would lead me to Barry's. Where was my car? I told her tonight I was on foot. In truth I had taken the bus, having parked in a lot by the stop a mile from my house. There'd be no traffic or anything com-plicated when I got back, stoned or otherwise. We walked the two blocks, one long, one short, to Barry's: a one-bedroom apartment on a third floor reached by a side-entrance staircase. The door to his place shook with "Gimme Shelter." Nance knocked at the door with what appeared to be coded knocks, then inserted a key and let us in.

Inside there was nothing I hadn't seen in other apartments kept by eighteen- to twenty-year-olds: lighted candles, cruddy old furniture, psy-chedelic posters, Fender Stratocaster in a far corner, speakers strung this way and that, a mattress or two on the bare floor, ashtrays with cigarette butts and hash pipes. A window fan with colored streamers circulated humid air. "Man, you made it!" Barry bobbed forward on the broken-down sofa where a barefoot Gretch huddled in bliss. We clasped hands Power style. Then sitting back he parted the foil wrapper of a small brown hash cake, cut a slice with the cupped appendage of a Swiss Army knife, deposited it in a small silver pipe, lit and passed the pipe. "Peace," he intoned. With the second toke I could feel my thighs begin to elevate. By now we were listening to "Machine Gun" from *Band of Gypsys*. I looked at Barry in the room's cross light, one-part candle to two-parts glare radiating from a fluorescent tube in the kitchen toward the back. Yes, he looked like me. He had this place and it was his own, and Gretch would stay the night.

My eyes kept returning to Gretch. She was a bowl of ice cream enfolded with something sweet and warm. She had tucked her blonde hair behind an ear and dozed like a child in her young woman's body, exposed at thigh and midriff. I closed my eyes and saw her body still: full lower lip, soft inner thigh, magnified. Time passed in wayward increments. "Barry," Gretch whispered, "I've got to crash." At this my mind refocused. I desperately did not want her to leave, but at least she would have to step by me on her way to the bedroom, and thus the invisible field of her body would sweep across mine. "Good night," she said, touching my cheek, and it was almost like being kissed.

I rather liked Barry. He had an interesting collection of British R&B and was on to the Velvet Underground, and he had this charmingly immature way of living for the moment. Prompted by spasmodic reflex, he'd draw a cigarette from his shirt pocket, as though suddenly recalling he was free to smoke, and he'd do so having snubbed one out only five minutes earlier. He had characters running about in his head: Shandy Corkstroker, a drunk who periodically "fucked up" his amp, Mindy Maw Warp, a giant female amoeba who raided his fridge just before dawn, and others. Objectively, he drove a forklift in a plumbing-supply warehouse, practiced his guitar, and sold marijuana. Most of the money he made from dealing went into the First Federal savings account he had opened when he was ten. He had gone through three bank books and one evening proudly displayed them, all the while singing the First Federal jingle: "Hardworkin' dollar, what a dynamo! Even while you're sleepin' he makes your money grow—oh!" He'd spent some of the money just that spring on a five-day trip to Bermuda, having quit his job in a sandwich shop. While there he had sent postcards to his friends and one to himself: on the photo side a girl in a bikini, on the other a message reading, "Dear Barry, Wish you were here, wait, you are!" He'd pass it around for a laugh when people were good and stoned. His dad taught high school in one of the city districts, and his mom worked in the same building as a receptionist. They wanted him to attend the college at Geneseo, and he planned to do so someday, but first he wanted to live free, play his guitar, and idolize Gretch.

It was really Gretch who drew me back to his place. If Barry and I looked so much alike—and it was getting to be too much remarked: hey, here come the twins! hey, I just saw your doppelgänger!—if Barry and I looked so much alike, and Barry could have Gretch, wasn't there someone like that for me? But would I want to go out with someone to whom every Adam's son was drawn by irresistible hormonal magnetism? She was not my girl, yet I still felt alarm at the knot of guys clustering about her at the Hilltop—more so, perhaps, than Barry, stoned beyond prudence. What was it about her? She and Nance looked much alike. Nance was pretty but lacked a quality that emanated from Gretch. There was something urgent about her eyes and luminous about her skin. Her body curved beneath light cotton fabrics. She put out a perfume you could smell and one you could not. She could dress in blue jeans and a baggy sweatshirt, and you would still sense the naked body under the clothes. In a bid to quit smoking she had taken up running. One day I was over at Barry's when she came back from a run in eighty-degree heat, bathed in sweat. Her body exhaled a rank sweetness. Inwardly embarrassed, I couldn't get enough of this. To entertain these stimuli was highly inappropriate. I admonished myself: this is my friend's girl, but still I registered them. Another time the three of us went to a movie, and she was the one in the middle, holding the popcorn. "Here, take some," she whispered as the house lights went down, and for the rest of the movie I retained the sensation of her hot breath against my ear.

Barry and I were at the coffee shop a block away from his place. He was very stoned and off-the-wall voluble. Among his remarks was

"Gretch thinks you're cute and we should tie you down and tickle you." It would dawn on me six hours later that this had been a proposition. Some kids I knew did these things. For me group activities held no appeal, but for access to Gretch might I not have gone along? But by then the question was almost moot. Gretch was already a lost possibility, for Barry and me both. A month and a half into our acquaintance things went to pieces.

They had gone to pieces before I had come into their circle. From time to time Gretch would announce she was heading to Canandaigua to visit her mom or over to Brighton to check on her dad, and it would get back to Barry that she was seeing an old boyfriend, a new boyfriend. He would kick a hole in the wall or in one of his speakers, and she would come back and scold him for being possessive. Nance's boyfriend, Clark, Barry's ex–best friend, filled me in on this pattern. On my lunch break I'd see him sometimes with Nance at the diner across from work, and one afternoon when he wasn't with Nance he left the counter to join me at my table. Clark had recently cut his hair and enrolled in business college. He worked in a tire store where he was required to wear a bright-red polyester shirt with the store's logo. But he had taken to wearing that shirt when he was off duty. He knew this made him the butt of jokes but in the way of martyrs was making a statement. He had repudiated everything associated with hippies and looked at Barry as a case of arrested development. "Everyone's moving on," he observed in his tone of smug concern, "except Barry." Gretch was returning to William Smith for her sophomore year, Nance and he were thinking of getting married, I was heading back to Ohio. Barry would be left behind with his weed and set of shadowy friends: the "hard-drug blacks from the North Side," the ones who carried guns. At Clark's mention of guns my eyes must have widened: "Guns, you bet!" I knew Barry must have underworld contacts but had never visualized them so. The message was clear: everyone was abandoning Barry, and you should too before "the goons come 'round to his place some night to collect on a back payment." To dump Barry for fear of "goons" seemed a little cowardly, but I tried to think well of Clark. I had not known him in his longhair days, but he seemed so reformed and responsible. He was even attending a youth-oriented church. It would come as a shock later to learn that Nance was pregnant and Clark had moved on.

Barry had grudgingly accepted the fact that Gretch would return to college. Geneva wasn't far, and he could drive down on weekends, those on which she wasn't writing papers, although such, she pointed out, might be few. They were experiencing a kind of pre-separation honeymoon, but it was odd the way they wanted me around for meals and drinks, as though I were some kind of buffer. I felt as though I were the double, the look-alike, Jerry Sundown, whom I knew now wasn't a real person, but one of the cast of cartoon personalities populating Barry's marijuana brain. Gretch was full of sisterly caresses. I think they were sisterly; at least they seemed not to pose a threat to Barry. Threat took the form of some-one named Serge, a heavy-set guy with walrus mustache and shoulder-length hair whom we used to see at the Hilltop before the owner asked to see my driver's license, "the real one." Serge was on the horizon; he was outside on the sidewalk; his face appeared at the window. Gretch had never appeared lovelier, sitting on Barry's sofa in running shorts and T-shirt, a new and unexplained ankle bracelet catching the evening light, talking rapturously about her fall classes and plans for the junior year in Spain. I gazed at the bracelet and thought about the leg, thigh, little peach buttocks, strangely illuminated face and eyes, and saw that Serge had made his mark—that Gretch was as good as gone. These, I knew, must be Barry's thoughts as well, and the only difference between us would be the anguish he especially would feel. He sat in a chair apart from her with a look between resignation and dread.

Not long afterward Barry called to say she'd left. But his exact phrase was "Gretch has left *us*," and with that last word I felt the vacuum. I drove right over to find Barry sitting on the floor beside an overturned chair and pieces of a broken ceramic lamp, and between sobs he told me the details. Gretch had come in to announce that Serge was stopping by with his truck to retrieve her stuff for the drive to Canandaigua, preparatory to her return to school. (All these guys with trucks, I thought with perfect irrelevance: the stalker from the DMV, Clark and his big tire-store truck, and now Serge and his.) In ten minutes she and her personal items were gone. She'd left behind a tube of gel that she used to shave her legs. Barry clutched this item with such pathos that I had to take it from him and lay it aside. He drew heavily on a blimplike reefer and moaned, "Oh, oh, oh,

Gretch!" I took the reefer and snubbed it out. I made him walk outside; I took him to a coffee shop, newly opened, for espresso shots. I told him he had to stop: everyone, I said, was moving on, and it wasn't too late to enroll in fall classes. Without the least effort to sound convincing I told him I'd met some Geneseo girls and they were outasight.

Thus I did my duty by Barry. I might have done more, but it was time for me to pack. He would call to talk in his stoned-out way, and I'd resent the fact that he and not Gretch had called. He'd tell about seeing Gretch go by on the back of Serge's motorcycle, and I'd feel personally betrayed, and then mad at Barry for enlisting me in jealousies not properly my own. Two minutes later he'd ask for a loan of fifty dollars. I'd agree to twenty-five, meet him at the new coffee shop, and sit with him for an hour while he sat and stared at the wall. That was it. I needed to separate from this person who suddenly, to my view, did not look like me at all.

BUT STILL I HAUNTED CITY PLACES with the hope of meeting Gretch (or equivalent—surely she had a twin). Why did I persist in thinking about her?

"I know you." The raven-haired girl materialized in the glare of over-head fluorescent tubing: a complete stranger, in fury, vengeance.

"Oh yeah?"

"You're friends with that doper and his princess."

"Yeah, so?"

"You're really friends with her. She's from Brighton and so are you."

"Not quite. Do you care to know the facts?"

"I want to know why you come up here, why you treat this place like your place. What are you reading?"

"It's a book by Herman Hesse. Have a look."

"I've read that. I'm in MENSA. Why do you come here?"

"Why do you ask?"

"Because you don't belong here. Unless you're planning to ask me out."

"I don't really know you."

"No, but you think you know me. You people are all alike."

"I really don't think I know you."

"My hair is black because I dye it, my mascara makes my eyes bright green, and you don't belong here."

"Okay. So you're asking me to leave? Or ask you out?"

"You want to fuck my pussy. Say that."

"I'm not saying that."

"Say it."

"I'm not saying that."

"Then get the fuck out."

Downtown, at Main and Stone, I sometimes caught sight of myself stepping full-length from a panel of canted plate glass, the corner facet of an old-time display case that mirrored and magnified approaching passersby. The figure loomed up in jellied distortion, but the shoulder-length hair and photo-gray glasses were mine. It would nonplus me every time, this familiar, alien image to which my mind ventured a hesitant recognition. Surely, I did not look that monstrous. The shop dealt in secondhand medical supplies, items guaranteed to repel a young person: in the dimly lit window, if you cared to look, lay an assortment of braces, wheelchairs, and oxygen tanks. Simply to dwell on planet Earth, the old needed to be equipped like astronauts. I hurried on in my errand, objectless as it might be.

I had a host of such errands, circuitous tours the object of which was to absent myself from the house. Five out of seven nights spent at home might pass unnoticed, but more than that begins to look pathetic, even to parents who enjoy your company. What was the chance of crossing paths with Gretch? It was getting too late to form additional summer friendships. The barroom had lost its attraction (always the same boy-girl patter and stale beer-and-tobacco stench). I was tired of every option. To walk the streets of downtown, making the rounds of secondhand bookstores or perusing the shelves of record shops; to decide to visit some bar and then bail a step or two from the door; to drive aimlessly through suburb and city or ride the bus when the cars were in use meant going through the motions of an old and discarded self. It was time to be a new person, to step into a different body, one that didn't look ludicrous when appearing on some random reflective surface. I would cut my hair and set my jaw.

I would leave the old image on a panel of tarnished glass in a building slated for demolition.

I visualized myself elsewhere among other young people liberated from the suburbs of Rust Belt cities, from material acquisitions and Republican career paths. I could see myself in Oregon and California. I could imagine emigrating to the high desert of New Mexico and Arizona, working for the Park Service and living in a commune. I had never been west of the Mississippi but didn't doubt that white suburban bodies grew strong and lean in desert sun. I could visualize myself hoeing beans in a community garden. I could experiment with life in a remote compound with an arcane library and plurality of girlfriends. Or I could opt for something urban and coastal. A season at the Pacific beach made you a Californian, whereas years spent in Manhattan never made a New Yorker in the true sense. Party scenes pertained to each of these fantasies: drugs, drink, girls, and music in euphoric sidereal convergence, but I had seen a little of the vomit and tears, the zombie stupefaction that marked the party scene's sequel, and so the ecstatic moment in my dream of far places did not emphasize delights of the flesh. Rather, it was all about standing high on a ridge and meeting the sun's full nuclear glare, a world of endless interlocking canyons spreading below in all directions. Or it involved surveying a deserted beach as the mist rose from the ocean surface and stars appeared in a sky that went on forever. Such scenes compelled you to leave behind everything you had known and to contemplate a magnificent reflective surface that didn't return your image. I would find those places, even if I couldn't dwell in them; I would stand at those ultimate thresholds. Then I'd determine how and why such experience should make my life something other than a variation of my parents'.

Meanwhile, there was college, a six-hour drive west and south. Ohio was as nowhere as western New York. And more immediately there was the problem of remnant summer weeks.

Downtown afforded a poor excuse to get out of the house. The flat nasality of overheard talk was repellent. The shopping districts had become an anxious shuffle of haves and have-nots. I got tired of panhandlers, many of whom were kids my age just out of jail who saw in me an easy mark: "My man, my man! Need some bread to make a new life! You got some, I know you got some! Hey, come back!"

One evening three of them stalked me until I turned into a liquor store, the only thing open for blocks. There was, I saw, a fine line between panhandler and mugger, and thus I no longer went downtown after six for idle strolling. I could satisfy my taste for urban scenes in the more prosperous blocks around Oxford and Park. But in that neighborhood there was always the risk of running into Barry.

Riding the Monroe Avenue bus back to Brighton, I rarely got into conversations anymore. I'd gaze abstractly across the aisle, focusing on my disembodied image in the semitransparent windows, a face among others dissolving together in the cross-lighted glass. The bus offered refuge for a journey's duration, one or two stops for some, end of the line for others, during which everyone consented to be a self-contained object routed and shipped. We were city and suburb dwellers, white, tan, black, and brown, and of a half-dozen generations. The bus grew malodorous in the universal way of late-day public transport. Yet I imagined a kind of aura enclosing the burly, impassive middle-aged men as well as the tired young women wearing Rexall and Woolworth uniforms, eyes down and hair bound back. There we were, strangers awash in a collective fatigue, all headed for domestic scenes, supper, TV, sex, sleep, dream, death. The process owed everything to ingrained habit; in twenty years the passengers would all be replaced and this bus sit in some junkyard. I liked being part of this anonymous group. Moments of passage had become for me inherently symbolic.

At the suburban plaza, by contrast, individual constituents of the trooping crowd seemed atomized beyond possibility of bond, or no more bond than preexisted the visit, shambling units taking the form of family groups and teenage cliques. Certain plazas had begun to morph into malls, the enclosed, antinatural inscape of which lent shoppers the air of consumer automatons, bodies snatched for life on a mercantile planet. Five minutes in such a place made you feel dead. Everywhere you looked there was a shiny metal surface, and the white-light fluorescence converted one's image into that of a wax figure. Badly behaved teenagers offered the only sign of life. Letters to the editor of the suburban weekly called for their banishment, but I was old enough to surmise a ruse. The mall barons saw in the shouting, sulking, shoplifting teen a lucrative future and were willing to indulge his, and more commonly her, contempt for the law. To the far-seeing mind the important point was the teenager's attraction to merchandise, a desire that would long outlast her petty-larceny phase. It would long outlast her sexual desire and reproductive years. She'd have her children and bring them here. Occasionally, I'd catch sight of a pregnant teenage girl, a witless-looking teen-child with absurdly bulging abdomen, and it would dawn on me that kids two and three years my junior had made this enormous start on life. Perhaps, I thought, the inception of each member of the human mob, from babe in arms to octogenarian, shares a similarly doubtful genesis. Naturally, the children on Whitewood Lane were the elite issue of planned pregnancies and self-regulating demographics, with family trusts in place to direct the flow of wealth. But if that were the case, it was the great exception. Seeing, in the space of one week, at random, six or seven expectant moms younger than I, it was clear to me that one generation is brought forward by the folly of another.

The shore of Lake Ontario offered other occasions for solitude. Sometimes, on overcast days, I'd drive up to Kanatota Park, leave my shoes in the car, and stroll about the strand. The water at such times was an anemic yellow-green, but it extended as far as eye could reach, and what the eye desired was simply unbounded expanse. The fluid heaviness stilled my mind, and I fantasized losing consciousness beneath it as under a heavy blanket. Even in chilly conditions this stone-and-driftwood beach drew girls, members of a social or family unit, but as such totally unapproachable. I still kept watch for Gretch or her double, but did so with a sense of futility. I might equally watch for UFOs.

Still, I thought of her.

Gretch had escaped the suburb. And she had left without burning the bridge back. That alone lent her fascination. But there was so much more. Gretch didn't submit to flattened dimensions. She entered a room and commanded the scene. By disposition sweet and ostensibly passive, her body compelled and bullied young men. Barry had been a stage in her self-liberation, but I, not liberated, was the one who could read her soul.

Surely she must know? Taking a hit from the blimp-shaped reefer I had rolled from leftover seeds and stems, I gazed at the wall and studied the imaginary photo album enshrining her image. How I longed to sit with her, talk one-on-one, confirm our mutual understanding.

"Oh, oh, oh, Gretch!"

Yes: life again had contracted, and for an eternal month I would be stuck. Whitewood Lane was living death. Here, structurally, there could be no romance. None at least that wasn't part of a fully rationalized routine. This was the suburb: everything, including fun, had to have purpose. I was too old or too young for purpose. I embraced isolation. Here, the only folks truly at home were middle-aged people with chemical lawns. Some of the neighborhood's older residents had begun to depart for retirement colonies. Into their houses moved young couples with small children and more on the way. Closer in years to me than my parents, immersed in study to become middle-aged, these couples had clearly renounced youth. When my folks invited one such couple over for cocktails, I noted the young wife's chubby arm, the husband's waistline heft. She'd had her hair cut and permed, exposing a once lovely nape. He ventured the mere suggestion of sideburns, and his red flesh glistened through a newly shorn scalp. This is what happens between twenty-five and thirty. Bodies didn't exist for them except as infant factories. Bodies didn't exist for old people except as engines of misery—sources of pain, objects of medication. The magic of another's voice, eye, skin tone, scent: gone. There were no secrets left. Nothing remained but capital possessions and afternoon naps.

THERE WAS ANOTHER NOT-GRETCH who approached as I sat reading and drinking a milk shake.

"Looking for a good time?"

"Maybe. Who's asking?"

"I'm Serena. It's my Christian name. This is our pamphlet."

On the cover a radiant butter-colored cross arose from a nightmare collage: earthquake, mushroom cloud, grim-faced world leaders, angry minorities, puzzled-looking whites.

"Oh, I have a church."

"Yes, but do you go to it?"

"It's there when I need it."

"You need it now."

"How do you know?"

"Because tonight you shall die! Smile, Christian! That's a good thing!"

"Why is it good?"

"Because death is the door to eternal life."

"So, okay, what is your church?"

"The Double Church of Victory and Praise. It's for young people like you and me. What are you reading?"

"Poems. By William Blake."

"Oh, he's a Christian!"

"I guess."

"Anyway, we're having a free concert tonight at the church."

"Some sing-along thing or a real concert?"

"A real concert, with electric guitars! The group is called the Ark."

"What about girls—will there be cute girls?"

"I'm a cute girl."

"Will you be there?"

"Yes."

"Does your minister eyeball the kids all the time? I went to a church school. I know about these things."

"Our pastors truly understand kids. Lots of us meet other kids at the church. They're not antisex! Really! Jesus teaches that sex is beautiful. Sex is Jesus's special gift to couples who have sanctified their love in his name."

"Where does he teach that sex is beautiful?"

"In one of our pamphlets all about love and how to make it work." She smiled like one caught in a bluff. "I'll give you a copy if you come tonight."

"You just said tonight I will die. I think it's a plot."

"Maybe. Come and find out."

She had long, straight, dense blonde hair. When she stood and turned her head, the mass swept over my face. But it was soft and smelled of the era's fruit shampoo, one called Garden of Eden. I was better for the contact.

"I'm sorry. I do that all the time!"

But I didn't go to her church. I was much too conservative on the question of church music. If I was going to church, I needed the authority of a pipe organ. I needed God, the strong father. Guitars—electric, acoustic—smacked of diluted faith.

The second time we met I explained it to her in just those terms. She said she understood.

"Invite me to your church."

"Yes—good idea."

But I had things to do on each of my three remaining Sundays. So we did other things on days when church services weren't scheduled. We went on long walks in two of the city parks. The cicadas trilled in the late-summer trees. Her eyes held a mesmerized expression, as if to say, I am waiting for you to make a move. But three seconds later her eyes as plainly said, better not. That was all right. Abstention has its own wistful beauty. Serena was not Gretch, but for twenty-one days I thought about her, too.

We walked and held hands. I think we were both content with that.

I HAD TAKEN LEAVE before I had left. I left and returned to take leave once more. I was used to the notion of residing in places that were not Rochester, city or suburb. Still, for years I had imagined someone worth meeting just over the city limits. No such person ever quite appeared. By the end of summer I had abandoned this fantasy. I had likewise abandoned all hope of Gretch (the person if not the type, assuming there to be a type). I had drawn the conclusion that there was no one within a thousand-mile radius who would play a significant role in my life. Yet, in after years, inevitably, I'd dream back over those sites and occasions of hoped-for contact as though I had missed an encounter, or not kept an appointment, detained by hesitation and self-consciousness, or for other essentially unknowable reasons unable to connect with what I had sought. The conviction of missed opportunity might have come from my sense of social failure (my class narrowness and lack of generosity) or from the simple human capacity to imagine more lives than one person can lead. Of the many lives I could plausibly lead, is this the right one? How will I know? But like anyone else I had encounters, appointments, for which—happily or not—I appeared.

But disappearance from the scenes of childhood was ordained.

For a month or so, the sensation that I was away from home lurked beneath every other. It wasn't as though I'd never been away. But now I was seriously and irretrievably away. The sensation was one of liberation and sadness. Day after day I'd awake to the thought that I am not home on Whitewood Lane. When that idea ceased to be novel, when it no longer recurred, even then the old street remained in my life: the address I had significantly vacated, the house to which, though I return on vacation, I would never truly return. I might close my eyes and see color photos of the house enveloped in snow or surrounded by trees in full leaf. Never truly to return: there was something final and sad to that thought, but it was my first reflection as I settled into the dorm freshman year. My parents had said good-bye, and I watched the Caprice disappear down the drive, one in a parade of family sedans, and knew I had crossed a threshold. Not that I wouldn't see them again, not that I wouldn't follow the road back, but my relationship to home had changed.

But this is nearly everyone's experience.

DECEMBER I COULD GO HOME. As my birthday falls on the tenth, this for me is the month of origin, homecoming, reconciliation, and the more snow, the better. Birthday, Christmas, New Year's: it was always a small miracle to reach the back door, inhale the familiar entryway scent, arrive safe and sound between snowstorms, before the airport closed and the thruway shut down. On the little TV in the kitchen the weatherman forecasts another foot. Travel is strongly discouraged. But I am through, for now, with my travels. Let it snow, heavily and forever.

Perhaps it was something about winter and snow. In the new-fallen snow's moonlike pall I admired the houses on Whitewood Lane. I liked the assurance of solid walls and glowing windows and the sight of blazing logs in the fireplace. The fire imparted a wood-smoke scent to the finely penetrating arctic air, and the person outside with a key to the door benefited the most. I might walk for an hour, careless of my mom's tendency to worry. Let her worry: it will simply enhance her pleasure at my return. Besides, what could be safer than these bland streets? I visualized wine in wrought-iron racks and premium scotch on marble counters.

Late-season football luxuriated across the large color television. I knew these houses inside and out: they were simply incarnations of the one house, a Platonic ideal of the good life in the United States circa 1972. Just off the kitchen was a powder room with miniature soap and small hand towels, and a carpeted staircase led to rooms where the hush of central heating lulled occupants to a dreamless sleep. I stood in the snow and thought about these things. These were the houses of doctors and lawyers, bankers and corporate vice presidents, mechanical engineers promoted to management. They were also the houses of their wives: educated women, occasionally professional, who possessed power and a hard, intriguing beauty. Each house had a cabinet or desk with a drawer containing financial documents: here you will find bank and brokerage statements articulating wealth (the real if ever intangible wealth) in six and seven figures. I desired to possess on my own terms such self-contained, such well-maintained, affluence: warmth and comfort in the deep-winter night. I would have it all but reserve every right. From a just arraignment of the privileged class I held myself exempt. I might own things but not become old. I would read the world by the light of youthful sympathies. The years would thin and silver my hair, and I'd awake one day to something resembling my father's face in the bathroom mirror. But I'd not become someone other than who I'd been and always would be. On that I made vows.

11

Home and Away and Home Again

Sunlight poured through the picture windows. From late spring through early fall it touched the walls with the green of the lush backyard, the trees and bushes my father planted in an effort to create his half-acre Canaan.

This was our living room. At some point around age twelve, I sat in the room and thought about the phrase. "Living room": a place for people relieved of compulsory doing. Ours surely had perfected that idea. Among living rooms I had known as a guest, none rivaled its generous space and none approached its variability of mood. In the bleak afternoons following New Year's, light pierced the room with icy wrath, and at night the windows went completely black. My father sat in an upholstered chair asleep in the winter night, a glossy void on the other side of the double-paned glass. Inspecting the room as she walked to the kitchen, my mother stepped behind his chair and drew the heavy drape.

I always liked that room. Depending on the season, it could be open and airy or sealed tight against the wind. Sun and cloud plunged the room into alternate worlds. A white carpet enhanced the sense of interior space, large enough to situate the piano out of direct sun. You felt the solidity of the house in this room. The walls neither admitted drafts nor winced beneath thunderclaps. The fireplace held big blazing logs. The room was furnished according to a taste not quite in keeping with its horizontal lines. The chairs had come, via Walden Road, from my mother's home on Birr Street. A half-dozen paintings and quality prints depicted rural and seaside vignettes or else the vaguely Oriental themes of the last century. Here and there my mother placed crafted objects featuring a golf or beach motif. On the coffee table lay four or five of the most recent issues

Winter neighborhood. Courtesy of the author.

of the *New Yorker*. Music flowed from stereo speakers behind the piano. The records my parents listened to consisted mostly of piano concertos, Mozart, Chopin, Rachmaninoff, although, by herself, my mother would play the easy-listening station. Nothing about the room was cheap or obviously extravagant. Its privacy was beyond price. From picture windows in living and dining rooms you saw nothing that wasn't ours.

"Picture window." I thought about that phrase. Life as a photograph: perfection on both sides of the glass.

As a child, when no one was watching, I might sit in the dark with secret guests: in one chair my aunt Emma Ellwanger, in the other my grandfather Culp. Gramps had died that past June, Auntie Emma the June before. They sat again in their preferred chairs, and this gave me time to reason with death. As a teenager, as a college student, I returned to the room with a memory of the boy conducting this timid séance. But by then he too had vanished.

Even when no longer a child, I could come back from the world and hide out in this room. I could close the drapes, put up my feet, and doze to the white noise of the central heating. I could stretch out on the sofa and read forever.

Back at college or out on the road, I visualized my dad in this room. He might sit there in late middle age and behold the fruits of his labor. The chief objects of life had been attained. Here was a home and a way of living more nearly approaching utopian conditions than he dared consciously expect. The golden years of golf and travel await. The mortgage is paid and the children are grown, well on their way to becoming respectable citizens. In the Bible this would be the part of the story where, after exodus and adventure, trial met with courage and probity, you lived out your years in the home you had made, children and grandchildren ministering to your need, and then you died.

Grown children do not willingly discern a parent's decline. They are too caught up in the turbulence of their own lives to notice much beyond obvious change in others. I resisted evidence of my parents' mortality. A parent has to keep on living, if at a necessary remove, as financier and intercessory or simply as an elderly voice on the other end of the long-distance call, picking up between the third and fourth ring. The child's life can be disorderly, open-ended, subject to revision, but the parent's life and ways must be set in stone.

MY FATHER IN MIDDLE AGE was a figure of strength: six feet tall, two hundred pounds. At 7:30 a.m., in a dark suit with burgundy tie and polished dress shoes, he strode through the kitchen alert, immaculate, out the door and off to work. Weekends found him in flannel shirt and cotton work pants vigorously raking leaves in the yard, mounting the ladder to clear the gutters. There he is, at the end of our driveway, advising a younger neighbor. Or here, at his desk, beneath the plaque honoring his thirty years' service at Kodak, writing checks that pay the bills, happy to pause and chat with a son. There is nothing remarkable in the fact that he can rise from the chair and walk to the garage; there, he gets down on his knees to make an adjustment to the lawnmower's cutting blade. In the backyard he has filled two aluminum buckets with leaves and twigs. He places one inside the other, lifts them both, and carries them to the street for the Tuesday pickup. He hitches the ladder on his shoulder and disappears around the side of the house.

He announces that he is off to the gas station, hardware store, nursery—did I want to go? Yes. I liked the fact that he had his own ways of getting to a destination, different from my mother's. I admired his manner—never pompous, always firm, his most ordinary errand proceeding with a certain inevitability. The clerk at the hardware store has to track down the premium battery for the smoke detector—this other won't do. My dad notes the price and counts his change; he smiles and says thank you. In late April we drive three miles to a pocket of hilly countryside not yet invaded by suburban development where the old Dutchman De Visser runs a nursery, and while Dad consults with the nurserymen about plantings and fertilizers, I wander about the greenhouses, inhaling their warm, earthen, fecund, fetid scents. My dad speaks my name: he can use a hand, if I'm offering, with the bags of fertilizer. The lawnmower needs repair; he can use my help getting it into and out of the trunk. He can use help generally with the fall cleanup, stowing the patio furniture away for the winter. At the gas station he asks the mechanic to check the alignment; leaving the car, we walk across the parking lot cleared of last night's snow to the pharmacy for his prescription and then to the liquor store so he can purchase bourbon and wine. I am anxious on his account about slick patches beneath the slush. This summer, when I'm home for a week, he'll do the steadying, and I'll be the one on the ladder clearing the gutters and trimming the hedge. It's time to refill the propane tank for the backyard grill. Do I want to drive? And now he needs me to take him to the optician's to be fitted for glasses following cataract surgery.

He preferred that people comment neither on his strengths nor his weaknesses. His vision of what he had to do was so sure that approbation seemed irrelevant. Several days before spring vacation my sophomore year at Saint Peter's, I came down with the flu and was laid up in the infirmary. After work on a Thursday, he drove the three hundred miles from Rochester to Peekskill, checked into a motel, and next morning came by to sign me out. After arranging the car so that I would be comfortable, we drove back to Rochester. He did so as though there were nothing to it, a simple performance of duty. The fact that he took off work was beside the point, as was my gratitude. It wasn't that you should not express thanks. Your gratitude was something for you to feel; it reminded you of your connectedness. But you must amply accept as you amply give. You don't ask to be congratulated for doing the right thing. A man fulfilled his responsibilities because they were his.

The summer before my senior year we took a road trip, just the two of us, to visit college campuses. My brother was attending college in the Midwest and was doing quite well, so it was decided I would look at campuses in Ohio, Illinois, and Wisconsin. The outskirts of Rochester are really an eastward extension of suburban Middle America, so it made as much sense to go west as go east. We took turns behind the wheel, and for the first time I ventured west of the Niagara frontier. The interstate highway beckoned. We traversed the countryside of Ohio and Indiana and the industrial suburbs of Chicago. In the late afternoon, after a long day of driving, we'd check into a motel and drink the cold beer that we'd buy from a package store drive-up window, then go out for an early dinner. One time, as we left the motel restaurant, my dad remembered he needed to pick up some toiletry. While I mounted the outside staircase to our second-level room, he proceeded to cross the four-lane highway to the little store on the far side. I watched with concern; his right leg dragged a bit, and the traffic was fast, local people turning sharp and accelerating hard. I could see him picked off for all his caution, and stood vigil until he was safely back on the motel side. At night we watched the Democratic National Convention taking place in Chicago, not far from where we were making our campus tours, and sat wordless at the spectacle of street violence. It blended with images of Soviet tanks rumbling through Prague earlier that week. I remember little else from that trip. The small liberal arts colleges were all the same, or differed only in the color of stone in the oldest building.

THE COLLEGE IN RURAL OHIO was a six-hour drive from suburban Rochester. Destined to be part of a Greater Columbus, the towns dotting this western shelf of Appalachian plateau had been planted by New Englanders and retained a cleanly Calvinist air. Turned 'round in your journey you might think you had entered a village in the Berkshires. Nearly everyone at the college had grown up on Whitewood Lane or its equivalent. And in 1969 nearly all thought they were trying to get as far away from Whitewood Lane as possible. How I envied my first college girlfriend, an art major and flower child from western Massachusetts. She was a step or two ahead of me—had dropped mescaline, been briefly incarcerated, and slept in mud at Woodstock while I was at home on Whitewood Lane reading about the Manson murders. Her real boyfriend, a poet, was in jail for drug possession. It was hard to compete with credentials like those, but the year would offer many opportunities to acquire experience. After a month I bailed out of my first dorm room, leaving a roommate who knew from age ten he wanted to be a golf pro, and moved in with Chip, whose first name—Chadwick—was a maternal surname. His version of Whitewood Lane was in Bethesda, Maryland, and this came in handy later that semester when kids on campuses all over the region mobilized to converge on Washington, DC, for a mass rally and march against the war.

That fall the country was absorbing reports of the My Lai massacre and in a short writing assignment for Western Civ we were asked to consider the degree to which Lieutenant Calley should be held responsible. There was no easy answer, but the consensus favored laying it at the politicians' feet. Here, on the one hand, was a soldier who had abandoned military discipline to go on an ecstatic bloodletting rampage, while there, on the other, was a group of old and middle-aged men who had managed to construct, in Vietnam, laboratory conditions guaranteed to produce paranoia and atrocity. The great fear of Vietnam lay not so much in the physical trials of jungle warfare or the hazards of booby-trap combat, but in the settled conviction that in going to war, you would cease to be your parents' son, cease to be the young adult you were fashioning apart from your parents' expectation but still, fundamentally, much in their image. In going to Vietnam you assumed a role in a plot that had no end, or rather ended with death and dismemberment, yours or some peasant civilian's. The My Lai massacre made the November Washington rally a generational duty.

Someone from the college had fitted up a truck, and a lot of kids, including my girlfriend, were planning to ride on the covered bed from central Ohio to Washington and back. Chip and I had another idea. We would hitchhike to Bethesda, spend the night at his parents', get up early, and bus into DC. On Sunday we would drive his Barracuda back to Ohio. Setting out in cold weather we were lucky in our rides, for after a short hop with a village teen down to the interstate we were picked up by a grandfatherly man in a big car who lectured us in his twangy way on everything from the dangers of hitchhiking to the misguided views of the protest movement. He was taking us as far as he was going—Wheeling, West Virginia—not because he wanted us on the streets of the nation's capital but because he didn't want to see some nut get ahold of us and leave us dead in a ditch. Maybe we could persuade our parents to thank him if we were planning to let them know where we had spent the weekend and how we got there. Sitting in the back of his boxy sedan, we felt like little kids caught in a misdeed. And here was his address and phone number if we got stuck. Our next ride—and we practically leaped from the one car to the other—was with college kids from Youngstown State. We were elated to squeeze into the backseat, shoulder to shoulder with other young people, and hear John Lennon on the tape deck sing "Come Together." The driver wore a kind of Rough Rider's hat, had a mustache like Teddy Roosevelt's, and sported wire-rim glasses. We were at Chip's house in what seemed to be no time. After politely declining Chip's offer to crash in his parents' living room, the kids in the car disappeared. "See you on the Mall."

That night Chip and I wandered the streets of Georgetown, and it was clear already the floodgates had burst. Young people thronged every corner, and a dangerous energy—our energy in aggregate—disturbed the air. A block away some protesters with flares had assembled a bonfire, and the police had stepped in. Let there be confrontation! We, or our massed presence, and our scorn of Nixon and Agnew, and everything they stood for, would end this war. Everything they stood for! Boxy car, steak dinner, country club, polyester wardrobe, *Reader's Digest*, Sunday sermon, Lawrence Welk, Big Lie, insulated living room. The embalmed, timid, self-satisfied citizenry. The napalm-dealing, son-sacrificing, minority-oppressing, sex-detesting, so-called silent majority. Next morning Chip and I arose early, bused to DC, and massed with the human confluence toward Constitution and Pennsylvania Avenues. I was astonished that so many people, spilling in columns from every street, tens and tens of thousands, like waters rising and swelling, could make so little noise, as though the press of numbers reduced the voice to a whisper. There were contingents led by people holding signs: actors from New York, nurses from Bridgeport. A group of Vietnam veterans, a class of men of whom I had formed only the most speculative conception, marched beneath a hand-lettered banner. The solemnity reminded me of JFK's funeral procession, although that was television and this was here and now, and the present solemnities concerned something larger than a president. We—if the plural first person can represent such a multitude—were well behaved, and I remember feeling contempt, passing the White House, at the sight of rows of yellow school buses barricading the residence of the world's most powerful man. We were cold all day, and while all those bodies might in theory have raised the ambient temperature, it was only the hours of marching that made one forget how chilled one's hands and feet remained. Later, back in Bethesda, Chip and I watched TV coverage of the rowdiness at the Justice Department Building. In the morning we drove back to school.

That evening, in the weekly call home, I made a point of telling my dad where I had been. I wanted to be honest and open, consistent with my love and respect for him, but I also wished to defy. He responded with predictable disapproval, falling back on the parental reflex that would vainly seek to preserve the child from any and all experience. But beyond that he just couldn't understand that to oppose the war and march against it didn't require radicalization. You had to be strange—a college Republican in the Nixon era—not to want to go to Washington and march against this war. I didn't care to hear how he wasn't paying tuition so that I could go off with a bunch of hippies, et cetera, and rang off abruptly. I hadn't convinced him my attitudes were sane and my choices reflected ideals of fairness learned at home. I resolved to find ways of demonstrating what I deemed my emerging maturity of judgment.

My career as a hitchhiker wasn't over, however. The first week of December one of the guys on the hall, Mark, a bit of a goof but—so I thought—okay, was looking for someone to hitch with him to Vermont to visit "a lady friend" at a girls' college there. Having just broken up with my art major, I jumped at the chance. To be out on the road, rambling about, meeting people, trying to forget someone—why, half the folk songs not protesting the war were on this theme. So one cold morning we stepped downhill to the highway back of campus and waited for the first ride. Mark would prove to be an alarming companion: on the empty road between rides he paced and gulped and ranted under his breath, pulling himself together only as cars approached. Some eight hours after starting this journey, we cruised along the New York State Thruway in the rattle-trap car of a soldier who looked as though he might nod off any moment. As we passed the series of Rochester exits, I was struck by how my life had diverged (however temporarily) from the paths my parents envisioned— it seemed strange, and sad, not to be getting off the thruway to go home and sleep in my bed. I contemplated my supreme irresponsibility and felt stoutly burdened by Mark, who had subsided from his daylong agitation into a sound sleep in the back of the car and looked as though he might have to be carried. We spent that night sleeping in the lounge of a high-rise dormitory on the state university campus in Albany, having damaged a window to gain access, and then rode up to Vermont next morning. The girls were impressed with the epic nature of our trek, but the trip was more memorable as an experience of cold weather and a hitch mate's multiple personalities. On the return trip we had good fortune, two rides to the Angola rest stop, where we immediately connected with some upper-classmen from Denison. A week later Mark had a psychotic episode and disappeared from campus for good. That was it: I had logged more than a thousand miles, hadn't died in a ditch or in someone else's car crash, hadn't been obliged to institutionalize my fellow traveler, and thought it best now to retire.

Besides, things on campus had become interesting. I had a new girlfriend, a bright-eyed if moody physician's daughter from Indianapolis who had experimented with cocaine, something that lent intrigue to an otherwise typical suburban girl. In an effort to pad my own outlaw résumé I was helping a sophomore distribute periodic shipments of hash. But I had begun to notice that some kids entering those smoke-filled rooms didn't come out for days. I was trying to read Joyce and Wittgenstein, both of whom promised a sort of intoxication for which you had to keep a clear head. The dope people talked revolution but wobbled about a stuffy room like paramecia. Then there was the object lesson of the upperclassman whose drug-grungy habits had driven out his roommate. He slept on a bare mattress and rarely left his den. One evening, smoke drifted from his room: steeped in a barbital marinade he had fallen asleep with a lighted cigarette. The guys on the hall tugged the rotten, smoldering mattress out of the building and got him aired out. He thanked us for saving his life and shook our hands. Two hours later smoke again seeped from his room. He had gone back to sleep with a new cigarette on his former roommate's mattress, and so a second smoldering heap had to be dragged down the hall and thrown clear of the dorm's back door. And he was said to be a smart kid with prospects of pursuing a graduate degree at the University of Chicago.

Another casualty of the campus drug scene was a guy everyone referred to as Fetus: a prematurely balding, baby-faced senior. Amid the stratus haze of marijuana and tobacco smoke he looked like a cross between a lost child and a vegetable deprived of sunlight. I found it odd that I'd never meet him outside the circle of tokers, but when I heard his story I understood why. Despite the appearance of feckless innocence, Fetus had known something like genuine evil. Hitchhiking at night in Mexico (afoot with a wallet of traveler's checks on some Leary-inspired mushroom quest), he'd accepted a ride with an elderly man who drove, according to custom, without headlamps so as not to attract bandits. Toward dawn the man, having passed through a village, misjudged a curve and struck a bicyclist. This was bad enough, but rather than stop and render aid or at least flee the scene, the man whipped the car around and in a cloud of dust and exhaust finished the boy off. That way, no witness—unless this gringo counted as one. I never accepted the account at face value (it was one of those stories bathed in the aura of déjà vu: something you've heard before and will hear again), but I never doubted that Fetus, for whatever reason, was a wounded man. He had scored 800 on the math SAT. But he was afflicted with baldness and a very bad episode that left him with nightmares for a lifetime. His nickname added to the horror, as it was impossible, looking at him, not to think *Aborted* Fetus.

These lessons impressed kids on the floor, many of whom were intellectually ambitious. To have what is called a life of the mind seemed inherently oppositional and attractively dangerous. I would gaze at portraits of people like Karl Marx, James Joyce, and Allen Ginsberg, and think, here are men whose very minds are bombs. I pictured myself as one who gave his life to learning, who questioned everything, who upset factitious order. I aspired to be a college professor, a calling that seemed to support revolution while preserving the tie to Whitewood Lane. For the first time I adopted a schedule of compulsory study, six days a week, and invited Chip to partake. Having become something of a political theorist, he was receptive to the idea. Chip and I reinforced one another in a resolution to limit consumption of bourgeois escape products that he now pronounced "reactionary." He was getting his own house in order, assignments completed on time, books and papers stacked neatly on a shelf. He had established a set of twelve empty Coke bottles on his dresser in some complex pattern, and this seemed to help with his stress.

Chip could be cheerful and drolly talkative.

"Man," he queried, looking up from his book, "ever think about who makes all the shit we buy?"

"You mean like General Electric, General Motors, General Foods?"

"I mean the guys who work the factories and the women and children overseas who gather the raw materials."

"Well," I replied, "I know to look for the union label."

"Damn straight! But like the tires we drive on—that's what Vietnam is all about! Rubber trees! The domino theory is a joke!"

The door to our room being open, a hall resident foraging food or cigarettes might overhear such remarks and take exception to their import:

"It's only a joke till the domino falls on you! Wake up, Chip! Dominate or be dominated! It's already World War III!"

Chip, red in the face, was out of his chair. "Yeah, it's the United States of General Motors and Dow Chemical against the People! That's the war, dumb ass!"

By now three or four residents had positioned themselves between the two. Five minutes later tempers were pacified. But getting riled up seemed good for Chip. He returned to his book, convictions honed.

The big event of spring semester was a campus uprising known as the Black Demands. There couldn't have been more than thirty African Americans at the college, but they felt the humanities curriculum didn't adequately reflect black experience, which it didn't, and there were other conditions they wanted changed. Prodded by the New Left younger faculty, the overwhelmingly white student body had been itching for a harness, and this was it. Putting aside his books, Chip rushed to the forefront. For two days there were committee meetings and mass gatherings, teachers and classmates speaking through bullhorns, gradations of revolutionary posturing, all of it keenly sincere. Then, on the third, before the sleepy administrators stirred the cream in their morning coffee, a full-scale building occupation was in progress—the Student Union, not the president's office suite. A manifesto and an assortment of strawberry statements were issued, and the demands were instantly met. The administration, although caught off-guard, deftly exercised options. A parallel alternative college was instituted with black classmates as teachers—very serious and conservatively professorial in manner. I learned about Reconstruction, read essays by W. E. B. DuBois and poetry by Don L. Lee.

The semester was drawing to a close when my girlfriend was summoned home to Indiana. A high school friend—a not quite but almost boyfriend—had hanged himself, and she needed to attend the funeral. That would be on a Thursday. On Saturday the Jefferson Airplane were scheduled to play Bloomington in the football stadium. Coming out of retirement on one last lark, I hitched to Indianapolis the day after the funeral and arrived at Annie's place in time for tuna casserole. That night, a VW van stuffed with art and theater majors along with a visiting French graphics professor pulled up to the house without notice. Everyone just camped in the living room of the parents' spacious suburban home. Saturday morning Annie's mom served powdered eggs and Spam, and right after breakfast we all managed to wedge into the yellow VW. Guy (short for Guillaume) overslept and therefore boarded the van with breakfast on a paper plate, but no sooner did we hit the highway than he rolled down his window and scraped the plate's contents into the adjacent lane to see if the Spam would bounce. A half hour later we arrived in Bloomington, where we rallied en mass in the stadium. The warm-up band came on and bored us for a good hour. Then B. B. King, not at all boring, appeared with "Lucille," but his musicianship was probably lost on the crowd until the Airplane, an hour late and minus the male lead singer, detained by "the pigs" in Detroit, stumbled onstage like people who had pulled an all-nighter. Here was Grace Slick, herself, recounting their adventures in a sleepy voice and asking whether anyone there had "medication" to zap a headache. Up from the kids in front popped something—a reefer?—but she tossed it back. "I can't get off on this!" Laughter and cheers. Then came the songs, on instruments barely tuned, in voices scarcely awake: *got a revolution got to revolution!* This was shabby, and I felt like an extra in a low-budget youth film. No one after Altamont could maintain exalted views of rock concerts, free or pay. But there was no avoiding the impression that, if this crowd and that band were any measure, the Movement was dead. That night, while the van people posed on Annie's back patio in a series of erotic tableaux at the bidding of Guy, who alternately sketched and took snapshots, Annie's physician dad took her mom, Annie, and me out to the club for a lobster dinner. We were like kids rewarded for vague good behavior. Next day Annie and I drove her dad's pewter El D back to school for the last two weeks of spring term. Along I-70 in western Ohio Annie cranked the Caddy to 85.

Meanwhile, Chip had taken to wearing a black beret and shades indoors. He had become obsessed with the Black Panthers and was convinced there was a place for him, white as he was, in their organization. He wanted to write them but at what address? I told Chip they'd never accept him. You'd have to hook up in the line of fire and practically take a bullet before they'd believe you were anything but an infiltrator or a fool. I told him there were probably loads of white guys just like us who had entertained the same idea. This last suggestion seemed to wound him. He was sore at me anyway for spending all my time with Annie. Abandoning his resolve to abstain, he had been sucking pretty hard on the weed and was 90 percent sure he wouldn't return for sophomore year. He would prove correct on that score. There were many members of the freshman class sucking on the weed, including a group of three or four ultralong-hairs and about as many girls who were also into chemical drugs and free love. They had managed to rent a dumpy house in the student section of the village. One afternoon they'd gotten drunk, stoned, and naked, and playing the *White Album* backward (Charlie M. style) had conceived the idea of piling up all their paper money, some two hundred dollars, and burning it, laughing hysterically as they did so. I found this distressing. The stories of group sex didn't bother me as much as the account of the money fire. In a moment of puritan self-scrutiny I wondered: what did this say about what really matters to me?

Not that I was above getting drunk and stoned, stoned and drunk, strung out on stress and caffeine tablets, miserable to be with. In some such state I remarked to Annie: "Maybe you could give me a little space."

"Oh," she replied, "if it's space you want, I'll give you space." She brushed past me to the hall, heading for the elevator. "It's never you that's fucked up. It's always others!"

I couldn't stand for her to leave on that note. I was raised to suture wounds, those especially I had inflicted; I could hardly tolerate an open gash. Annie met up with two others in the hall, and by this point she was shouting: "He's all fucked up. Don't get anywhere near him!"

I implored her to wait. The situation had rapidly slipped from control. As the elevator door closed, I punched it with something like three months' worth of related and unrelated anguish. Even in the act a part of me couldn't believe I was so out of it; then, holding my right hand, I would have given anything to go back ten seconds in time.

Retreating to my room, I at once focused on Chip's set of empty Coke bottles, there on his dresser, meticulously arranged like soldiers at sentry. This had always annoyed me: he wasted more time lining them up just so! The display made me itch. There was nothing to do but knock them down like so many bowling pins with my fisted left hand. One of them bounced off my ankle: there was nothing to do but seize it and smash it against the steel post of our bunk! Maybe then I could hurl the neck through the dorm window, showering glass over Annie and my so-called friends. But at that point the cool rational self that had been observing this rage unfold intervened. Closing my eyes and counting to twelve I made myself stop. Then I checked out a broom from the hall closet and as my right hand swelled swept up the glass. I spent fifteen minutes restoring the bottles to what I thought were Chip's OCD specifications, and even went down to the vending machine for a single that, emptied, could replace the one I had smashed. With the lame explanation that I had caught my hand in the elevator door I went to student health next day. The nurse referred me to a town physician who X-rayed the break and put the hand in a cast. There were fingers sufficiently functional to hold a pen and write final exams. Annie and I met that afternoon to put the incident, and then our relationship, behind us.

School was nearly out by the time of the Kent State shootings. A carload of juniors and seniors had gone up to Kent and returned deeply shaken. They broke the story on campus before it became national news. It seemed hardly credible—National Guardsmen firing on unarmed college kids, girls and guys alike. On the peripheries of attention given to end-of-term projects, kids had been learning of the US invasion of Cambodia, and it had begun to seem as though no amount of protest would deflect Nixon's course. What happened at Kent State terrorized the suburban protester. It was terrible beyond conception, yet one needed to put it off to the side and get through exam week. I would process the horror back home. I watched follow-up stories on television and read about the shooting's aftermath in *Time,* just as I had processed Manson and company the year before, sprawled on the sofa in the Whitewood Lane living room, comfortably insulated, far from friends and front lines. It was 1970; the sixties were over. Nixon and his goons behaved outrageously yet with each new caper seemed only emboldened the more. After a year or two of believing that youth could change the world, I felt the paralysis. Marching accomplished nothing, nature offered only false refuge, and hedonism made for contemptible political expression. The only credible voices belonged to the vets, the most sadly estranged of all, but the Movement commonly viewed these guys as so many Lieutenant Calleys. The war went on. Other anxieties began to make headlines: the Population Boom, the Middle East Time Bomb, Nuclear Asia.

My three remaining college years were pleasant and instructive but not remarkable. My dad paid tuition and expressed satisfaction with my good grades. There were fine teachers and good friends; there were excellent girlfriends I would not go on to marry. The breakups were not deeply traumatic. Life was always in rhythmic flux, and each semester saw progress toward a degree. Nothing exceeded the bounds of normal development. I acquired a sense of vocation. The people I admired most were teachers; they taught because they had taken the time to examine the underlying pattern of things. This was an idealized but not wholly unreasonable view. I was drawn to a certain kind of professor: one who was rational, confident, a little aloof, who had thought hard to attain such beliefs as he or she could defend, who duly noted life's absurdities yet responded fiercely to the world's injustice, and who, moreover, condescended to reassure those nearly adult children, the students. I, for one, required such assurance. I needed to be told that political action must not be thought futile. Vote, my teachers implored. Do so with your whole person in everything you do. I found meaning in that advice even as, for the first time, in 1972, I cast a ballot for the losing side. Soon after, the Watergate scandal broke, and finally it seemed the political system was embarked on corrective paths. A mild faith began to displace a gathered if shallow cynicism.

Before long I'd be out on my own, the interstate highway my path. At night I'd arrive in places calculated to awe the Rochester native—the mountains east of Laramie, the high desert of northern Arizona, San Francisco by way of Golden Gate Bridge, illuminated like a great harp against the backdrop of a paper city. One measure of a place's interest was its obvious distance from anything resembling Whitewood Lane. But after a while, mountain and plain, rural setting and small college town, became the norm. I had plotted and made my escape. The big city was not my destination, but chance had favored life in settlements too small or unique to produce the American suburb. Rochester, increasingly sub-merged beneath associations of past time, would be two and sometimes three flights away.

I WAS AWAY when my father underwent hip-replacement surgery. For ten years arthritis had been establishing residence in his joints, and no sooner had he retired from Kodak than inflammation in his hip and back nar-rowed his range of motion. Golf and travel were out of the question, and strangers had to be hired to do yard work. During the day he would sit in his study and fall asleep trying to read. After supper he dozed in the liv-ing room. Eventually, he'd get up, have a bourbon highball, and an hour or so later go to bed, sleep a while, then lie awake half the night. To replace a hip joint was serious, and the procedure hadn't been around long, but he went into it with courage, confidence, an inveterate trust in science and technology. There would be the surgery itself, a four-day hospital stay, and a month or more of physical therapy. My brother and sister-in-law were minutes away if help were needed. No reason, I was told, to cancel activities and come home.

Back then joint replacement was a bloody business requiring multiple transfusions. The anesthetized body had to surrender its normally secure borders. No doubt doctors went over this part of the script with my dad. But no one guessed he'd contract hepatitis, much less lie in the post-op ward braced and trussed and out of his mind on the weird mix of toxins and medications that coursed through his bloodstream. After three days his head cleared; he recognized family members and pieced together why he was there in the first place. Six months later he was playing golf again, better than before but not great, and not without pain. My parents took a programmed tour of the Canadian Rockies. That went well, so the next year they bought into another package and finally crossed the Atlantic to Ireland, Scotland, Wales, and England. In Dublin, my dad was leaving a restaurant, missed a step, and dropped to the sidewalk. My mother's first thought was, my God, he's gone. But he picked himself up and was taken by cab to a Catholic hospital where the nuns read his vitals, patched his arm and forehead, and sent him on his way. He proceeded to Wales next morning with the rest of the group as though nothing had happened.

"You are certainly having your adventures," I said to him over lunch in the Whitewood Lane kitchen during a rare October visit.

"Like you," he replied, "I go away and come back. But I'll try to be more predictable. Let's get back to those leaves."

He moved slowly and warily, but he moved. We had high hopes for his retirement as the last five years at Kodak had been tough. The firm was under pressure—from Japanese competitors, stockholders, the EPA. Each year brought a fresh humiliation. But with his secure pension and health benefits, all Dad had to do was live.

Some three years later I was the one in Europe, awakening in the middle of the night from the immovable conviction that he had died. Pieces of dream came together: forgetting I was abroad, my mother had dialed my Midwest number. The telephone in my second-floor apartment rang and rang. I could see the black rotary before my eyes, but was unable to grasp the receiver because I was in Dublin. One read about the certainty with which people skeptical of paranormal phenomena still felt the death of a family member just as it was taking place. I waited until next day, after the plane had touched down at Logan Field, to call home. I thought about contacting my brother first but decided to ring the home number. "Hello," Dad answered placidly. Something like this happened again the following year when I was camping along the Continental Divide in Colorado. I was at my mother's deathbed: she said good-bye, and then, as at the flip of a switch, the light in her eyes went out. The next evening, back in the Midwest, I decided to call home before unpacking, and picked up the phone. There was no dial tone, only a remote female voice saying "Hello? . . . Hello? . . ." into electronic space. I had picked up the receiver in the precise interval before her call had produced a ring. It was like hearing a voice from the land of the dead. After a moment my dad got on, and I told them both about the trip to southern Utah. They seemed happy to hear about my excursions but were mostly relieved I was back safe in my shoe-box apartment in a university town. They worried about me: unlike my settled, responsible brother, I had neither wife nor steady job, and I enjoyed hiking the slick-rock deserts in blistering heat. They feared I might die on one of my treks, but only later, after I married, did I learn that they had planned for my death. For the duration of my bachelorhood they had reserved, in the crypt of Saint Paul's Church, a drawer for my ashes, should it be needed, next to the drawers reserved for their own.

On a bright July day during a weeklong visit the month before I married, the three of us drove to Watkins Glen in my parents' big green Chevrolet Caprice. Our plan was to drive south along the east side of the lake to the Glen, walk a little beyond the parking lot on the paved path, have lunch at a famous old roadhouse, and then proceed west, stopping, as time permitted, at the little village of Bradford, reached by curving blacktop roads, where my father's great-great-grandfather lay buried. Bradford center was simply a crossroads—post office, city hall, corner bar, ministore, Methodist church. Just south of the center we spotted the sign, white letters on a green ground: CEMETERY. Bradford's necropolis extended over several acres—far more people in this suburb of the dead than in the live village. I scouted the field and found our name inscribed in seven stones, faded but still legible. Here were Dennis and Mary, there was George, their teenage grandson. In the newer part were Burr and Laura, cousins surely. These folks, complete strangers who bore our name, had been rural people, descendants of the Dutch patriarch. My grandfather Merrill had left this place far behind, running off to Geneva, Rochester, Detroit, and later Boston to work on the early cars and airplanes. My dad and I conversed about these nearly forgotten people. The day trip was destined to slip, in its turn, into the recent and then distant past. We took a few snapshots, first he, then I. So I stood with my dad on this side of the grave. The present moment was already a memory.

Premonition has a way of proving true. "Your dad's not well." With this my mother opened her Thanksgiving Day phone call. He had been bothered in October by a urinary infection, but the problem had cleared up. Now he was having delusions. He would go to the base of the stairs and call my name, and my mom would have to remind him that I lived in Wyoming with wife and infant son, their grandson, that I had grown up and was teaching at a university. Next day she found him upstairs, where the boys' bedrooms were, looking for the flight to the third-floor attic. He was sure an attic had been part of the original plan. After supper that evening he had stood up, put on his hat and coat, and announced that he'd had a pleasant time but that he really needed to get back to his wife.

After forty years of marriage, her husband looked her straight in the eye and didn't know her, didn't know who he was or where he was going. She couldn't control him; he was a danger to himself. Their doctor took charge and consigned him to a nursing home. Tom, reporting from the scene, had grown increasingly skeptical of the doctor's judgment—that nursing home, of all places, was no place for our dad. But there he stayed, breathing the sour, overheated air, roommate to a man who spent his nights shrieking, while my mother and the doctor monitored his progress and thought about a next move. He had begun to exhibit moments of lucidity. He knew that he had a real home and this bedlam wasn't it. By the time I arrived with wife and child for Christmas, he was all but himself—except for the grief of having been removed from his home. He couldn't fathom why he had awakened to find himself in hell.

So the first day back I drove with my brother through the snow and slush of a December morning to collect Dad from the home. He seemed clear-headed if emotional, aggrieved at having been enveloped in this nightmare but elated to leave it. Frail as he was he evinced his wonted self-command. By now the doctor had figured it out: the drugs my father had been taking for the infection induce in some patients a delusional withdrawal stage. He was past that stage and could resume normal life. I tried not to ponder the curious fate of reaching your middle seventies only to lose your sense of where you are and who is who—to be turned out of your home by a conviction proceeding from deep within that you aren't in the right place. I suspended those thoughts and joined with the others in the genuine if old-time-movie celebration that my dad, whom we'd thought lost, had found himself and returned in familiar form—had come home, just in time for Christmas.

He got to keep his mind, and for that we would be grateful. But in the year ahead he would gradually lose his capacity to breathe. The condition was identified as pulmonary fibrosis, although my father-in-law, an internist on the West Coast, explained that there were various diseases that produced that condition, including arthritis, and had there been a diagnosis? Not that I could gather from anything anyone was willing to discuss. Years would pass before Tom and I began to suspect his half-century exposure to asbestos at Kodak Park as the cause of this slow asphyxiation.

As for my dad, the voice at the other end of the weekly call was good for only a minute of panting conversation before my mom would get on, and then she would not want to talk about the details of his health. During the summer visit I would see firsthand how it exhausted him to leave his chair and come to a meal—how laborious the details of daily living were for someone progressively starved of oxygen. By Christmas he went from room to room trailing a wheeled tank. Except to see one or another specialist he didn't go out. The winter was a hard one with near falls and a bout of shingles. In the evening of good days he and my mom sat in the living room playing gin, tank at his side.

It is what they did in the evening. It is what my mom and I do in the evenings when I visit her in the Fairport condominium with all the furniture from Whitewood Lane, including the parlor grand. So deep are our habitual reflexes, so apt are we to merge with one another and forget the passage of time, that she has on more than one occasion startled me and herself by calling me by my father's name.

He reached his seventy-eighth birthday on February 12, two days after his grandson's second birthday. He had been in the hospital and now was home, but things remained tentative.

The phone call I had been expecting came in March.

Tom spoke straight to the point: "He's back in the hospital and probably won't last the week. Get home, fast."

Good fortune provided a clear road from Laramie to Denver and clear flying through Chicago to Rochester. By Monday morning his out-of-town family was at his side, and he managed to clasp the hand of his two-year-old grandson—the small child hand that, dislocated from anything it had known, was grasping at anything and everything, including the IV tubing. They were on two different planets, yet I was struck at that moment by how alike they were in the face. Whereas my brother and I resemble my mother, my son inherits my father's nose, mouth, and jaw. Both required care. Tuesday, as I arrived in the morning, Dad's physician drew me aside to tell me my father was dying. To me it was so obvious that my first response was annoyance, but then it occurred to me that some people resist the recognition as long as they can. He explained to me that his body would fail for want of oxygen despite the mask and the O^2 supply. He would die of a heart attack. When I stepped into the room I found him submerged in the steady current of morphine but nevertheless agitated. As he fought for breath he constantly tried to remove the mask, as though that were the problem, and when tired of futilely working the mask his left hand pulled at the IV anchored in the back of his right. I held his hand still; I had to keep it from grasping at things. At one point in my eight-hour vigil, after repeatedly having to keep the left hand from the tube, I called him by my son's name. The parent-child relationship was in flux.

I arrived Wednesday morning at eight to find country-and-western music blaring from the radio in his room. I summoned a nurse and asked her to keep the music off unless my father requested it be on. After silencing the radio, she, a woman in her early twenties, had to deal with his catheter, and so semiconscious was he that I had to feel on his behalf the indignity that he, Harold, the most private man in the world, exemplar of self-command, should have felt. My mother came in a little later. He was more subdued today; he could barely speak, but asked for his grandson, and asked to go home. We stayed there all day, my mom leaving about six, and I lingered until seven or so, when Tom and Barbara arrived. In the lengthening shadows of late afternoon I held his hand and watched his eyes open and close. He had lost so much weight that I could see and admire the beautiful symmetry of the bones in his face. Toward nightfall his eyes turned but remained open; he continued to breathe but did not respond when I spoke. He had, I think, entered a coma. My brother and sister-in-law arrived. "Good-bye, Dad," I said, and left.

The phone rang at six next morning. When the phone rings at that hour under those circumstances, the message can only be one thing. My mom and I got up and within an hour left for the hospital. When we arrived in his room I was struck by how quiet it was with the compressor off. My mother said, "Good morning, dear," as though forgetting what she had been told. We left his room and went down the hall, and I called my brother, who was just about to depart for the hospital. When he arrived we gathered in my dad's room. It was the last time our family of four would be together, and already we were three. The nurse came in and drew the drape around my father's bed.

I CROSSED A THRESHOLD as I left the hospital, the same hospital on the city's south side where I'd entered the world thirty-four years earlier. I had seen my father die piecemeal over the course of ten or more years; now he was deceased, but finality doesn't register all at once. How normal it would seem just to go home and find him sitting in his study, wondering where we had been. Institutional experiences are parenthetical, a break from the daily narrative, never quite real, and this trip, dominated by the hospital room, felt like one giant parenthesis. From the many occasions I had flown in and out of Rochester, I was used to seeing the medical complex off to the side as the plane followed the Elmwood Avenue corridor to and from the airport. I was eager to see the week elapse and to view the hospital and its maze of streets from the angular vantage of the departing flight, the aircraft climbing over the suburbs and in no time at all cruising above farmland and open water. We'd connect in Chicago with the flight to Denver and sometime that evening, in the afterglow of mountain sunset, proceed across the magnificent plain to our two-bedroom house on a quiet street in Laramie, Wyoming. There, the various duties we had put aside awaited us. For a while the world would feel palpably diminished, and then it would seem just itself.

12

Home and Away

June 1995. We left home, in Oklahoma, and flew to Rochester for a visit. Like many Americans I had settled in a region far removed from my place of birth. Reunion with family meant two days of travel, coming and going. Not quite routine, this sojourn had a fixed place on our summer calendar. But that year normal events transpired with a certain estrangement.

We drove seventy miles south on I-35 across rolling plains that flatten as you approach Oklahoma City. The lush green of vernal prairie yellows under assault of south wind and sun. Over these lanes of interstate highway a nondescript man ferried a load of ammonium nitrate and gasoline. That was in April, and the shell of the Alfred P. Murrah building testified to the effect. Yet life resumed and roads remained open, and nothing in the blank, permissive pavement bespoke a malevolent purpose. We passed the amusement park at the city's north end, turned west where the interstate divides, then exited onto a boulevard lined with pawnshops and dead gas stations. Our plan was to drop our aging Volvo at the downtown dealership for service and storage and catch the van to the airport. All went forward according to plan. Then two blocks from the lot I happened to look up: *there* was the lacerated YMCA, curtains billowing from blown-out casements, and I knew we were at Fifth and Robinson, the bomb site. Our driver, a woman in her thirties with a lot of frosted hair, began her narration: how she'd entered the freeway a block from the federal building when the earth rocked and jolted her vehicle onto the shoulder. The world, she thought, had come to an end—a silence broken by sirens and gasps. All the way to the airport, across miles of inner-city expanse, stockyards and blighted streets and drifters under the railroad overpass, she

Broad Street Bridge. Courtesy Communications Bureau, City of Rochester.

talked about the bombing and how it had changed the city. She had trouble believing it wasn't foreigners but "just a guy" who did this.

We checked our bags and proceeded to the gate. Among business travelers and couples with children sat passengers in cowboy boots, and the overheard speech was twangy. The plane ambled out on the runway, idled a moment amid flat terrain—the horizontal vacancies of harvested wheat fields—then hurtled full throttle skyward. At Chicago we deplaned and walked the long corridor to the gate for the Rochester flight. Here western attire would seem outlandish. Most of the passengers were dark-suited men who reminded me of my father's colleagues. Their talk was monotone and weary. We had crossed a threshold. I felt almost there.

Almost home, where I hadn't lived for thirty years. Neither sickness nor death motivated this visit. It was simply time. The trip home, the reunion with family, carries with it an understanding: life is tentative; next times are not guaranteed. Such visits begin in celebration and end in a sorrow masked by hollow assurance: see you again before long, talk to you tonight. In another ten years I'd be the parent with an empty house occasionally enlivened by a son's return. At least the promise that concluded the last visit—we'll do this again *next* year—would now be fulfilled. The plane descended over western New York farmland, soil and greenery so much darker than that of Oklahoma. Then suburbs, expressways, innumerable streets of two-and-a-half-story houses with narrow side yards. We're on the ground and taxiing to the terminal; welcome to Rochester, local time is 5:30 p.m.

In the rental car we drive south and east on the expressway's outer loop. For my wife and sons the landscape is characterless: ranch houses clustered in the usual tracts, franchise restaurants flanking the arterials, low-rise office buildings clad in smoked glass. For me, however, there's something more: I recall the fields and wooded hills, sagging barns and dilapidated farmhouses that preceded the subdivisions and great white malls. The once-new construction shows signs of age. To observe layers of past time: is this not a sign of incipient seniority? My wife similarly sees a lost world when we visit California: the pastures and plum orchards of Santa Clara County that made way for freeways and industrial parks soon after her family moved up from Santa Barbara. Yet to me the West Coast remains ever new, whereas places in and about the Great Lakes evoke a personal and historical past. Native if nonresident, I read in the undulating landform the glacial geology of western New York State. I know the canal's serpentine path and can visualize the parade of beggars and opportunists spilling into the region two centuries ago. The road winds north; we enter a stretch where concrete curtains divide the expressway from residential backyards. When we come in view of a particular overpass I know we're exactly two-thirds of a mile west of Whitewood Lane. Three minutes later, now headed east, we slip within hailing distance of the house on Walden Road. We continue south for another three miles to Fairport village, where my mother lives in a condominium one block from the canal, two miles away from my brother and sister-in-law and their children.

Thus, the overflights and expressway traffic I once associated with leaving Rochester have brought me back. I entertain illusions that I've never left. Decades of adult life spent elsewhere never happened. My vowels flatten in sympathy with the local speech.

IN TWENTY MINUTES we are settled as guests: kids playing electronic games, wives grouped with my mother in the kitchen. My niece and nephew have begun to look teenaged. My mother and sister-in-law each wear new glasses. I accompany Tom as he barbecues chicken in the large semiwooded backyard. His place reminds me a little of Whitewood Lane but perhaps a bit more of Walden Road, given the size of his trees. Following the path of our grandfather Culp he has led a career in local advertising, and life on the whole has been good. We enter a rapport of affection and intimacy, an old emotional integument, exchanging information about kids and jobs. I'm in the presence of my oldest and most trusted friend. Rather delicately, he alludes to the bombing. Other years it might be the tornado; this year it's the bombing. They all have the image freeze-framed on their mental TV screens: the broken husk that was the Murrah building, U-shaped blast zone with pancaked floors, maimed children and blood-capped adults, black smoke rising into the pristine sky of an April morning. Seventy miles north, in Stillwater, I was no more aware of what had happened in Oklahoma City than were people twelve hundred miles away in Rochester. It wasn't until I overheard the special report on the office radio and came home to see what CNN broadcast from our own backyard that I discovered what already half the world was coming to know. The bombing took place on a Wednesday. I tell my brother about how, that Friday, while driving along a rural road at the edge of town, I looked up to see helicopter after helicopter streaming to the north. Soon afterward, news broke that in a town nearby a man jailed two days earlier on a weapons charge had been identified as a suspect. The state of Oklahoma is a small town. Having lived there nine years as people with normal middle-class connections, we know a blast victim, a fireman who picked through the rubble, and a paralegal secretary employed by the firm defending the principal accused. Degrees of separation hardly exist. If you yourself don't personally know someone killed in that blast, you surely know people who do.

As family men with an obvious stake in public safety, my brother and I speak the banalities good folk burble in the wake of such unthinkable events. The guys who did this were out of their minds, grudge-bearing dorks who chose to target an average, defenseless humanity. They fit the profile of losers, small men with thick portfolios of failure and spite. Our comments are not far off the mark. Yet we also agree that their crime was unthinkable—truly so—only in the sense that no one could have predicted the time, place, and means. And maybe in the sense that nobody wants to think through the details of what it's like to be caught in an edifice collapsing in flame. But as a discrete probability the event was thinkable and from a certain perspective—our perspective as middle-aged men: husbands, fathers, amateur actuaries—all but ordained. You cannot exist forty-plus years and fail to notice patterns. The world abounds with individuals looking to annihilate pieces of everyday life—people for whom the world is an artifice in need of fire and death. Their beliefs may differ, but all such agree that violence speaks a compelling language. In that regard they are not so very different from legally constituted states whose artifice exists to protect good citizens like ourselves. But for lives destroyed as a result of its exercise, violence is violence, isn't it? Bombs and assassinations, an Elysium of flame, hostages in buses and airplanes more or less doomed: in 1995 it was as convenient as ever to presume that such emanated from without. The sanctity of our middle-class homes cohered around the televised image.

New trauma stirs old trauma; forgotten episodes reel into focus. People our age are apt to recall ephemeral details of past routines by a public tragedy's lurid light: through time I see my leaky scrawl on the social studies quiz I had just completed when informed that President Kennedy had been shot. Strangely private and public events, grim interruptions of scheduled programming, they play out on TV and in our dreams and preoccupy one's waking abstraction. They conform to a sequence, and as men at midlife my brother and I could discern it, theme and variation. First come words, like *bomb* or *has been shot*, followed by a wave of contradictory accounts culminating in the industrial extended coverage. As facts become "known," the damage is always worse than first thought—worse generally by far. The sequel proceeds like a chemical reaction: spasms of incredulity, wakeful sleep, sadness alternately dull and acute. A maudlin psychosis of communal sorrow. A pledge that we shall never forget. Conspiracies are proposed and evidence comes to light. Witnesses appear or a roll of film is found to have captured a detail, but years pass and no one's convinced that anyone knows the whole truth. There is in fact no "whole truth," none we can ever know.

So what was distinctive about this event? It had something to do with the homegrown, homemade quality of it all: the bomb fashioned of materials at hand in any farm community, set off by citizens who could pass invisibly through any middle-class suburb. The size of the bomb was distinctive: conceived on a scale out of proportion to the usual measure of white discontent—hard-cider rage toiling away at a basement workbench until one fine day the house explodes, leaving the neighborhood more or less intact. This was a genuinely visionary undertaking. One thing is certain: the suburb, not the training camp in Arkansas or Idaho, still less South Asia, was the place where people resembling ourselves dreamed this bomb into life. Its detonation vented Caucasian fantasies rioting in darkness all over the country. That, along with the spectacular devastation, made the event stand out.

We talk about the bomber: product of the nearby Buffalo suburbs. His sister, father, and parish priest talk to the media in our flat-voweled accent. Surely we know him: didn't we watch that boy grow up? An average, decent, unremarkable kid, with nothing much to say for himself: now mowing the neighbor's lawn, now bagging your groceries, not a psychopath. He went to war and came back and then drifted. He observed his government's heavy-handed ways with citizens challenging its monopoly of righteous violence. Not content to fume at his television, he stood vigil at the standoff in Waco. He and his band sought something to assail and happened upon the Murrah building. He spent time reconnoitering the site, so he had to know about the child-care center. Our average kid had become a monster without, on the surface, ceasing to be an average kid. Good people of Oklahoma City, at a loss to explain what has happened, accept the vapidities of the television anchor, consent to become victims of a "terror in the heartland," residents of a city that has "lost its innocence." What do they know about our neighbor Tim? As for innocence: no city could have been less innocent of violence inflicted on women and children than this midsize urban crossroad nestled in Bible Belt America. In the week leading up to the bombing, local media had fixated on a man who had thrown gasoline and a lighted match on his former girlfriend and her daughter as they walked down a city sidewalk. That item had been preceded by the more conventional story of a suburban husband shooting his family and then himself.

Atrocity, for anyone born in the fifties, hardly begins with this bombing. Menace environed the storybook prospects of earliest life. With the providence of quiet streets and ready-made places for us to inhabit came knowledge that the world can alter radically without advance notice. The Kodak Moment evinces the period's deepest anxieties. Sometimes consciously, most often not, we lived in reference to the eradicating firestorm of the nuclear blast. Surmise of something structurally amiss became a perpetual condition. Day after day the sun rose on our east-facing kitchen, the ordinary activity of Whitewood Lane replicating the activity of any other morning, the newspaper full of distant bad news. Even in our teens we noticed the contrast. This ordinary, placid, unchanging scene for which our parents had worked and saved: what right did it have to exist in the face of violence, want, and upheaval? What manner of hypocrisy did it represent? What list of privileges *here* necessitated want and violence *there*? In the lives of mystics or political revolutionaries, such moments inaugurate abrupt shifts and fatally renegade careers, and for my brother and me they were more, I think, than isolated moments of doubt. But as points of departure such moments wouldn't figure on the map: my brother and I, in keeping with the trends of our oppositional generation, became family men with the parental obligation to seek safe harbor in middle-class homes. The vulnerable, idealized bodies of our children compelled assent to this program. Or at some level, true to our origins, we felt thus compelled. Seeing no real alternative, preferring the familiar, we accepted this model of comparative serenity. Not that we ever lost sight of the fact that safety is nine-parts illusion. But basic middle-class notions of need contained the impulse to oppose—and stilled the urge to escape. Or they did with us. We with our mortgages and school-age children, we in our cars and seasonal clothes, were inextricably part of this world.

For Timothy McVeigh, product of a later, nostalgic, conservative generation, conditions were equally amiss. But for him the problem concerned the loss of home values, ingratitude toward veterans, persecution of whites wishing to secede, big government negating the patriotic small-town republic. For those formed in the 1960s, the young man with the fifties hair seemed profoundly old-fashioned. With slight adjustments he could have coached Little League, served on town council, sold insurance—or so it might seem. Like most extremists he was moved by ideals and an inflexible idol of justice. He saw with pernicious certainty. He lusted after martyrdom. He made a big statement, trite as the day is long. But no cliché, his or ours, will ever explain who he was or what he did.

For twenty minutes in a summer backyard my brother and I discuss such things.

The meat is grilled. We close the conversation with reference to what we know, have always known, as siblings: our first home and mortal parents and what we have come in our own middle age to understand of their lives. On balance they managed admirably. Theirs was not an ideal time to start a family. As they lived in the world their children were destined to slog through the world's trouble. Our parents' marriage remained intact. There was meaning in the choice they made when they chose each other. To parent, for them, involved the production of respectable citizens who by trial and error learn to govern and transcend impulse. In the qualified ways of human success they made good on those goals. Prudent and methodical as they fancied themselves, Depression-era sober as they would always remain, utopian expectation guided their path. Perhaps it was inevitable their sons should marry and raise children of their own.

What else in the course of a five-day stay will we talk about? Our mother, our families. The new cars each of us covets. The economy, taxes. The wounded—perhaps dying—god that is Eastman Kodak. Rochester and its problems. Fathers at forty speak of such things. We've arrived at midlife in spite of our generation's repudiation of age. We're on course to be old and gray. But younger generations seem infinitely older, don't they? More staid, conservative, than we can imagine ourselves becoming. Our status as fathers, home owners, employees with pension plans, men concerned with an aging mother notwithstanding.

THERE WAS NOTHING unprecedented about the bombing, yet it shook the foundations. A Stillwater neighbor thought that he felt a shock wave pass through his woodworking shop, and several parents at a Little League game agreed that a tremor stole through town at 9:03, the time of the blast, followed seconds later by a puff of wind. I didn't find such stories credible. Still, there were ways in which the destruction of an entire city block and the deaths of 168 people (very ordinary people: men, women, children, native, black, white) terrorized those who resided just up the interstate. It made one look upon everyday life as a set of arrangements holding together in spite of powers large and small that willed their demise. Flying to Rochester two months later, I thought about all the fragile adjustments that kept the plane in the air. I looked upon the Rochester family as though I had never before traversed such distance coming home. I was home and not home.

However unlikely, what happened in Oklahoma City could take place in anyone's stagnant downtown. In youth I habitually, indeed compulsively, fantasized about annihilation sudden and complete. For years it hadn't occurred to me to look at my home and the nexus of familiar places and imagine their abrupt negation. Yet in 1995—for a little while at least— I resumed that questionable practice. I recalled how, as a child, I visualized Rochester and environs as a Soviet target. How I pondered the rain of ICBMs: one to take out Kodak Park, others to atomize thruway and rail line, places like Whitewood Lane caught in the middle. Perhaps everyone pondered accordingly, if in secret. Morbid expectation attached to TV screens: before the sirens, before the blast, we'd learn of our fate while watching TV. In the snowy depths behind *Dobie Gillis,* onset of war lurked as a news flash heralded by the frame *Special Bulletin.* Walter Cronkite would come on to say, "We interrupt this program," then proceed to announce our impending doom. On *Meet the Press* irritable men spoke of the inevitable nuclear exchange, as if to say it's coming, so don't let's blink. They spoke of plans for rebuilding a world rid of the USSR. The long-term gain would be worth the sacrifice of major cities and several million citizens. How did we live with that kind of talk? People my age had to resist or face paralysis, and the animosity one felt for the elders, less as individuals than in the abstract, pertained to their know-it-all prognostications. Naturally, we abhorred the thought of annihilation. It colored and qualified every other thought. To despise these old, cankered, demonic men mitigated anxiety. But no such recourse offered here. The Murrah blast did not preexist as a nightmare to which you became inured. It came out of nowhere, everywhere, the endless hinterlands, our fellow citizens' deep malaise. No ready category yet existed for that.

1995: The Cold War was over. The cloud overhanging the streets of my childhood, the specter darkening the clear blue sky, was gone. No more Berlin Wall, no more Soviet Union. Iron and Bamboo Curtains ceased to exist. Only six years had passed since this change had come about. Such fixtures had structured the world, and without them everyone needed to find a new order, but it was hard to shake the past. Pastors and politicians were eager to name a next big enemy, and new pompous know-it-alls scanned the horizon for threats. During our visit I thought back to the old Missile Crisis days. What had become of the Whitewood Lane fallout shelter? I imagined rows of freeze-dried foods, canisters of sealed water, a stack of *Reader's Digests* and *Highlights for Children*, all under layers of antiseptic dust, still awaiting refugee families—a cellar stocked with a time capsule's inventory. But if the Cold War were history, Auschwitz remained a point of reference as the Balkan wars and Ugandan genocide reprised civilian massacre, images of slaughtered Bosnians and Tutsis flooding the cable news. New urban warfare broke out everywhere; bombed-out Murrah buildings reappeared globally. All this seemed intensely present but hygienically remote. For professional people like myself, product of Depression Era parents, schooled to spend little and save much, life was getting unexpectedly good: well-being measured by purchasing power, the stock market's rising tide. Our assets sufficiently ample, we might think seriously about buying a new car. And we could go ahead with improvements to the house.

In Oklahoma, from May to October, unless you farm or work construction, life unfolds beneath an air-conditioned dome. In Fairport we sleep with the windows open, and the humid heat wraps the body like a blanket you can't throw off. For me this makes for light sleep. The children stay with their cousins while my wife and I overnight at my mother's. A short walk from her condominium, across the canal, the Conrail corridor intersects Main Street. In the small-town quiet of a June night, train whistles pierce one's slumber, and long successions of container cars jostle the somnolent village. Such dreams as I have in this room are vivid and retrospective. Often they involve my father. I meet him in the kitchen on Whitewood Lane or the side yard on Walden Road. It is five in the morning; he wears a flannel shirt and can't stay long. The whistle shrieks. In the time remaining he has little to say. His face exhibits the perplexity of one who had thought he'd fulfilled the checklist of a life's responsibilities. But now he worries about acts of omission he cannot name. The state of the world has not improved. He and the men just like him, all those hardworking, scrupulous, citizenly fathers, back from the war or the militarized home front—in what precise way had they failed? Why had the world rejected their wisdom? Why did it sneer at their zealously preserved virtue?

Or I myself am on the train, any train, destination New York, London, Paris, Amsterdam, Berlin. I peruse the graffiti along the rail corridor. For a moment it seems I can almost make sense of the endless spray-paint cuneiform screed exploding in color mile after mile, as though explanation of the world's anonymous anguish resided therein.

WHAT I COULD NOT DISCERN, that summer and afterward: was this set of responsibilities I had assumed, this cultivation of conventional virtues, this reaping of predictable material rewards—was this an evasion of the true responsibility? Had there been a call to leave father and mother, wife and child, to serve the interest of some great change, a call I chose not to hear? Or heard and wisely ignored . . . ?

AS LEISURED VISITORS in a working family's house, we have to find things to do. Two museums and a planetarium occupy two afternoons. Bookstores, libraries, and suburban mall shopping expend a third. Niagara Falls isn't far, and Seneca Lake makes a nice outing on a warm day. The Adirondack Park beckons but that entails distance. To get to the museums we can take the expressway north to downtown or follow Fairport Road until it becomes East Avenue, seven miles from village to city. That will take longer, but the view from a slower road permits survey of local detail. The suburbs are old and the houses lining the boulevard pretentious: very large and fluid neocolonial residences of wood and brick, an art-deco palace, then the stately Queen Anne and Greek Revival mansions inside the city limits, all culminating in the columned spectacle known as the George Eastman House. Here, the founder of Eastman Kodak lived with his mother and huge pipe organ. Somewhere amid all that ostentation, an old man suffering from spinal stenosis, he ended his life with a pistol shot. The interior revels in dreamlike space, and its photographic galleries make it a stop on the museum trail. But in 1995 we continued north toward downtown until we came to the city museum and planetarium. Exhibits here are permanent. The third floor is devoted to local history. The displays—dioramas of old Rochester, scenes from an early dry-goods store and dentist's office, the interiors of a Seneca wigwam—hadn't changed since I was a boy.

That day the planetarium show didn't concern planets. Instead, it featured stunt bicyclists on parabolic ramps for forty minutes on a concave screen, narrated by an enthused nineteen-year-old, the kid next door, himself a contestant. This is his life story, shaped and disciplined in quest of the ultimate rush, endless hours of practice, injury, and rehab. His helmet has been fitted with a camera so that viewers can sense the speed and vertigo and then the triumph of besting the competition. The young man, situating himself among contrary forces, had taught himself to fall and get back up. At the show's conclusion we feel a little airsick.

We need light, oxygen, and exercise, and as a native I know just where to go. In five minutes by neighborhood streets we ascend Cobb's Hill, a reservoir and park just inside the southeast city limit. Attaining the summit the eye commands Rochester and environs, lake to the north, moraine hills south, an old-time postcard panorama. We note the major thoroughfares, the patchwork of industrial and residential districts, and old boxy neighborhoods, street after street of two-and-a-half-story wood-frame houses, variants of the American "four square." Far off we make out the redbrick complex of Kodak Park, while much closer stands the multiwing hospital where I was born and my father died. In the sixties and seventies Rochester developed a skyline on a par with those of other midsize cities: three genuine but undistinguished skyscrapers amid a cluster of merely tall buildings. Two structures put up in the thirties provide the signature profiles: Kodak Office, which has the roofline of a Renaissance *Stadthaus*, and the Times Square Building, the top of which is crowned by a pair of bronze folded wings. Coming home as a young man from New York City or Chicago, I'd scorn this skyline's lack of aerial density. But my provincial city, as I thought of it then, was and is an intensely urban place, historically layered and geographically extensive. Indifferent to the myopic, mundane, frantic, and sometimes violent lives of its residents, the skyline rises from midtown Rochester with a serenity best appreciated from the large oval pool that crowns Cobb's Hill, where couples, old people, and families seek refuge and office workers quietly lunch. Returning home in my student days, I ran laps on the path around the reservoir at different hours and in all kinds of weather. I liked it best under a layer of snow.

Downtown had changed, however, and just in the past five years. The old department and clothing stores have been shuttered: no more Sibley's, Foreman's, McFarlin's, the very names of which invoke whole chapters of immigration and entrepreneurial history. And Midtown Plaza had become a mausoleum. To see the dentist, against her family's wishes, my mother still insisted on driving downtown, summer and winter: a woman in her eighties parking a car amid snowdrifts, hiking across icy pavements to the Temple Building's mostly deserted lobby. Drive-by shootings have become so routine they often don't make the paper, my sister-in-law explained, and she would know from her life as an inner-city school administrator. She makes home visitations in the most distressed neighborhoods and intervenes on behalf of their child inhabitants. Venturing down some of those streets you could get killed quite by accident, and some combatants might offer apologies. Just south and east of downtown we saw clubs catering to young professionals committed to a season of urban living. But much of the city core was dead or dormant. The restaurants—those an out-of-town visitor sees at a glance—were fast food. No more Manhattan and Eddie's Chop House. We lunched in the museum café and then returned to Fairport via the expressway.

My brother had tickets to a Red Wings game. That would take care of another afternoon and allow my sons to see Silver Stadium, one of the grand old Minor League baseball parks, before the Red Wings move to a multipurpose facility named for a local IT firm, and the old venue, named for a man, one Morrie Silver, local baseball enthusiast and patron, met the wrecking ball. On Norton Street Silver Stadium stands just north of the

Seventh Ward. We parked on Remington Street, from which, my brother assured me, we could hear gunfire after dark and maybe before. I had splendid childhood memories of this park: warm nights under the canopy of stadium lights, full moon rising over left field, innings with frequent hits and infield plays, the gregarious smell of hot dogs and draft beer.

Saturday morning we arose early and drove up to the public market, east of downtown by the Conrail mainline. We parked on another residential side street showing signs of decay: the half-block stretch of vacant dwellings—plywood panel at window and door—broken sidewalk, and uncut grass. A century ago this neighborhood was Italian working class, across the tracks even then. The market itself is situated on a rise and like all such markets presents the opportunity of buying direct from the producer, although remainder brokers occupy much of the space. There are long aisles of seafood and meat on ice, displays of local produce and baked goods, a table of spices and new-age soaps, racks of ball caps sporting team logos, geezer slogans, bathroom humor. There is a clutch of vendors serving fried ethnic foods filling the air with hot, fragrant odors. On a Saturday morning there are droves of shoppers ambling about in family groups. Here were all the people I'd go downtown in my youth to see: Italians, Poles, Ukrainians, Puerto Ricans, joined now by folks from East and South Asia. Going to the central market seems like an Old World ritual, an alternative to shopping the mall emporia where cameras monitor your every move and odors are strictly policed.

On April 19, after the truck bomb took out the federal building in Oklahoma City, measures were taken to secure the perimeter of the federal building in downtown Rochester. Federal buildings all over the country hardened their borders. This domestic embassy instantiates everything from the Welfare State to illegal wiretaps of social activists, and many are architecturally consistent with a 1960s Brutalist aesthetic. Rochester's federal building dates from the Nixon era. In 1995, it was mostly right-wing people whose rancor focused on federal buildings. Very angry white people dwell in the city's far suburbs; they write letters to the *Democrat and Chronicle* complaining about taxes, food stamps, and the influx of foreigners. They complain of a federal government run by liberals dispensing coin to people who work no job, but rather devote themselves to propagating the species. None of the letter writers advocates the bombing of federal buildings; few perhaps have much stomach for physical violence of any sort. But they rant like stuck records against big government, social programs, legal protection of what they consider a freakish humanity, and they generally bemoan the erosion of middle-class virtue. They want to go back to the way things were. Federal buildings are magnets to the left behind, indigent, lost, the gathering point for veterans of unpopular wars, the contact zone between mammoth bureaucracy and raw human need. The nation, through such offices, struggles to recall and make good its ideals as well as to rationalize its betrayals. In my adolescent wanderings I passed the old federal building many times and never without noting its little congregations of impoverished people.

So there was a home feeling, strangely alienated, to the city and environs as I moved about them in 1995. It was like beholding images on a screen. At any turn the sight of something—street corner, intersection, river view, bridge—stirred memory, or rather stimulated the mind's endless desire to recall an image no longer there. For no clear reason there are moments in which you find yourself observing the world as though you were leaving it. My last look at Rochester, if such were the case, locked it in sad impression. The problems and failures seemed chronic, with little in view but further decline. Portions of Kodak Park itself, source of our family's wealth and pride, faced the prospect of wrecking ball or—more likely—the festive ignominy of televised implosion. The suburbs stood aloof as ever. The city proper had grown older, poorer; a shadow city ringed the downtown and extended to the industrial perimeters, with here and there a pocket of restoration, a determined stand for community values against the crack house. To what degree is this place of my making? What gives me leave to move on? I could stay here, I thought, or come back after having completed a life. I could sojourn in this city as a retired person whose every other foothold has collapsed. I could purchase a grand nineteenth-century house in a gentrifying city neighborhood or settle in Fairport and begin the day with a walk along the canal. I could grow old and see my memory of leading a life elsewhere fade, and I could contemplate dying in the blank page of a Rochester winter—departing in a scene identical to that of my arrival in December 1951.

MY SONS LIKED BEING THERE. It took us out of the heat of summertime Oklahoma, and the cousins absorbed them into their activities. For them the trip culminated in an afternoon spent at Sea Breeze Park, where I was rarely taken as a child, partly because it was a long drive from our southeast suburb up to the lake, partly because my father disliked crowds. But the crowd at the amusement park was the chief distraction for those who waited while the cousins rode the roller coaster or subjected themselves to other engines of vertiginous motion. I liked hearing neighborhood variations of the local speech and contemplating tattoos adorning the shoulders of thirty-something moms. While the children stood in line or whirled about, my sister-in-law updated me on the condition of family members. The old folks continued to age, naturally, while the middle-aged enjoyed their time of apparent calm. Meanwhile, I took all possible solace in the mildness of the day. Lake Ontario sat to the north, deep blue in noontide sun. I recalled the excitement of seeing the lake come into view toward the end of the long drive to my aunt Jane's house on Rock Beach Road. After passing through the city's outskirts and the shade of a heavily wooded park, there, across a highway and a railroad right-of-way, lay the lake, free blue space that merged with sky on the northern horizon. One's childhood soul instinctively hurled itself into such space. At the roller coaster's apex, perhaps the souls of my children dwelt for a time in that element.

"PLEASE, NO PICTURES . . ." My mother, youthful and photogenic well into middle age, figures now as the dowager in family photos, a penalty of living so long. But we are ruthless, sacrificing her old woman's vanity to the three-generation portrait that will serve as memento of this visit. A month after we return to Oklahoma, an envelope will arrive with a half-dozen snapshots, compendium of the recent past. So many occasions and photographs: one learns to be grateful to those who have jotted dates and names on the back. What thought do we give, as the shutter clicks, to the life and use of snapshots, what care as to who will inherit, study, preserve, or throw them away? Toward the end of the visit I leaf through an old photo scrapbook my mother keeps on her window seat and peer at relatives two and three generations removed—grouped for graduations and weddings, picnicking in heavy clothes. Here is a picture of my mother at seven, a pretty child still in her pajamas, and there she is at twenty on my grandfather's sloop. There is my father in the role of suitor, a young man with a thick head of hair, bouquet in hand, the honorable intention incarnate. I select three duplicate copies to take home: one of my dad, two of my mom, chosen on the basis of facial expressions I think I see in my sons. The copies will supplement our own photo album, haphazardly maintained and occasionally viewed. I think of all those family photos, fated to mean less and less as the identity of each face contends with the tide of anonymity, until anyone's old snapshots merge with those of everyone else, lost in a move, a fire, or a war. In the aftermath of historic Oklahoma tornadoes, photographs from leveled houses have been known to land two and even three counties away. They weigh very little and, given the chance, float above the clouds.

NEARLY EVERY YEAR I drive over to the Walden Road and Whitewood Lane neighborhoods. When I get to the deeply shaded streets that lead to Walden and Greenway Roads, it is as though I slip through a seam and enter a place that exists out of time, or so it feels for a moment or two, but after noting long-familiar sights, the profile of houses or a hydrant positioned at the junction of two streets, I become aware of new things—blue paint on a house I remembered as yellow, large plastic toys in a driveway, a satellite dish on a porch roof. When I turn into Walden Road I slow to a crawl, conscious that were I to see an intruder thus inspecting my own neighborhood I'd be suspicious. Such a person could only be an outsider, corporate or government agent in mortal enmity with my own interests. Without relation to the life of this neighborhood, I am the outsider. I bring nothing to these streets but rapidly receding private memory: here a corner I turned as a kindergartner headed home at midday, there the window of a bedroom that was once my own. But I have no claim on the present moment, and the young man mowing his lawn has every reason to be wary of my presence. He averts his eyes yet maintains his surveillance. On the very spot of the Walden Road driveway where my father parked his '56 Biscayne stands this home owner's immaculate black Saab. The lot to the north that my father bought to extend our privacy remains empty, although a subsequent resident paved part of it and erected a basketball hoop. The Walden Road neighborhood is small and in a matter of minutes I have done with it, satisfied that it remains intact and no further revision is needed. But what I recall is no longer the life we led here four decades ago but what has become my periodic revisitation, my ritual reminiscence. When I completed this tour in 1995, I had nothing by way of fresh recollection; empty-handed, empty-minded, I exited the web of residential streets.

Five minutes and two traffic lights later I turned left onto Whitewood Lane. First thing that struck me was the size of the sycamores, just then in full leaf, but really they had achieved their growth twenty years before when my parents still lived there. The houses seemed closer to the street than I remembered, and their characteristic aspect—low front with high-pitched roof, massive chimney and small dormer window aloof from the world—made them seem impregnable. Additions had been made to some of the houses, converting them into pretend mansions, and the '60s neocolonial look had acquired a shallow antiquity. As an adult I could see what as a child I mostly intuited: this street talked money—new cars and manicured lawns told of corporate profit. The stock portfolios underwriting this life had steadily appreciated, cushioning residents against the local economy's prolonged stagger. Behind these doors, good times and bad, there was wine in abundance. There was a self-sufficiency I found repellent even as I coveted it. Like many a son or daughter of the upper middle class, a part of me wanted to break down the door and loudly summon the grieving world to pillage and destroy. Nor in good conscience could I exempt this house, four houses up from the corner: 125. From the street it looked unchanged, although I understood from my mother that the people who bought it had expanded the kitchen and made other changes that rendered the interior strange.

I inspected the front porch, recalled the feel of the latch as it sprung and the sound of the door swinging on its hinge, recalled the smell of the house and the expectation of familiar contact beyond the threshold. I imagined passing over the threshold into a life that persisted unchanged in its temporal warp. I thought of the meals and holidays, mornings and evenings, the glad vacancy of the house when I had it to myself summer afternoons. I thought of winter nights I lay awake hearing far-off sirens. Then I reflected that what lies therein, upstairs and down, is alien, pertaining to other lives that have made this place their own. Strangers have resided long enough at this address to have their own deep memories, their own stories. Number 125 is a closed door, in a neighborhood of closed doors and impregnable walls where no obvious notice is taken of my passage. Nothing could be more irrelevant to this place than my presence here, except perhaps my memory of it.

Like Walden Road, Whitewood Lane remained intact. It would take fire or a bomb or natural disaster to alter it greatly. Ruin in some form is assuredly ordained, but in the years ahead I'd perform this ritual and know beforehand what I'd see and recall. For the time being I was content to rejoin my wife and sons, whose relation to this place was simple and whose place connections were to a world remote from Rochester, New York. We'd keep to the safety of surfaces. The visit thus far had gone well. Tomorrow we'll spend the day at the lake. And the day after that we'll depart.

Towpath, Fairport. Courtesy of the author.

Epilogue

Seven years later, a wholly idle Internet search of suburban Rochester real estate brought to the screen images of 68 Walden Road. I
had begun to hear encouraging news of the city's resurgence—its rein-
vention as a hub of small start-up businesses that continued the tradition of Rochester as a center of imaging. Number 68 Walden Road lent
itself beautifully to digital presentation. There was its center entrance,
classic colonial curbside view, there the back and side yards, and there
the interiors I hadn't laid eyes on since 1959: living and dining rooms,
kitchen, staircase, upstairs bedrooms, including the one I was quite sure
had been my own, clean utopian clickable thumbnails of a very well-
cared-for house, and I might buy it except for the fact that I lived twelve
hundred miles away and was unlikely to move back to Rochester except
in my dreams. I did, however, have the money, and the thought that I
could make the house mine gave me the sensation of purchasing power
over my past. Gazing into the computer screen at clear electronic images
of space associated with my infancy made the passage of time seem
illusory. How could those interiors survive all that time and remain so
unchanged? In the lapse of forty years, none of the world's violence had
made its way through those doors, or at least not to scorch and deface.
I found one image particularly haunting: a wide-angle shot of the living room, fireplace to the side, and in the far corner a window at which
I could recall standing, hearing an airplane circle for what seemed all
time. I was afraid of the airplane, but my fascination was greater than my
fear. Peering by any number of oblique perspectives, I still couldn't manage to see it. For some reason I'd been forbidden to go outside. I couldn't
have been older than five.

I saved the images to my computer's hard drive and established the living room as my desktop. But every time I booted up I lingered too long in auld lang syne, so I had to replace it with an image of something monotonous: snowdrifts on an endless plain, a gray open sea. I kept meaning to e-mail the images to my brother, anticipating his pleasure and surprise. But I never got around to it, and when the hard drive crashed I discovered I hadn't backed up the file. It was as though I had squandered a gift that had arrived by providential means.

I persuaded myself that it makes little difference. Images of the unfurnished house return no more than outline, frames from which our lives have been erased. Digital figure on illuminated screen simulates a daylight that pertains very little to anything that has been. The shadows, in any case, provided the depth, and words alone might suggest their place in our lives. Nothing, I surmised, could henceforth assist my somnolent and fading power to possess the past.

Acknowledgments

F or reading portions of the manuscript or supporting the project in other ways, the author wishes to thank the following: Jon Billman, Sarah Dabney, Elizabeth Grubgeld, Britton Guildersleeve, Joanne Jacobson, Carol Mason, Art Redding, Tony Stoneburner, and Jeff Walker. Daniel Crutcher provided indispensable help in digitalizing old images. This book found ideal friends at Syracuse University Press, and special thanks are due the following: Jennika Baines, Mary Selden Evans, Annelise Finegan, Mona Hamlin, Lynn Hoppel, Victoria Lane, and Fred Wellner. Annette Wenda copyedited the manuscript with an admirably sharp eye. Finally, the author thanks the anonymous readers commissioned to review the manuscript.